Introduction to Metaphysics

MARTIN HEIDEGGER

Introduction to Metaphysics

New translation by Gregory Fried and Richard Polt

 YALE NOTA BENE

Yale University Press   New Haven & London

Originally published as *Einführung in die Metaphysik* by
Max Niemeyer Verlag, Tübingen.
Published as a Yale Nota Bene book in 2000.
Copyright © 2000 by Yale University.

For information about this and other Yale University Press publications, please
contact: U.S office   sales.press@yale.edu
Europe office   sales@yaleup.co.uk

Designed by Rebecca Gibb. Set in Galliard type by Keystone Typesetting, Inc.
Printed in the United States of America.

Library of Congress Cataloging-in-Publication Data
Heidegger, Martin, 1889–1976.
[Einführung in die Metaphysik. English]
Introduction to metaphysics / Martin Heidegger ; translated by Gregory Fried
and Richard Polt.
p. cm.
Includes bibliographical references and index.
ISBN 0-300-08327-0 (Hardcover : alk. paper) —ISBN 0-300-08328-9 (pbk.)
1. Metaphysics.   I. Title.
BD111 .H42 2000
110—dc21   99-088479

A catalogue record for this book is available from the British Library.

10 9 8 7 6 5 4 3

Contents

Translators' Introduction

IN 1953, in the preface to the seventh edition of his masterwork, *Being and Time*, Martin Heidegger suggested that for an elucidation of the question of Being raised by this text, "the reader may refer to my *Einführung in die Metaphysik*, which is appearing simultaneously with this reprinting."[1] Heidegger had originally presented this *Introduction to Metaphysics* as a lecture course at the University of Freiburg in the summer semester of 1935. It attests to the

---

1. *Being and Time*, trans. John Macquarrie and Edward Robinson (New York: Harper and Row, 1962), 17. The 1953 edition of *Einführung in die Metaphysik* was published by Max Niemeyer Verlag (Tübingen). Niemeyer has continued to publish the book, and it has also been published in the series of Heidegger's collected works as *Gesamtausgabe*, vol. 40, ed. Petra Jaeger (Frankfurt: Vittorio Klostermann, 1983). The *Gesamtausgabe* edition notes the Niemeyer edition's pagination, and in our translation, we have also noted this pagination for the reader's convenience. In citing the *Introduction to Metaphysics*, we will use the abbreviation IM, followed by a page reference according to the Niemeyer edition, which will allow the reader to find the passage in both our translation and the two German editions.

importance he attached to this work that Heidegger chose this course, from among the dozens of manuscripts of lecture courses held over the decades of his teaching career, as the first to present for general publication, and that he saw fit to present this *Introduction* as a companion—indeed, as a rightful heir—to *Being and Time,* the book that established him as one of the preeminent philosophers of the twentieth century. Although this text consists of a series of classroom lectures, it is composed with great care. Heidegger writes in an intricate, nuanced style. Nearly every paragraph contains a series of plays on words that exploit the sounds and senses of German, and often of Greek, in order to bring us closer to a genuine experience of primordial phenomena—Being, truth, and *Dasein* (human beings insofar as they relate to Being).

In the English-speaking world, the importance of *Introduction to Metaphysics* was in part established by the fact that in 1959 it became the first book-length work by Heidegger to be translated into English, three years before a translation of *Being and Time* itself appeared.[2] In effect, the *Introduction to Metaphysics* introduced Heidegger to the English-speaking world. Ralph Manheim undertook the daunting task of translating Heidegger's highly idiosyncratic prose, and if we judge the results in view of the fact that he had few models to work with, Manheim's effort stands as a landmark. He succeeded in presenting Heidegger's often turgid style in a readable and idiomatic English.

Nevertheless, all important philosophical works are standing invitations to new translation, for translation is one of the means by which such works are continually reappropriated by their interpreters. Furthermore, after forty years, Manheim's translation is showing its age. To begin with, in these intervening years, a broad

---

2. *An Introduction to Metaphysics,* trans. Ralph Manheim (New Haven: Yale University Press, 1959).

consensus has developed for rendering key concepts in Heidegger's philosophical lexicon. Although no serious translation should allow such consensus to dictate its labors, a contemporary rendering should take this consensus into account so that, as far as possible, the reader may endeavor to place the arguments of this book in the context of Heidegger's wider body of work now available in English. Secondly, Manheim's felicitous translation of Heidegger at times obscures, by its very fluidity, important philosophical issues; this is because an idiomatic translation may sacrifice terminological consistency or precision in a turn of phrase for the sake of a more natural-sounding English expression. We have tried to maintain a high degree of consistency in conveying key concepts, retreating from this standard only when sense absolutely dictates otherwise. The point of this procedure is to let readers form their own interpretations of Heidegger's words, based on their knowledge of all the contexts in which they appear. To some readers this fidelity will result in what sounds at times like an unnatural English, but it is important to recognize that Heidegger's language can be just as alien to a native German speaker.

A common objection against so-called literal translations is that a single word can have many meanings, depending on the context. This is true, and it is especially true of Heidegger. But the best way to suggest the shifting pattern of the meanings of a German word is to use one word in English that is amenable to undergoing a similar series of uses. For example, when we consistently use "fittingness" to translate *Fug,* we do not mean to imply that the word should always be understood according to some single formula, such as a dictionary definition. The various meanings of "fittingness" in this text must be gathered from its successive contexts, just as one would understand the senses of *Fug* if one were reading the German text. If we used several different renderings, it would become impossible to see the connections among the various uses of *Fug* —

for there are many such connections, even if no single, formulaic definition of the word is possible. Having said this, we must also acknowledge that it has not always been possible to employ a single English word to render some of Heidegger's terms.

Because Heidegger places such a great emphasis on the importance of language and the use of language for the question of Being and its history, the attentive reader should learn enough about Heidegger's philosophical terminology to form a judgment concerning the best way to render Heidegger's key words in English. Because we have endeavored to maintain a high degree of terminological consistency in our translation, we hope this version of the *Introduction to Metaphysics* will aid this process of reflection. To assist the reader further, especially the reader who comes to Heidegger for the first time with this book, we offer here a brief discussion of important words in Heidegger's philosophical vocabulary, restricting ourselves to the most difficult and characteristic terms used by Heidegger in this work. We also recommend a study of the more comprehensive glossary accompanying this translation. The reader must understand that what follow here are sketches, not definitions, and that only closer study through an engaged process of familiarization can develop the fuller meaning of these words. There are no solutions to genuine problems of translation, only temporarily satisfactory placeholders for what thoughtful readers should themselves take up as a question about language.

Das Seiende: beings; what is; that which is. Heidegger's expression *das Seiende* is broad enough to refer to any entity, physical or otherwise, with which we may have dealings, whether real, illusory, or imagined. One helpful passage in this text (IM 58) suggests the range of things that may count as beings, including vehicles, mountains, insects, the Japanese, and Bach's fugues. *Das Seiende* (or the equivalent *Seiendes*) also often refers to beings in general and as a whole, as in the opening question of the book, "Why are there beings [*Seiendes*] at all instead of nothing?" It should be noted that the German expression, unlike the English "beings," is not plural, and is translated most literally as "what is" or "that which is." Occasionally, Heidegger refers to something as *seiend,* and we have translated this word as "in being." This is meant to function as a verbal adjective and does not mean located *inside* a being or thing. Finally, *Seiendheit* means "beingness," that which characterizes beings as beings, in general. For Heidegger, much of the history of philosophy has focused on this beingness rather than inquiring into the happening of Being itself.

Das Sein: Being. For Heidegger, Being is not any *thing.* It is not *a* being at all. *Introduction to Metaphysics* often gives the impression that Being is the same as beingness. However, Heidegger's ultimate question is how it is that beings in their beingness become available to us in the first place, or how we come to understand what it means *to be.* The question of Being, in this sense, inquires into the happening, the event, in which all beings become accessible and understandable to us as beings. Being is thus essentially verbal and temporal. Literally translated, *das Sein* would be "the *to be,*" but this would be far too clumsy a rendering. Among Heidegger scholars there is considerable controversy on how best to translate *das Sein* into English. Many prefer the lowercase "being" in order to fend off the impression that Heidegger means some Supreme Being standing above or holding up all other beings; *das Sein* must not be mistaken for a subject deserving the substantiation that capitalization can imply in English. (In German, all nouns are capitalized, so there is no such implication.) Still, in our judgment, to render *das Sein* as "being" risks confusion, especially with "beings" as the translation for *das Seiende,* and so we resort to the capitalized term.

Dasein: A word left untranslated in almost all renderings of Heidegger's work, *Dasein* denotes that being for whom Being itself is at issue, for whom Being is in question. For the most part, in Heidegger, this being is us, the human being, although Dasein is not *equivalent* to human beings; Heidegger insists that Dasein is not an anthropological, psychological, or biological concept. We can think of Dasein as a condition into which human beings enter, either individually or collectively, at a historical juncture when Being becomes an issue for them; in this sense, Heidegger often speaks in this text of "historical Dasein," "our Dasein," "human Dasein," or "the Dasein of a people." In everyday German, the word *Dasein* is used just as we use the word "existence"; readers may always substitute "existence" for "Dasein" in order to get a sense of how Heidegger's statements would have sounded to his original audience. But Heidegger consistently sees the Latin term *existentia* as misleading and superficial (see IM 49, 138), so it is preferable to interpret *Dasein* in terms of its root meaning. This root meaning is usually rendered in English as "Being there," but when Heidegger hyphenates *Da-sein*, we have employed the equally valid translation "Being-here." Dasein is the being who inhabits a Here, a sphere of meaning within which beings can reveal themselves as meaningful, as significant.

Das Nichts: Nothing. As the first sentence of *Introduction to Metaphysics* indicates, the question of "nothing" will be a recurrent theme of this work. For Heidegger, there is a deep connection between *das Nichts* and *das Sein*, and once again, the reader must beware of taking the capitalized *Nothing* as a substantive thing. Neither Being nor Nothing is *a being* for Heidegger. We have resorted to capitalization again to avoid confusion between Heidegger's use of *das Nichts*, which as Nothing is the counterpart to *das Sein*, Being, and his use of *Nichts* or *nichts*, without the article, which generally means "nothing" as employed in more ordinary language.

Gewalt: violence. *Gewalt* belongs to a family of words used in this work that present considerable difficulties for translation. In ordinary German, *Gewalt* can mean violence in the sense of arbitrary and willful force, but it can also mean the legitimate force employed by the institutions of the state. We have decided to translate this word uniformly as "violence," in part for the sake of consistency, but also because Heidegger seems to want to underline the radically transformative work of the *Gewalt-tat* and the *Gewalt-tätiger* — the act of violence and the doer of violence — without minimizing the danger and even the terror of such work. Still, the reader should keep in mind the ambiguous meaning of *Gewalt* in German.

Walten; das Walten: hold sway; the sway. Related to *Gewalt* are the words *walten* (a verb) and *das Walten* (a verbal noun). In ordinary German, *walten* means to prevail, to reign, to govern, to dominate. Heidegger interprets the Greek word *phusis,* which is usually translated as "nature," as a Greek name for Being itself — that is, the "emergent-abiding *Walten*" of beings as such. We believe the expression "the sway" suggests this powerful upsurge of the presence of beings. That Heidegger seeks to interpret *phusis* as this "sway" is an undertaking to which the reader must lend special attention.

Grund: ground; reason; foundation. Like its English cognate, "ground," the German *Grund* can mean both the earth beneath our feet and the reason upon which we establish a position. As such, *ein Grund* can be a foundation, and it is opposed to *ein Abgrund,* an abyss. For Heidegger, every serious "Why?" — such as the question, "Why are there beings at all instead of nothing?" — strives to reach such a *Grund,* although a genuine question may well run up against an *Abgrund*. We translate *Grund* and related words in a variety of ways, as indicated here, because no single English word can adequately capture its range of meaning.

Der Mensch: humanity; human beings; humans; the human being; the human. In German, *Mensch* means human being, irrespective of gender, and so, with a very few exceptions, we have sought to preserve this gender neutrality, especially because Heidegger discusses all human beings as Dasein.

Volk: a people; the people. The German word *Volk* has a troubled history. In official Nazi ideology, the *Volk* is the race, the bearer of a specific historical destiny, both biological and spiritual. But in ordinary German, *Volk* has no necessary connection with race. It can mean a people or a nation, or "the people" as the basis for sovereignty (as in the American "We the people"), although *Volk* usually does not mean "people" in the informal sense of "folks around here." Heidegger uses the word *Volk* in *Being and Time,* and there it is best translated as "community." But in the 1930s, especially during his involvement with the Nazi regime, Heidegger discusses the *Volk* in a manner that clearly endeavors to come to grips, for better or worse, with the politics of his time.

Beyond the question of terminology, as our discussion of *das Volk* suggests, it is crucial to take into account the historical context of *Introduction to Metaphysics.* Manheim's translation at times blunts the edge of the political references and implications of Heidegger's work. When Heidegger delivered the original lecture course in 1935, Adolf Hitler had been in power for two years. Heidegger had himself joined the National Socialist party in May 1933 and served the regime as the rector of the University of Freiburg from April 1933 until his resignation in April 1934, when he determined that he had lost an internal power struggle concerning the direction of educational policy.[3] Readers must judge for themselves how Heidegger

3. The question of Heidegger's political involvement has generated great controversy in several cycles of discussion since the end of the Second World War. For reliable biographies, readers may consult Hugo Ott, *Heidegger: A Political Life,* trans. Allen Blunden (New York: Basic, 1993), and Rüdiger Safranski, *Martin Heidegger: Between Good and Evil,* trans. Ewald Osers (Cambridge: Harvard University Press, 1998). For further discussion, see Richard Wolin, ed., *The Heidegger Controversy: A Critical Reader* (Cambridge: MIT Press, 1993); Tom Rockmore and Joseph Margolis, eds., *The Heidegger Case: On*

had come to view the historical meaning of the regime by 1935, but to render *Führer* as "chancellor," as Manheim does (IM 27), to take one example, makes this reckoning more difficult, because the reader is not fully confronted with the political connections of this book. The implications of Heidegger's references, as when he makes approving use of Knut Hamsun for an example of talk about Nothing (IM 20) or when he criticizes Theodor Haecker's *What Is Humanity?* (IM 109), may well escape the contemporary reader: Hamsun, a Nobel Prize–winning writer, was a Nazi sympathizer; Haecker's book advanced a clearly anti-Nazi argument.

Some in Heidegger's German audience of 1953 recognized the significance of this *Introduction to Metaphysics,* although perhaps not in the way Heidegger had expected or hoped. The young Jürgen Habermas, himself recently a student of Heidegger's, wrote a letter to the editors of the *Frankfurter Allgemeine Zeitung,* declaring his outrage that Heidegger could publish in 1953, without comment or retraction, his words of 1935 hailing the "inner truth and greatness" (IM 152) of the National Socialist movement.[4] This passage, appearing toward the end of the book, has remained one of the most controversial and oft-quoted sayings in Heidegger's corpus since it was first published. The sentence reads in full as follows: "In particular, what is peddled about nowadays as the philosophy of National Socialism, but which has not the least to do with the inner truth and greatness of this movement [namely, the encounter between global technology and modern humanity], is fishing in these

---

Philosophy and Politics (Philadelphia: Temple University Press, 1992); and Gregory Fried, *Heidegger's* Polemos: *From Being to Politics* (New Haven: Yale University Press, 2000).

4. Jürgen Habermas, letter to *Frankfurter Allgemeine Zeitung,* July 25, 1953, trans. in Wolin, *The Heidegger Controversy,* 190–197. See also Wolin's introduction to the Habermas letter for an overview of the history of the passage in question.

troubled waters of 'values' and 'totalities.'" Particularly problematic has been the status of the phrase within the brackets. In the 1953 edition, this phrase stood in parentheses, indicating by Heidegger's own convention that he had added the phrase in 1935. During the controversy that arose around Habermas's 1953 demand for an explanation, Christian Lewalter published a letter in *Die Zeit* arguing that the passage in question means that "the Nazi movement is a symptom for the tragic collision of man and technology, and as such a symptom it has its 'greatness,' because it affects the entirety of the West and threatens to pull it into destruction." Heidegger himself then wrote to *Die Zeit* to confirm that Lewalter's "interpretation of the sentence taken from my lecture is accurate in every respect." In brief, a concerted attempt was made to characterize this passage as a condemnation of the hubristic aspirations of movements such as National Socialism that sought a monstrous "greatness" on the basis of a total control of humanity and nature through conquest and technology; the "inner truth" of the movement could then be taken as the historical truth of a phenomenon whose profound, if unsettling, significance defines the nihilism of the times.[5]

The trouble with this explanation is that Heidegger did not add the parenthetical remark in 1935 or soon thereafter, whether as a silent criticism or anything else. In his prefatory note to *Introduction to Metaphysics,* Heidegger claims that material in parentheses was added at the time of the lectures and that material in brackets was added during later reworking of the text; in his 1966 interview with

---

5. On the letters by Lewalter and Heidegger, see Wolin, *The Heidegger Controversy,* 187–188. For further discussion of the textual history, see Otto Pöggeler, *Martin Heidegger's Path of Thinking,* trans. Daniel Magurshak and Sigmund Barber (Atlantic Highlands, N.J.: Humanities Press International, 1987), 276–278; Petra Jaeger's afterword to *Gesamtausgabe,* vol. 40, 232–234; and Dominique Janicaud, "The Purloined Letter," in Rockmore and Margolis, *The Heidegger Case,* 348–363.

Der Spiegel, Heidegger explicitly asserted that the parenthetical remark "was present in my manuscript from the beginning" but that he did not read it aloud for fear of party informers.[6] Nevertheless, subsequent scholarship has shown that many of the passages in parentheses should have been in brackets, and the insertion about "the encounter between global technology and modern humanity" is one of these.[7] The reader must judge the meaning of this passage in consideration of the fact that Heidegger did not, at least in 1935 when the lectures were originally delivered, explain the significance of National Socialism in terms of the parenthetical remark.

In our translation, we have indicated wherever parentheses in the 1953 edition have now been revised to brackets to show that the material was added not in 1935 but thereafter.[8] We have not taken lightly this decision to impose on Heidegger's text, but we believe that for the sake of a full understanding of the context of the book, such interventions are necessary. We have also provided bibliographical references for literary and philosophical works that Hei-

6. Martin Heidegger, "'Only a God Can Save Us': *Der Spiegel*'s Interview with Martin Heidegger," in Wolin, *The Heidegger Controversy*, 104.

7. Otto Pöggeler attests that the parenthetical remark was very deliberately added in 1953 as the lectures were being prepared for publication: Pöggeler, *Martin Heidegger's Path of Thinking*, 278; see also Wolin, *The Heidegger Controversy*, 188. The three student assistants who worked on the page proofs of *Introduction to Metaphysics* upon its publication have all asserted that this insertion was not part of the original text, and furthermore that Heidegger changed the phrase "greatness of N.S." [National Socialism] to "greatness of this movement": see Hartmut Buchner, "Fragmentarisches," in Günther Neske, ed., *Erinnerung an Martin Heidegger* (Pfullingen: Neske, 1977), 47–51, esp. 49. For further discussion of this textual question and its larger context, see Theodore Kisiel, "Heidegger's Philosophical Geopolitics in the Third Reich," in *A Companion to Heidegger's Introduction to Metaphysics,* ed. Richard Polt and Gregory Fried (New Haven: Yale University Press, 2001).

8. More recent German editions of Heidegger's text, including the *Gesamtausgabe* edition, have revised such passages, changing parentheses to brackets, and we have relied on such corrections in preparing our translation.

degger mentions, and we have occasionally commented on the contents of these works when we believe that such commentary would enhance the understanding of his lectures. Furthermore, in addition to scholarly and contextual references, where Heidegger's language becomes especially difficult or where the sense depends in part on the German itself, we have provided either interpolations of the German words or, where the language is ambiguous or especially complex, a footnote for entire phrases or sentences. We have also provided the pagination from the Niemeyer edition in the margins of this translation so that readers may easily find the German whenever they have questions about the translation.

Our practice has been to transliterate individual Greek words, such as *phusis, logos, on, einai, polemos,* and *technē,* so that readers unfamiliar with the language may track the use of these terms. We have used the Greek alphabet in longer citations, on the assumption that any readers who study the details of these longer passages will know Greek and will not need a transliteration. In footnotes, we have also frequently provided conventional translations of Greek passages, because Heidegger's own interpretative translations often depart from what scholars would generally recognize as a conventional rendering, and the reader should have the opportunity to judge the extent of Heidegger's departure.

Aside from all issues of vocabulary, political context, and textual history, *Introduction to Metaphysics* remains, first and foremost, a powerful and provocative work of philosophy. Heidegger's impassioned lectures resonate with each other and with us, leaving us with a wealth of questions. What is the meaning of Being? Does it have a particular meaning for Westerners, and if so, how did it come to have that meaning? Does our ordinary disregard for such issues blind us to our history and condemn us to a superficial relation to the world? Do our ordinary science and logic separate us from the truth? What is truth in the first place? What is language? What is thinking? What is it to be human at all?

We prefer not to try to answer such questions here, or to venture farther into the difficulties of interpreting *Introduction to Metaphysics* as a whole. Instead, we hope that our translation will make it possible for thoughtful readers to enter the book on their own and form their own judgments. Our outline, glossary, and index may provide some assistance. Readers who are interested in further explorations of the many dimensions of this text may also consult the anthology *A Companion to Heidegger's Introduction to Metaphysics,* which is being published by Yale University Press as a sequel to this volume.[9]

9. For a general introduction to Heidegger's thought, see Richard Polt, *Heidegger: An Introduction* (Ithaca: Cornell University Press, 1999). Those who read German may also consult Heidegger's own notes on the lecture course, as well as an alternate draft of one section, included as an appendix to the *Gesamtausgabe* edition, 217–230. In his notes, Heidegger criticizes the lecture course for failing to develop the question of Being in its fullest breadth; the draft treats the topic of the etymology of Being, with some significant differences from the published lectures.

Outline of *Introduction to Metaphysics*

This is one possible outline of the text that the reader may find useful in following Heidegger's arguments. Page numbers refer to the German pagination.

Introduction to Metaphysics

Prefatory Note ⟨1953⟩

THIS PUBLICATION contains the text of the fully elaborated[1] lecture course that was held under the same title in the summer semester of 1935 at the University of Freiburg in Breisgau.

What was spoken no longer speaks in what is printed.

As an aid to the reader, *without any change in content,* longer sentences have been broken up, the continuous text has been more fully articulated into sections, repetitions have been deleted, oversights eliminated, and imprecisions clarified.

Whatever stands between parentheses was written during the elaboration of the lectures. Whatever is set within brackets consists of remarks inserted in subsequent years.[2]

1. By *vollständig ausgearbeitete,* Heidegger probably means that he finished writing the text in 1935, with the exception of the changes he notes below. (All footnotes are by the translators, with the exception of two notes by Heidegger that will be identified as such.)
2. The 1953 edition often did not follow the conventions Heidegger describes here: later insertions of a sentence or longer were usually printed in brackets,

In order properly to consider in what sense and on what grounds the term "metaphysics" is included in the title, the reader must first have taken part in completing the course of the lectures.

---

but later insertions consisting of a word or phrase were usually printed in parentheses. The *Gesamtausgabe* and the more recent Niemeyer editions use brackets for all the later insertions. We will observe the usage of these recent editions, while noting all occasions where parentheses in the 1953 edition have been revised to brackets. Translators' interpolations and references to the original German are printed in angle brackets: ⟨ ⟩.

The Fundamental Question of Metaphysics

WHY ARE THERE beings at all instead of nothing? That is the question. Presumably it is no arbitrary question. "Why are there beings at all instead of nothing?"—this is obviously the first of all questions. Of course, it is not the first question in the chronological sense. Individuals as well as peoples ask many questions in the course of their historical passage through time. They explore, investigate, and test many sorts of things before they run into the question "Why are there beings at all instead of nothing?" Many never run into this question at all, if running into the question means not only hearing and reading the interrogative sentence as uttered, but asking the question, that is, taking a stand on it, posing it, compelling oneself into the state of this questioning.

And yet, we are each touched once, maybe even now and then, by the concealed power of this question, without properly grasping what is happening to us. In great despair, for example, when all weight tends to dwindle away from things and the sense of things grows dark, the question looms. Perhaps it strikes only once, like the muffled tolling of a bell that resounds into Dasein[1] and gradually fades away. The question is there in heartfelt joy, for then all things are transformed and surround us as if for the first time, as if it were easier to grasp that they were not, rather than that they are, and are as they are. The question is there in a spell of boredom, when we are equally distant from despair and joy, but when the stubborn ordinariness of beings lays open a wasteland in which it makes no difference to us whether beings are or are not—and then, in a distinctive form, the question resonates once again: Why are there beings at all instead of nothing?

But whether this question is asked explicitly, or whether it merely passes through our Dasein like a fleeting gust of wind, unrecognized as a question, whether it becomes more oppressive or is thrust away by us again and suppressed under some pretext, it certainly is never the first question that we ask.

But it is the first question in another sense—namely, in rank. This can be clarified in three ways. The question "Why are there beings at all instead of nothing?" is first in rank for us as the broadest, as the deepest, and finally as the most originary question.

The question is the broadest in scope. It comes to a halt at no being of any kind whatsoever. The question embraces all that is, and that means not only what is now present at hand in the broadest sense, but also what has previously been and what will be in the future. The domain of this question is limited only by what simply is not and never is: by Nothing. All that is not Nothing comes into the question, and in the end even Nothing itself—not, as it were, because it is something, a being, for after all we are talking about it, but because it "is" Nothing. The scope of our question is *so* broad that we can never exceed it. We are not interrogating this being or that being, nor all beings, each in turn; instead, we are asking from

---

1. See the discussion of *Dasein* in our introduction.

the start about the whole of what is, or as we say for reasons to be discussed later: beings as a whole and as such.

Just as it is the broadest question, the question is also the deepest: Why are there beings at all . . . ? Why—that is, what is the ground? From what ground do beings come? On what ground do beings stand? To what ground do beings go?[2] The question does not ask this or that about beings—what they are in each case, here and there, how they are put together, how they can be changed, what they can be used for, and so on. The questioning seeks the ground for what is, insofar as it is in being.[3] To seek the ground: this means to get to the bottom ⟨*ergründen*⟩. What is put into question comes into relation with a ground. But because we are questioning, it remains an open question whether the ground is a truly grounding, foundation-effecting, originary ground; whether the ground refuses to provide a foundation, and so is an abyss; or whether the ground is neither one nor the other, but merely offers the perhaps necessary illusion of a foundation and is thus an unground.[4] However this may be, the question seeks a decision with respect to the ground that grounds the fact that what is, is in being *as* the being that it is.[5] This why-question does not seek causes for beings, causes of the same kind and on the same level as beings themselves. This why-question does not just skim the surface, but presses into the domains that lie "at the ground," even pressing into the ultimate, to the limit; the question is turned away from all   [3]

2. *Zu Grunde gehen* (literally, "go to the ground") is an idiom meaning "to be ruined."
3. See *seiend* in German-English Glossary.
4. "Allein, weil gefragt wird, bleibt offen, ob der Grund ein wahrhaft gründender, Gründung erwirkender, Ur-grund ist; ob der Grund eine Gründung versagt, Ab-grund ist; ob der Grund weder das Eine noch das Andere ist, sondern nur einen vielleicht notwendigen Schein von Gründung vorgibt und so ein Un-grund ist."
5. ". . . daß das Seiende seiend ist *als* ein solches, das es ist."

surface and shallowness, striving for depth; as the broadest, it is at the same time the deepest of the deep questions.

Finally, as the broadest and deepest question, it is also the most originary. What do we mean by that? If we consider our question in the whole breadth of what it puts into question, beings as such and as a whole, then it strikes us right away that in the question, we keep ourselves completely removed from every particular, individual being as precisely this or that being. We do mean beings as a whole, but without any particular preference. Still, it is remarkable that *one* being always keeps coming to the fore in this questioning: the human beings who pose this question. And yet the question should not be about some particular, individual being. Given the unrestricted range of the question, every being counts as much as any other. Some elephant in some jungle in India is in being just as much as some chemical oxidation process on the planet Mars, and whatever else you please.

Thus if we properly pursue the question "Why are there beings at all instead of nothing?" in its sense as a question, we must avoid emphasizing any particular, individual being, not even focusing on the human being. For what is this being, after all! Let us consider the Earth within the dark immensity of space in the universe. We can compare it to a tiny grain of sand; more than a kilometer of emptiness extends between it and the next grain of its size; on the surface of this tiny grain of sand lives a stupefied swarm of supposedly clever animals, crawling all over each other, who for a brief moment have invented knowledge [cf. Nietzsche, "On Truth and Lie in the Extramoral Sense," 1873, published posthumously].[6]

6. In parentheses in the 1953 edition. Nietzsche's essay begins: "'In some remote corner of the universe, glimmering diffusely into countless solar systems, there was once a planet upon which clever animals invented knowledge. It was the proudest and most mendacious minute in "world history"; but it was only a minute. After nature had taken a few breaths, the planet grew cold,

And what is a human lifespan amid millions of years? Barely a move of the second hand, a breath. Within beings as a whole there is no justification to be found for emphasizing precisely *this* being that is called the human being and among which we ourselves happen to belong.

But if beings as a whole are ever brought into our question, then the questioning does come into a distinctive relation with them — distinctive because it is unique — and beings do come into a distinctive relation with this questioning. For through this questioning, beings as a whole are first opened up *as such* and with regards to their possible ground, and they are kept open in the questioning. The asking of this question is not, in relation to beings as such and as a whole, some arbitrary occurrence amid beings, such as the falling of raindrops. The why-question challenges beings as a whole, so to speak, outstrips them, though never completely. But [4] this is precisely how the questioning gains its distinction. What is asked in this question rebounds upon the questioning itself, for the questioning challenges beings as a whole but does not after all wrest itself free from them. Why the Why? What is the ground of this why-question itself, a question that presumes to establish the ground of beings as a whole? Is this Why, too, just asking about the ground as a foreground, so that it is still always a *being* that is sought as what does the grounding? Is this "first" question not the first in rank after all, as measured by the intrinsic rank of the question of Being and its transformations?

To be sure — whether the question "Why are there beings at all instead of nothing?" is posed or not makes no difference what-

---

and the clever animals had to die? Someone could invent a fable like that, and he still would not have adequately illustrated how wretched, how shadowlike and fleeting, how pointless and arbitrary the human intellect appears within nature." Cf. *The Portable Nietzsche,* ed. Walter Kaufmann (New York: Viking, 1954), 42.

soever to beings themselves. The planets move in their orbits without this question. The vigor of life flows through plant and animal without this question.

But *if* this question is posed, and provided that it is actually carried out, then this questioning necessarily recoils back from what is asked and what is interrogated, back upon itself. Therefore this questioning in itself is not some arbitrary process but rather a distinctive occurrence that we call a *happening*.

This question and all the questions immediately rooted in it, in which this one question unfolds — this why-question cannot be compared to any other. It runs up against the search for its own Why. The question "Why the Why?" looks externally and at first like a frivolous repetition of the same interrogative, which can go on forever; it looks like an eccentric and empty rumination about insubstantial meanings of words. Certainly, that is how it looks. The only question is whether we are willing to fall victim to this cheap look of things and thus take the whole matter as settled, or whether we are capable of experiencing a provocative happening in this recoil of the why-question back upon itself.

But if we do not let ourselves be deceived by the look of things, it will become clear that this why-question, as a question about beings as such and as a whole, immediately leads us away from mere toying with words, provided that we still possess enough force of spirit to make the question truly recoil into its own Why; for the recoil does not, after all, produce itself on its own. Then we discover that this distinctive why-question has its ground in a leap by which human beings leap away from all the previous safety of their Dasein, be it genuine or presumed. The asking of this question happens only in the leap and as the leap, and otherwise not at all. Later, we will clarify what we mean here by "leap." Our questioning is not yet the leap; for that, it must first be transformed; it still

[5]

stands, unknowing, in the face of beings. For now, let this comment suffice: the leap ⟨*Sprung*⟩ of this questioning attains its own ground by leaping, performs it in leaping ⟨*er-springt, springend erwirkt*⟩. According to the genuine meaning of the word, we call such a leap that attains itself as ground by leaping an originary leap ⟨*Ur-sprung*⟩: an attaining-the-ground-by-leaping. Because the question "Why are there beings at all instead of nothing?" attains the ground for all genuine questioning by leaping and is thus an originary leap, we must recognize it as the most originary ⟨*ursprünglich*⟩ of questions.

As the broadest and deepest question, it is the most originary, and conversely.

In this threefold sense the question is the first in rank, first in rank in the order of questioning within that domain which this first question definitively opens up and grounds, giving it its measure. Our question is the *question* of all true questions — that is, of those that pose themselves to themselves — and it is necessarily asked, knowingly or not, along with every question. No questioning, and consequently no single scientific "problem" either, understands itself if it does not grasp the question of all questions, that is, if it does not ask it. We want to be clear about this from the start: it can never be determined objectively whether anyone is asking — whether we are actually asking this question, that is, whether we are leaping, or whether we are just mouthing the words. The question loses its rank at once in the sphere of a human-historical Dasein to whom *questioning* as an originary power remains foreign.

For example, anyone for whom the Bible is divine revelation and truth already has the answer to the question "Why are there beings at all instead of nothing?" before it is even asked: beings, with the exception of God Himself, are created by Him. God Himself "is" as the uncreated Creator. One who holds on to such faith as a basis can, perhaps, emulate and participate in the asking of our question in a certain way, but he cannot authentically question without giving himself up as a believer, with all the consequences of this step. He can act only "as if" — . On the other hand, if such faith does not continually expose itself to the possibility of unfaith, it is not faith but a convenience. It becomes an agreement with oneself to adhere in the future to a doctrine as something that has somehow been handed down. This is neither having faith nor questioning, but indifference — which can then, perhaps even with keen interest, busy itself with everything, with faith as well as with questioning.

[6]   Now by referring to safety in faith as a special way of standing in the truth, we are not saying that citing the words of the Bible, "In the beginning God created heaven and earth, etc.," represents an answer to our question. Quite aside from whether this sentence of the Bible is true or untrue for faith, it can represent no answer at all to our question, because it has no relation to this question. It has no relation to it, because it simply cannot come into such a relation. What is really asked in our question is, for faith, foolishness.

Philosophy consists in such foolishness. A "Christian philosophy" is a round square and a misunderstanding. To be sure, one can thoughtfully question and work through the world of Christian experience — that is, the world of faith. That is then theology. Only ages that really no longer believe in the true greatness of the task of theology arrive at the pernicious opinion that, through a supposed refurbishment with the help of philosophy, a theology can be gained or even replaced, and can be made more palatable to the need of the age. Philosophy, for originally Christian faith, is foolishness. Philosophizing means asking: "Why are there beings at all instead of nothing?" Actually asking this means venturing to exhaust, to question thoroughly, the inexhaustible wealth of this question, by unveiling what it demands that we question. Whenever such a venture occurs, there is philosophy.

If we now wanted to talk about philosophy, giving a report, in order to say what it is in more detail, this beginning would be fruitless. But whoever engages in philosophy must know a few things. They can be stated briefly.

All essential questioning in philosophy necessarily remains untimely, and this is because philosophy either projects far beyond its own time or else binds its time back to this time's earlier and *inceptive* past. Philosophizing always remains a kind of knowing that not only does not allow itself to be made timely but, on the contrary, imposes its measure on the times.[7]

Philosophy is essentially untimely because it is one of those few things whose fate it remains never to be able to find a direct resonance in their own time, and never to be permitted to find such a resonance. Whenever this seemingly does take place, whenever a philosophy becomes fashion, either there is no actual philosophy or else philosophy is misinterpreted and, according to some intentions alien to it, misused for the needs of the day.

Philosophy, then, is not a kind of knowledge which one could [7] acquire directly, like vocational and technical expertise, and which, like economic and professional knowledge in general, one could apply directly and evaluate according to its usefulness in each case.

But what is useless can nevertheless be a power — a power in the rightful sense. That which has no direct resonance ⟨*Widerklang*⟩ in everydayness can stand in innermost harmony ⟨*Einklang*⟩ with the authentic happening in the history of a people. It can even be its prelude ⟨*Vorklang*⟩. What is untimely will have its own times. This holds for philosophy. Therefore we cannot determine what the task of philosophy in itself and in general is, and what must accordingly

---

7. Heidegger puns on *zeitgemäß* ("timely"), meaning literally "in measure with the times."

be demanded of philosophy. Every stage and every inception of its unfolding carries within it its own law. One can only say what philosophy cannot be and what it cannot achieve.

A question has been posed: "Why are there beings at all instead of nothing?" We have claimed that this question is the first. We have explained in what sense it is meant as the first.

Thus we have not yet asked this question; right away we turned aside into a discussion of it. This procedure is necessary, for the asking of this question cannot be compared with customary concerns. There is no gradual transition from the customary by which the question could slowly become more familiar. This is why it must be posed in advance, pro-posed ⟨vor-gestellt⟩, as it were. On the other hand, in this pro-posal of and talk about the question, we must not defer, or even forget, the questioning.

We therefore conclude the preliminary remarks with this session's discussions.

Every essential form of spirit is open to ambiguity. The more this form resists comparison with others, the more it is misinterpreted.

Philosophy is one of the few autonomous creative possibilities, and occasional necessities, of human-historical Dasein. The current misinterpretations of philosophy, which all have something to them despite their misunderstandings, are innumerable. Here we will mention only two, which are important for clarifying the situation of philosophy today and in the future.

One misinterpretation consists in demanding too much of the essence of philosophy. The other involves a distortion of the sense of what philosophy can achieve.

[8]   Roughly speaking, philosophy always aims at the first and last grounds of beings, and it does so in such a way that human beings themselves, with respect to their way of Being, are emphatically interpreted and given an aim. This readily gives the impression that

philosophy can and must provide a foundation for the current and future historical Dasein of a people in every age, a foundation for building culture. But such expectations and requirements demand too much of the capability and essence of philosophy. Usually, this excessive demand takes the form of finding fault with philosophy. One says, for example, that because metaphysics did not contribute to preparing the revolution, it must be rejected. That is just as clever as saying that because one cannot fly with a carpenter's bench, it should be thrown away. Philosophy can never *directly* supply the forces and create the mechanisms and opportunities that bring about a historical state of affairs, if only because philosophy is always the direct concern of the few. Which few? The ones who transform creatively, who unsettle things. It spreads only indirectly, on back roads that can never be charted in advance, and then finally — sometime, when it has long since been forgotten as originary philosophy — it sinks away in the form of one of Dasein's truisms.

Against this first misinterpretation, what philosophy can and must be according to its essence, is this: a thoughtful opening of the avenues and vistas of a knowing that establishes measure and rank, a knowing in which and from which a people conceives its Dasein in the historical-spiritual world and brings it to fulfillment — that knowing which ignites and threatens and compels all questioning and appraising.

The second misinterpretation that we mention is a distortion of the sense of what philosophy can achieve. Granted that philosophy is unable to lay the foundation of a culture, one says, philosophy nevertheless makes it easier to build up culture. According to this distortion, philosophy orders the whole of beings into overviews and systems, and readies a world picture for our use — a map of the world, as it were — a picture of the various possible things and domains of things, thereby granting us a universal and uniform orientation. Or, more specifically, philosophy relieves the sciences of their labor by meditating on the presuppositions of the sciences, their basic concepts and propositions. One expects philosophy to promote, and even to accelerate, the practical and technical business of culture by alleviating it, making it easier.

[9]   But—according to its essence, philosophy never makes things easier, but only more difficult. And it does so not just incidentally, not just because its manner of communication seems strange or even deranged to everyday understanding. The burdening of historical Dasein, and thereby at bottom of Being itself, is rather the genuine sense of what philosophy can achieve. Burdening gives back to things, to beings, their weight (Being). And why? Because burdening is one of the essential and fundamental conditions for the arising of everything great, among which we include above all else the fate of a historical people and its works. But fate is there only where a true knowing about things rules over Dasein. And the avenues and views of such a knowing are opened up by philosophy.

The misinterpretations by which philosophy remains constantly besieged are mainly promoted by what people like us do, that is, by professors of philosophy. Their customary, and also legitimate and even useful business is to transmit a certain educationally appropriate acquaintance with philosophy as it has presented itself so far. This then looks as though it itself were philosophy, whereas at most it is scholarship about philosophy.

When we mention and correct both of these misinterpretations, we cannot intend that you should now come at one stroke into a clear relation with philosophy. But you should become mindful and be on your guard, precisely when the most familiar judgments, and even supposedly genuine experiences, unexpectedly assail you. This often happens in a way that seems entirely innocuous and is quickly convincing. One believes that one has had the experience oneself, and readily hears it confirmed: "nothing comes" of philosophy; "you can't do anything with it." These two turns of phrase, which are especially current among teachers and researchers in the sciences, express observations that have their indisputable correctness. When one attempts to prove that, to the contrary, something does after all "come" of philosophy, one merely intensifies and secures the prevailing misinterpretation, which consists in the prejudice that one can evaluate philosophy according to everyday standards that one would otherwise employ to judge the utility of bicycles or the effectiveness of mineral baths.

It is entirely correct and completely in order to say, "You can't do anything with philosophy." The only mistake is to believe that with this, the judgment concerning philosophy is at an end. For a little epilogue arises in the form of a counterquestion: even if *we* can't do anything with it, may not philosophy in the end do something *with us,* provided that we engage ourselves with it? Let that suffice for us as an explication of what philosophy is not. [10]

At the outset we spoke of a question: "Why are there beings at all instead of nothing?" We asserted that to ask this question is to philosophize. Whenever we set out in the direction of this question, thinking and gazing ahead, then right away we forgo any sojourn in any of the usual regions of beings. We pass over and surpass what belongs to the order of the day. We ask beyond the usual, beyond the ordinary that is ordered in the everyday. Nietzsche once said (VII, 269): "A philosopher: that is a human being who constantly experiences, sees, hears, suspects, hopes, dreams extraordinary things . . ."[8]

Philosophizing is questioning about the extra-ordinary. Yet as we merely intimated at first, this questioning recoils upon itself, and thus not only what is asked about is extraordinary, but also the questioning itself. This means that this questioning does not lie

8. *Beyond Good and Evil,* §292. Heidegger's references to Nietzsche cite the edition of his works published in Leipzig by C. G. Naumann, 1899–1905.

along our way, so that one day we stumble into it blindly or even by mistake. Nor does it stand in the familiar order of the everyday, so that we could be compelled to it on the ground of some require- ments or even regulations. Nor does this questioning lie in the sphere of urgent concern and the satisfaction of dominant needs. The questioning itself is out-of-order. It is completely voluntary, fully and especially based on the mysterious ground of freedom, on what we have called the leap. The same Nietzsche says: "Philoso- phy . . . means living voluntarily amid ice and mountain ranges" (XV, 2).[9] Philosophizing, we can now say, is extra-ordinary ques- tioning about the extra-ordinary.

In the age of the first and definitive unfolding of Western philos- ophy among the Greeks, when questioning about beings as such and as a whole received its true inception, beings were called *phusis*. This fundamental Greek word for beings is usually translated as "nature." We use the Latin translation *natura,* which really means "to be born," "birth." But with this Latin translation, the originary content of the Greek word *phusis* is already thrust aside, the authen- tic philosophical naming force of the Greek word is destroyed. This is true not only of the Latin translation of *this* word but of all other translations of Greek philosophical language into Roman. This translation of Greek into Roman was not an arbitrary and innocu- ous process but was the first stage in the isolation and alienation of the originary essence of Greek philosophy. The Roman translation then became definitive for Christianity and the Christian Middle Ages. The Middle Ages trans-lated themselves into modern philos- ophy, which moves within the conceptual world of the Middle Ages and then creates those familiar representations and conceptual terms that are used even today to understand the inception of West-

[11]

9. §3 of the preface to *Ecce Homo*.

ern philosophy. This inception is taken as something that we have left behind long ago and supposedly overcome.

But now we leap over this whole process of deformation and decline, and we seek to win back intact the naming force of language and words; for words and language are not just shells into which things are packed for spoken and written intercourse. In the word, in language, things first come to be and are. For this reason, too, the misuse of language in mere idle talk, in slogans and phrases, destroys our genuine relation to things. Now what does the word *phusis* say? It says what emerges from itself (for example, the emergence, the blossoming, of a rose), the unfolding that opens itself up, the coming-into-appearance in such unfolding, and holding itself and persisting in appearance — in short, the emerging-abiding sway.[10] According to the dictionary, *phuein* means to grow, to make grow.[11] But what does growing mean? Does it just mean to increase by acquiring bulk, to become more numerous and bigger?

Phusis as emergence can be experienced everywhere: for example, in celestial processes (the rising of the sun), in the surging of the sea, in the growth of plants, in the coming forth of animals and human beings from the womb. But *phusis,* the emerging sway, is not synonymous with these processes, which we still today count as part of "nature." This emerging and standing-out-in-itself-from-itself may not be taken as just one process among others that we observe in beings. *Phusis* is Being itself, by virtue of which beings first become and remain observable.

It was not in natural processes that the Greeks first experienced what *phusis* is, but the other way around: on the basis of a fundamental experience of Being in poetry and thought, what they had to

10. See the discussion of *Walten* in our introduction.
11. The noun *phusis* corresponds to the verb *phuein.*

call *phusis* disclosed itself to them. Only on the basis of this disclosure could they then take a look at nature in the narrower sense. Thus *phusis* originally means both heaven and earth, both the stone and the plant, both the animal and the human, and human history as the work of humans and gods; and finally and first of all, it means the gods who themselves stand under destiny. *Phusis* means the emerging sway, and the enduring over which it thoroughly holds sway. This emerging, abiding sway includes both "becoming" as well as "Being" in the narrower sense of fixed continuity. *Phusis* is the event of *standing forth,* arising from the concealed and thus enabling the concealed to take its stand for the first time.[12]

[12]

But if one understands *phusis,* as one usually does, not in the originary sense of the emerging and abiding sway but in its later and present meaning, as nature, and if one also posits the motions of material things, of atoms and electrons — what modern physics investigates as *phusis* — as the fundamental manifestation of nature, then the inceptive philosophy of the Greeks turns into a philosophy of nature, a representation of all things according to which they are really of a material nature. Then the inception of Greek philosophy, in accordance with our everyday understanding of an inception, gives the impression of being, as we say once again in Latin, primitive. Thus the Greeks become in principle a better kind of Hottentot, in comparison to whom modern science has progressed infinitely far. Disregarding all the particular absurdities involved in conceiving of the inception of Western philosophy as primitive, it must be said that this interpretation forgets that what is at issue is philosophy — one of the few great things of humanity. But whatever is great can only begin great. In fact, its inception is always

---

12. "*Phusis* ist das *Ent-stehen,* aus dem Verborgenen sich heraus- und dieses so erst in den Stand bringen." Heidegger is playing on the etymological connection between *Entstehen* (genesis, growth) and *Stand* (a stand, state, situation, condition). The phrase *in den Stand bringen* ordinarily means to enable.

what is greatest. Only the small begins small — the small, whose dubious greatness consists in diminishing everything; what is small is the inception of decline, which can then also become great in the sense of the enormity of total annihilation.

The great begins great, sustains itself only through the free recurrence of greatness, and if it is great, also comes to an end in greatness. So it is with the philosophy of the Greeks. It came to an end in greatness with Aristotle. Only the everyday understanding and the small man imagine that the great must endure forever, a duration which he then goes on to equate with the eternal.

What is, as such and as a whole, the Greeks call *phusis*. Let it be mentioned just in passing that already within Greek philosophy, a narrowing of the word set in right away, although its originary meaning did not disappear from the experience, the knowledge, and the attitude of Greek philosophy. An echo of knowledge about the originary meaning still survives in Aristotle, when he speaks of the grounds of beings as such (cf. *Metaphysics* Γ, 1, 1003a27).[13]

But this narrowing of *phusis* in the direction of the "physical" did not happen in the way that we picture it today. We oppose to the physical the "psychical," the mind or soul, what is ensouled, what is alive. But all this, for the Greeks, continues even later to belong to *phusis*. As a counterphenomenon there arose what the Greeks call *thesis*, positing, ordinance, or *nomos*, law, rule in the sense of mores. But this is not what is moral but instead what concerns mores, that which rests on the commitment of freedom and the assignment of tradition; it is that which concerns a free

[13]

13. "Now since we are seeking the principles and the highest causes [or grounds], it is clear that these must belong to some *phusis* in virtue of itself. If, then, those who were seeking the elements of beings [*tōn ontōn*] were also seeking these principles, these elements too must be elements of being [*tou ontos*], not accidentally, but as being. Accordingly, it is of being as being that we, too, must find the first causes." —*Metaphysics* Γ, 1, 1003a26–32.

comportment and attitude, the shaping of the historical Being of humanity, *ēthos,* which under the influence of morality was then degraded to the ethical.

Phusis gets narrowed down by contrast with *technē* — which means neither art nor technology but a kind of *knowledge,* the knowing disposal over the free planning and arranging and controlling of arrangements (cf. Plato's *Phaedrus*).[14] *Technē* is generating, building, as a knowing pro-ducing. (It would require a special study to clarify what is essentially the same in *phusis* and *technē*.)[15] But for all that, the counterconcept to the physical is the historical, a domain of beings that is also understood by the Greeks in the originally broader sense of *phusis.* This, however, does not have the least to do with a naturalistic interpretation of history. Beings, as such and as a whole, are *phusis* — that is, they have as their essence and character the emerging-abiding sway. This is then experienced, above all, in what tends to impose itself on us most immediately in a certain way, and which is later denoted by *phusis* in the narrower sense: *ta phusei onta, ta phusika,* what naturally is. When one asks about *phusis* in general, that is, what beings as such are, then it is above all *ta phusei onta* that provide the foothold, although in such a way that from the start, the questioning is not allowed to dwell on this or that domain of nature — inanimate bodies, plants, animals — but must go on beyond *ta phusika.*

In Greek, "away over something," "over beyond," is *meta.* Philosophical questioning about beings as such is *meta ta phusika;* it questions on beyond beings, it is metaphysics. At this point we do

14. *Phaedrus* 260d–274b is devoted to determining how rhetoric can become a proper *technē* and what is required in general of a proper *technē.*
15. Cf. Heidegger's 1939 essay "On the Essence and Concept of Φύσις in Aristotle's *Physics* B, 1," trans. Thomas Sheehan, in *Pathmarks,* ed. William McNeill (Cambridge: Cambridge University Press, 1998).

not need to trace the history of the genesis and meaning of this term in detail.

The question we have identified as first in rank — "Why are there beings at all instead of nothing?" — is thus the fundamental question of metaphysics. Metaphysics stands as the name for the center and core that determines all philosophy.

[For this introduction, we have intentionally presented all this [14] in a cursory and thus basically ambiguous way. According to our explanation of *phusis,* this word means the Being of beings. If one is asking *peri phuseōs,* about the Being of beings, then the discussion of *phusis,* "physics" in the ancient sense, is in itself already beyond *ta phusika,* on beyond beings, and is concerned with Being. "Physics" determines the essence and the history of metaphysics from the inception onward. Even in the doctrine of Being as *actus purus* (Thomas Aquinas), as absolute concept (Hegel), as eternal recurrence of the same will to power (Nietzsche), metaphysics steadfastly remains "physics."

The question about Being as such, however, has a different essence and a different provenance.

To be sure, within the purview of metaphysics, and if one continues to think in its manner, one can regard the question about Being as such merely as a mechanical repetition of the question about beings as such. The question about Being as such is then just another transcendental question, albeit one of a higher order. This misconstrual of the question about Being as such blocks the way to unfolding it in a manner befitting the matter.

However, this misconstrual is all too easy, especially because *Being and Time* spoke of a "transcendental horizon."[16] But the

16. *Being and Time,* 39 (according to the pagination of the later German editions).

"transcendental" meant there does not pertain to subjective consciousness; instead, it is determined by the existential-ecstatic temporality of Being-here. Nevertheless, the question about Being as such is misconstrued as coinciding with the question about beings as such; this misconstrual thrusts itself upon us above all because the essential provenance of the question about beings as such, and with it the essence of metaphysics, lies in obscurity. This drags into indeterminacy all questioning that concerns Being in any way.

The "introduction to metaphysics" attempted here keeps in view this confused condition of the "question of Being."

According to the usual interpretation, the "question of Being" means asking about beings as such (metaphysics). But if we think along the lines of *Being and Time,* the "question of Being" means asking about Being as such. This meaning of the expression is also appropriate both in terms of the matter at stake and in terms of language; for the "question of Being" in the sense of the metaphysical question about beings as such precisely does *not ask* thematically about Being. Being remains forgotten.

But this talk of the "oblivion of Being" is just as ambiguous as the expression "question of Being." One protests quite rightfully at metaphysics does indeed ask about the Being of beings, and that therefore it is manifest foolishness to charge metaphysics with an oblivion of Being.

[15]

But if we 1ink the question of Being in the sense of the question about Being as such, then it becomes clear to everyone who accompanies us in thinking that it is precisely Being *as such* that remains concealed, remains in oblivion — and so decisively that the oblivion of Being, an oblivion that itself falls into oblivion, is the unrecognized yet enduring impulse for metaphysical questioning.

If one chooses the designation "metaphysics" for the treatment of the "question of Being" in an indefinite sense, then the title of this lecture course remains ambiguous. For at first it seems as though the questioning held itself within the purview of beings as such, whereas already with the first sentence it strives to depart this zone in order to bring another domain into view with its questions. The title of the course is thus *deliberately* ambiguous.

The fundamental question of the lecture course is of a different kind than the guiding question of metaphysics. Taking *Being and Time* as its point of departure, the lecture course asks about the "*disclosedness of Being*" (*Being and Time,* pp. 21 f. and 37 f.). Disclosedness means: the openedness of what the oblivion of Being closes off and conceals.[17] Through this questioning, too, light first falls on the *essence* of metaphysics, which was also concealed up to now.]

"Introduction to metaphysics" accordingly means: leading into the asking of the fundamental question.[18] But questions, and above all fundamental questions, do not simply occur like stones and water. Questions are not given like shoes, clothes, or books. Questions *are* as they are actually asked, and this is the only way in which they are. Thus the leading into the asking of the fundamental question is not a passage over to something that lies or stands around somewhere; instead, this leading-to must first awaken and create the questioning. Leading is a questioning going-ahead, a questioning-ahead. This is a leadership that essentially has no following. Whenever one finds pretensions to a following, in a school of philosophy, for example, questioning is misunderstood. There can be such schools only in the sphere of scientific or professional labor. In such a sphere, everything has its distinct hierarchical order. Such labor

17. "Erschlossenheit besagt: Aufgeschlossenheit dessen, was die Vergessenheit des Seins verschließt und verbirgt." This could also mean: ". . . of what closes off and conceals the oblivion of Being."

18. Throughout this passage, Heidegger plays on the connection between *Einführung,* "introduction," and *führen,* "to lead." Etymologically, *Einführung* means "leading into," as do the Latin roots of the English "introduction."

also belongs, and even necessarily belongs, to philosophy and has today been lost. But the best professional ability will never replace the authentic strength of seeing and questioning and saying.

"Why are there beings at all instead of nothing?" That is the question. To pronounce the interrogative sentence, even in a questioning tone, is not yet to question. We can already see this in the fact that even if we repeat the interrogative sentence several times over and over, this does not necessarily make the questioning attitude any livelier; on the contrary, reciting the sentence repeatedly may well blunt the questioning.

[16]

Although the interrogative sentence thus is not the question and is not questioning, neither should it be taken as a mere linguistic form of communication, as if the sentence were only a statement "about" a question. If I say to you, "Why are there beings at all instead of nothing?" then the intent of my asking and saying is not to communicate to you that a process of questioning is now going on inside me. Certainly the spoken interrogative sentence can also be taken this way, but then one is precisely not hearing the questioning. The questioning does not result in any shared questioning and self-questioning. It awakens nothing in the way of a questioning attitude, or even a questioning disposition. For this consists in a *willing*-to-know. Willing — this is not just wishing and trying. Whoever wishes to know also seems to question; but he does not get beyond saying the question, he stops short precisely where the question begins. Questioning is willing-to-know. Whoever wills, whoever lays his whole Dasein into a will, *is* resolute. Resoluteness delays nothing, does not shirk, but acts from the moment and without fail. Open resoluteness is no mere resolution to act; it is the decisive inception of action that reaches ahead of and through all action. To will is to be resolute. [The essence of willing is traced back here to open resoluteness. But the essence of open resoluteness ⟨*Ent-schlossenheit*⟩ lies in the de-concealment ⟨*Ent-borgenheit*⟩ of human Dasein *for* the clearing of Being and by no means in an accumulation of energy for "activity." Cf. *Being and Time* §44 and §60. But the relation to Being is letting. That all willing should be grounded in letting strikes the understanding as strange. See the lecture "On the Essence of Truth," 1930.[19]]

But to know means to be able to stand in the truth. Truth is the openness of beings. To know is accordingly to be able to stand in the openness of beings, to stand up to it. Merely to have information, however wide-ranging it may be, is not to know. Even if this information is focused on what is practically most important through courses of study and examination requirements, it is not knowledge. Even if this information, cut back to the most compelling needs, is "close to life," its possession is not knowledge. One who carries such information around with him and has added a few practical tricks to it will still be at a loss and will necessarily bungle in the face of real reality, which is always different from what the [17] philistine understands by closeness to life and closeness to reality. Why? Because he has no knowledge, since to know means *to be able to learn*.

Of course, everyday understanding believes that one has knowledge when one needs to learn nothing more, because one has finished learning. No. The only one who knows is the one who understands that he must always learn again, and who above all, on the basis of this understanding, has brought himself to the point where he continually *can learn*. This is far harder than possessing information.

Being able to learn presupposes being able to question. Questioning is the willing-to-know that we discussed earlier: the open resoluteness to be able to stand in the openness of beings. Because we are concerned with asking the question that is first in rank,

19. This essay is available in *Pathmarks*.

clearly the willing as well as the knowing are of a very special *kind*.
All the less will the *interrogative sentence* exhaustively reproduce the
question, even if it is genuinely said in a questioning way and heard
in a partnership of questioning. The question that does indeed
resonate in the interrogative sentence, but nevertheless remains
closed off and enveloped there, must first be developed. In this
way the questioning attitude must clarify and secure itself, establish
itself through exercise.

Our next task consists in *unfolding* the question "Why are there
beings at all instead of nothing?" In what direction can we unfold
it? To begin with, the question is accessible in the interrogative
sentence. The sentence takes a stab, as it were, at the question.
Hence its linguistic formulation must be correspondingly broad
and loose. Let us consider our interrogative sentence in this respect.
"Why are there beings at all instead of nothing?" The sentence
contains a break. "Why are there beings at all?" With this, the
question really has been posed. The posing of the question includes: 1) the definite indication of what is put *into* question, what
is *interrogated;* 2) the indication of that with regards to which what
is interrogated is interrogated—what is asked about. For what is
interrogated is indicated unequivocally: namely, beings. What is
asked about, what is *asked,* is the Why—that is, the ground. What
follows in the interrogative sentence—"instead of nothing?"—is an
embellishing flourish; it is just an appendix that inserts itself, as if
on its own, for the sake of an initially loose and introductory way of
speaking, as an additional turn of phrase that says nothing more
about what is interrogated and what is asked about. In fact, the
question is far more unequivocal and decisive *without* the appended
turn of phrase, which just comes from the superfluity of imprecise
talk. "Why are there beings at all?" But the addition "instead of
[18]   nothing?" is invalidated not just because we are striving for a precise formulation of the question, but even more because it says

nothing at all. For what more are we supposed to ask about Nothing? Nothing is simply nothing. Questioning has nothing more to seek here. Above all, by bringing up Nothing we do not gain the slightest thing for the knowledge of beings.[20]

Whoever talks about Nothing does not know what he is doing. In speaking about Nothing, he makes it into a something. By speaking this way, he speaks against what he means. He contra-dicts himself. But self-contradictory speech is an offense against the fundamental rule of speech (logos), against "logic." Talking about Nothing is illogical. Whoever talks and thinks illogically is an unscientific person. Now whoever goes so far as to talk about Nothing within philosophy, which after all is the home of logic, deserves all the more to be accused of offending against the fundamental rule of all thinking. Such talk about Nothing consists in utterly senseless propositions. Moreover, whoever takes Nothing seriously takes the side of nullity. He obviously promotes the spirit of negation and serves disintegration. Talking about Nothing is not only completely contrary to thought, but it undermines all culture and all faith.

---

20. Compare Heinrich Rickert, *Die Logik des Prädikats und das Problem der Ontologie* (Heidelberg: Carl Winters Universitätsbuchhandlung), 1930, p. 205. (Heidegger's note; present only in the *Gesamtausgabe* edition. Rickert writes: "With the help of the relative Nothing, we at best reach a distinctive alternative to the world, whose epistemic meaning does not seem to be essential for the Being of the world. On the one side of this alternative we have, then, the world that is, in its totality; on the other side, in contrast, we have only Nothing as the not-Being of the world. What does this alternative tell us as regards *knowledge of the world*? One will want to answer simply: nothing, and nothing *other* than just nothing! The world remains exactly what it was, and what it is, if we oppose Nothing to it as not-the-world." Rickert goes on to argue that there are, however, important logical points to be explored regarding the concept of Nothing. He concludes his book (226–236) with an analysis of Heidegger's "What is Metaphysics?" in which he identifies Heidegger's "Nothing" with *"the Other of the knowable world"* (229). In Rickert's reading of Heidegger, "the Nothing is the something *for which we have no predicates"* (231).)

Whatever both disregards the fundamental law of thinking and also destroys faith and the will to construct is pure nihilism.

Given such considerations, we will do well to strike from our interrogative sentence the superfluous turn of phrase "instead of nothing?" and restrict the sentence to the simple and precise form: "Why are there beings at all?"

Nothing would stand in the way of this, if . . . if in the formulation of our question, if in the asking of this question altogether, we had as much license as it may have seemed up to now. But in asking the question we stand within a tradition. For philosophy has constantly and always asked about the ground of beings. With this question it had its inception, in this question it will find its end, provided that it comes to an end in greatness and not in a powerless decline. The question about what is not and about Nothing has gone side by side with the question of what is, since its inception. But it does not do so superficially, as an accompanying phenomenon; instead, the question about Nothing takes shape in accordance with the breadth, depth, and originality with which the question about beings is asked on each occasion, and conversely. The manner of asking about Nothing can serve as a gauge and a criterion for the manner of asking about beings.

[19]   If we think about this, then the interrogative sentence pronounced at the start, "Why are there beings at all *instead* of nothing?" appears far more suitable to express the question about beings than the abbreviated version after all. Our introduction of talk about Nothing here is not a careless and overly enthusiastic manner of speaking, nor our own invention, but merely strict respect for the originary tradition regarding the sense of the fundamental question.

Still, this talk of Nothing remains contrary to thought in general, and leads to disintegration in particular. But what if both the concern for the proper respect for the fundamental rules of thinking as well as the fear of nihilism, which would both like to advise against talk of Nothing, rested on a misunderstanding? This is in fact the case. Of course, the misunderstanding that is being played out here is not accidental. Its ground is a lack of understanding that has long ruled the question about beings. But this lack of understanding stems from an *oblivion of Being* that is getting increasingly rigid.

For it cannot be decided so readily whether logic and its fundamental rules can provide any measure for the question about beings as such. It could be the other way around, that the whole logic that we know and that we treat like a gift from heaven is grounded in a very definite answer to the question about beings, and that consequently any thinking that simply follows the laws of thought of established logic is intrinsically incapable of even beginning to understand the question about beings, much less of actually unfolding it and leading it toward an answer. In truth, it is only an illusion of rigor and scientificity when one appeals to the principle of contradiction, and to logic in general, in order to prove that all thinking and talk about Nothing is contradictory and therefore senseless. "Logic" is then taken as a tribunal, secure for all eternity, and it goes without saying that no rational human being will call into doubt its authority as the first and last court of appeal. Whoever speaks against logic is suspected, implicitly or explicitly, of arbitrariness. This mere suspicion already counts as an argument and an objection, and one takes oneself to be exempted from further, authentic reflection.

One cannot, in fact, talk about and deal with Nothing as if it were a thing, such as the rain out there, or a mountain, or any object at all; Nothing remains in principle inaccessible to all science. Whoever truly wants to talk of Nothing must necessarily become unscientific. But this is a great misfortune only if one believes that scientific thinking alone is the authentic, rigorous thinking, that it alone can and must be made the measure even of philosophical thinking. [20]

But the reverse is the case. All scientific thinking is just a derivative and rigidified form of philosophical thinking. Philosophy never arises from or through science. Philosophy can never belong to the same order as the sciences. It belongs to a higher order, and not just "logically," as it were, or in a table of the system of sciences. Philosophy stands in a completely different domain and rank of spiritual Dasein. Only poetry is of the same order as philosophical thinking, although thinking and poetry are not identical. Talking about Nothing remains forever an abomination and an absurdity for science. But aside from the philosopher, the poet can also talk about Nothing—and not because the procedure of poetry, in the opinion of everyday understanding, is less rigorous, but because, in comparison to all mere science, an essential superiority of the spirit holds sway in poetry (only genuine and great poetry is meant). Because of this superiority, the poet always speaks as if beings were expressed and addressed for the first time. In the poetry of the poet and in the thinking of the thinker, there is always so much world-space to spare that each and every thing—a tree, a mountain, a house, the call of a bird—completely loses its indifference and familiarity.

True talk of Nothing always remains unfamiliar. It does not allow itself to be made common. It dissolves, to be sure, if one places it in the cheap acid of a merely logical cleverness. This is why we cannot begin to speak about Nothing immediately, as we can in describing a picture, for example. But the possibility of such speech about Nothing can be indicated. Consider a passage from one of the latest works of the poet Knut Hamsun, *The Road Leads On,* 1934 translation, p. 464. The work belongs together with *The Wayfarer* and *August*.[21] *The Road Leads On* depicts the last years and the end

---

21. Heidegger refers to these novels by the titles of their German translations. Hamsun's "August" trilogy begins with *Landstrykere* (1927), translated into

of this man August, who embodies the uprooted, universal know-how of today's humanity, but in the form of a Dasein that cannot lose its ties to the unfamiliar, because in its despairing powerlessness it remains genuine and superior. In his last days, this August is alone in the high mountains. The poet says: "He sits here between his ears and hears true emptiness. Quite amusing, a fancy. On the ocean (earlier, August often went to sea)[22] something stirred (at least), and there, there was a sound, something audible, a water chorus. Here — nothing meets nothing and is not there, there is not even a hole. One can only shake one's head in resignation." [21]

So there is, after all, something peculiar about Nothing. Thus we want to take up our interrogative sentence again and question through it, and see whether this "instead of nothing?" simply represents a turn of phrase that says nothing and is arbitrarily appended, or whether even in the preliminary expression of the question it has an essential sense.

To this end, let us stick at first to the abbreviated, apparently simpler and supposedly more rigorous question: "Why are there beings at all?" If we ask in this way, we start out from beings. They *are*. They are given to us, they are in front of us and can thus be

---

German as *Landstreicher* by J. Sandmeier and S. Ungermann (Munich: Albert Langen, 1928); Heidegger incorrectly calls the novel *Der Landstreicher,* in the singular. The most recent English translation is *Wayfarers,* by J. W. McFarlane (New York: Farrar, Straus, and Giroux, 1969). The second novel is *August* (1930), translated as *August Weltumsegler* by J. Sandmeier and S. Ungermann (Munich: Albert Langen, 1930) and as *August* by Eugene Gay-Tifft (New York: Coward-McCann, 1931). The conclusion of the trilogy, *Men Livet Lever* (1933), was translated as *Nach Jahr und Tag* by J. Sandmeier and S. Ungermann (Munich: Albert Langen/Georg Müller, 1934) and as *The Road Leads On* by Eugene Gay-Tifft (New York: Coward-McCann, 1934); the passage in question appears on p. 508 of the Gay-Tifft translation. We have translated it here from the German.

22. This and the following parenthetical interpolation are by Heidegger. He also inserts the dash after "here" at the beginning of the next sentence.

found before us at any time, and are also known to us within certain domains. Now the beings given to us in this way are immediately interrogated as to their ground. The questioning advances directly toward a ground. Such a method just broadens and enlarges, as it were, a procedure that is practiced every day. Somewhere in the vineyard, for example, an infestation turns up, something indisputably present at hand. One asks: where does this come from, where and what is its ground? Similarly, as a whole, beings are present at hand. One asks: where and what is the ground? This kind of questioning is represented in the simple formula: Why are there beings? Where and what is their ground? Tacitly one is asking after another, higher being. But here the question does not pertain at all to beings as a whole and as such.

But now if we ask the question in the form of our initial interrogative sentence — "Why are there beings at all instead of nothing?" — then the addition prevents us, in our questioning, from beginning directly with beings as unquestionably given, and having hardly begun, already moving on to the ground we are seeking, which is also in being. Instead, these beings are held out in a questioning manner into the possibility of not-Being. In this way, the Why gains a completely different power and urgency of questioning. Why are beings torn from the possibility of not-Being? Why do they not fall back into it constantly with no further ado? Beings are now no longer what just happens to be present at hand; they begin to waver, regardless of whether we know beings with all certainty, [22] regardless of whether we grasp them in their full scope or not. From now on, beings as such waver, insofar as we put them into question. The oscillation of this wavering reaches out into the most extreme and sharpest counterpossibility of beings, into not-Being and Nothing. The search for the Why now transforms itself accordingly. It does not just try to provide a present-at-hand ground for explaining what is present at hand — instead, we are now searching for a ground that is supposed to ground the dominance of beings as an overcoming of Nothing. The ground in question is now questioned as the ground of the decision for beings over against Nothing—more precisely, as the ground for the wavering of the beings that sustain us and unbind us, half in being, half not in being, which is also why we cannot wholly belong to any thing, not even to ourselves; yet Dasein is in each case mine.

[The qualification "in each case mine" signifies: Dasein is thrown to me so that my self may be Dasein. But Dasein means: care of the Being of beings as such that is ecstatically disclosed in care, not only of human Being. Dasein is "in each case mine"; this means neither that it is posited by me nor that it is confined to an isolated ego. Dasein is *itself* by virtue of its essential *relation to* Being in general. This is what the oft-repeated sentence in *Being and Time* means: the understanding of Being belongs to Dasein.]

Thus it is already becoming clearer that this "instead of nothing?" is no superfluous addition to the real question. Instead, this turn of phrase is an essential component of the whole interrogative sentence, which as a whole expresses a completely different question from what is meant by the question: Why are there beings? With our question we establish ourselves among beings in such a way that they forfeit their self-evidence *as beings*. Insofar as beings come to waver within the broadest and harshest possibility of oscillation—the "either beings—or nothing"—the questioning itself loses every secure foothold. Our Dasein, too, as it questions, comes into suspense, and nevertheless maintains itself, by itself, in this suspense.

But beings are not changed by our questioning. They remain what they are and as they are. After all, our questioning is just a psychospiritual process in us that, however it may play itself out, cannot concern beings themselves. Certainly, beings remain as they are revealed to us. And yet beings are not able to shrug off what is worthy of questioning: they, as what they are and how they are, could also *not* be. By no means do we experience this possibility as something that is just added on by our own thought, but beings themselves declare this possibility, they declare themselves as beings [23] in this possibility. Our questioning just opens up the domain so that beings can break open in such questionworthiness.

What we know about how such questioning happens is all too little and all too crude. In this questioning, we seem to belong completely to ourselves. Yet it is *this* questioning that pushes us into the open, provided that it itself, as a questioning, transforms itself (as does every genuine questioning), and casts a new space over and through everything.

It is simply a matter of not being seduced by overhasty theories, but instead experiencing things as they are in whatever may be nearest. This piece of chalk here is an extended, relatively stable, definitely formed, grayish-white thing, and, furthermore, a thing for writing. As certainly as it belongs precisely to this thing to lie here, the capacity not to be here and not to be so big also belongs to it. The possibility of being drawn along the blackboard and used up is not something that we merely add onto the thing with our thought. The chalk itself, as this being, *is* in this possibility; otherwise it would not be chalk as a writing implement. Every being, in turn, has this Possible in it, in a different way in each case. This Possible belongs to the chalk. It itself has in itself a definite appropriateness for a definite use. Of course, when we look for this Possible in the chalk, we are accustomed and inclined to say that we do not see it and do not grasp it. But that is a prejudice. The elimination of this prejudice is part of the unfolding of our question. For now, this question should just open up beings, in their wavering between not-Being and Being. Insofar as beings stand up against the extreme possibility of not-Being, they themselves stand in Being, and yet they have never thereby overtaken and overcome the possibility of not-Being.

Suddenly we are speaking here about the not-Being and Being of beings, without saying how what we call Being is related to beings themselves. Are they the same? The being and its Being? The distinction! What, for example, is the being ⟨*das Seiende*⟩ in this piece of chalk? Already this question is ambiguous, because the word "being" can be understood in two ways, as can the Greek *to on*. On the one hand, being means *what* at any time is in being, in particular this grayish-white, light, breakable mass, formed in such and such a way. On the other hand, "being" means that which, as it were, "makes" this be a being instead of nonbeing ⟨*nichtseiend*⟩, that which makes up the Being in the being, if it is a being. In accordance with this twofold meaning of the word "being," the Greek *to on* often designates the second meaning, that is, not the being itself, *what* is in being, but rather "the in-being," beingness, to be in being, Being.[23] In contrast, the first meaning of "being" names the things themselves that are in being, either individually or as a whole, but always with reference to these things and not to their beingness, *ousia*.[24]

[24]

The first meaning of *to on* designates *ta onta (entia)*, the second means *to einai (esse)*. We have catalogued what the being is in the piece of chalk. We were able to find this out relatively easily. We could also easily see that the chalk can also not be, that this chalk ultimately need not be here and need not be at all. But then, as

23. "... also nicht das Seiende selbst, *was* seiend ist, sondern 'das Seiend,' die Seiendheit, das Seiendsein, das Sein."
24. The Greek noun *ousia* is formed from the present participle of the verb *einai* (to be). Normally meaning "goods, possessions," it is developed by Plato and Aristotle into a central philosophical concept, and is usually translated as "essence" or "substance." Heidegger's *Seiendheit* (beingness) corresponds directly to the grammatical structure of *ousia*.

distinguished from that which can stand in Being or fall back into not-Being, as distinguished from the being—what is Being? Is it the same as the being? We ask this once again. But we did not include Being in our earlier catalogue of attributes—we listed only material mass, grayish-white, light, formed in such and such a manner, breakable. Now where is Being situated? It must after all belong to the chalk, for this chalk itself *is*.

We encounter beings everywhere; they surround us, carry and control us, enchant and fulfill us, elevate and disappoint us, but where in all this is the Being of beings, and what does it consist in? One could answer: this distinction between beings and their Being may at times have some linguistic importance, perhaps even some meaning; one can make this distinction in mere thought, that is, in re-presentation and opinion, without this distinction's corresponding to anything that is. But even this distinction made only in thought is questionable; for it remains unclear *what* we are supposed to think under the name "Being." Meanwhile, it is enough to be familiar with beings and to secure mastery over them. Distinguishing Being on top of this is artificial and leads to nothing.

We have already made some remarks about this popular question of what comes of such distinctions. Let us now simply reflect on our enterprise. We ask, "Why are there beings at all instead of nothing?" And in this question we apparently restrict ourselves only to beings and avoid empty brooding about Being. But what are we really asking? Why beings as such are. We are asking about the ground for the fact that beings *are,* and are what they *are,* and that there is not nothing instead. We are asking at bottom about Being. But how? We are asking about the Being of beings. We are interrogating beings in regards to their Being.

But if we persevere in the questioning, we are really already asking *ahead,* about Being in regard to its ground, even if this question does not develop and it remains undecided whether Being itself is not already in itself a ground and ground enough. If we pose [25] this question about Being as the first question in rank, then should we do so without knowing how it stands with Being and how Being stands in its distinction from beings? How are we even supposed to inquire into the ground for the Being of beings, let alone be able to find it out, if we have not adequately conceived, understood and grasped Being itself? This enterprise would be just as hopeless as if someone wanted to explain the cause and ground of a fire and declared that he need not bother with the course of the fire or the investigation of its scene.

So it turns out that the question "Why are there beings at all instead of nothing?" forces us to the prior question: *"How does it stand with Being?"*[25]

We are now asking about something that we hardly grasp, something that is now no more than the sound of a word for us and that puts us in danger of falling victim to the mere idolization of words in our further questioning. So it is all the more necessary for us to get clear from the outset about how it stands for us at present with Being and with our understanding of Being. Here it is important above all to impress on our experience again and again the fact that we are not able to lay hold of the *Being of* beings directly and expressly, neither by way of beings, nor in beings — nor anywhere else at all.

A few examples should help. Over there, on the other side of the street, stands the high school building. A being. We can scour every side of the building from the outside, roam through the inside from basement to attic, and note everything that can be found there: hallways, stairs, classrooms, and their furnishings. Everywhere we

25. *"Wie steht es um das Sein?"* This expression could be translated more colloquially as "What is the status of Being?" or even "What about Being?" We have kept the German idiom in order to preserve Heidegger's various plays on "standing."

find beings, and in a very definite order. Where now is the Being of this high school? It *is*, after all. The building *is*. The Being of this being belongs to it if anything does, and nevertheless we do not find this Being within the being.

Moreover, Being does not consist in our observing beings. The building stands there even if we do not observe it. We can come across it only because it already *is*. In addition, the Being of this building does not at all seem to be identical for everybody. For us, as observers or passers-by, it is not what it is for the students who sit inside, not just because they see it only from the inside but because for them this building really is what it is and how it is. One can, as it were, smell the Being of such buildings, and often after decades one still has the scent in one's nose. The scent provides the Being of this being much more directly and truly than it could be communicated by any description or inspection. On the other hand, the subsistence of the building does not depend on this scent that is hovering around somewhere.

How does it stand with Being? Can we see Being? We see beings — the chalk here. But do we see Being as we see color and light and dark? Or do we hear, smell, taste, or touch Being? We hear the motorcycle roaring along the street. We hear the grouse flying off through the mountain forest in its gliding flight. Yet really we are only hearing the noise of the motor's rattling, the noise that the grouse causes. Furthermore, it is hard and unusual for us to describe the pure noise, because it is precisely *not* what we generally hear. We always hear *more* [than the mere noise]. We hear the flying bird, although strictly speaking we have to say: a grouse is nothing we can hear, it is not a tone that could be registered on a scale. And so it is with the other senses. We touch velvet, silk; we see them without further ado as such and such a being, and the one is in being distinctly from the other. Where does Being lie and in what does it consist?

[26]

Yet we must look around us still more thoroughly and contemplate the narrower and wider sphere within which we dwell, daily and hourly, knowing and unknowing, a sphere that constantly shifts its boundaries and suddenly is broken through.

A heavy thunderstorm gathering in the mountains "is," or—it makes no difference here—"was" in the night. What does its Being consist in?

A distant mountain range under a vast sky—such a thing "is." What does its Being consist in? When and to whom does it reveal itself? To the hiker who enjoys the landscape, or to the peasant who makes his daily living from it and in it, or to the meteorologist who has to give a weather report? Who among them lays hold of Being? All and none. Or do these people only lay hold of particular aspects of the mountain range under the vast sky, not the mountain range itself as it "is," not what its real Being consists in? Who can lay hold of this? Or is it nonsensical, against the sense of Being in the first place, to ask about what is in itself, behind those aspects? Does Being lie in the aspects?

The portal of an early Romanesque church is a being. How and to whom does Being reveal itself? To the art historian who visits and photographs it on an excursion, or to the abbot who passes through the portal with his monks for a religious celebration, or to the children who play in its shadow on a summer's day? How does it stand with the Being of this being? [27]

A state—it *is*. What does its Being consist in? In the fact that the state police arrest a suspect, or that in a ministry of the Reich so and so many typewriters clatter away and record the dictation of state secretaries and ministers? Or "is" the state in the discussion between the Führer and the English foreign minister? The state *is*. But where is Being situated? Is it located anywhere at all?

A painting by Van Gogh: a pair of sturdy peasant shoes, nothing else. The picture really represents nothing. Yet you are alone at once with what *is* there, as if you yourself were heading homeward from the field on a late autumn evening, tired, with your hoe, as the last potato fires smolder out. What is in being here? The canvas? The brushstrokes? The patches of color?

In everything we have mentioned, what is the Being of beings? Really, how is it that we can run around in the world and stand around with our stupid pretensions and our so-called cleverness?

Everything we have mentioned *is*, after all, and nevertheless — if we want to lay hold of Being it is always as if we were reaching into a void. The Being that we are asking about is almost like Nothing, and yet we are always trying to arm and guard ourselves against the presumption of saying that all beings *are not*.

But Being remains undiscoverable, almost like Nothing, or in the end *entirely* so. The word "Being" is then finally just an empty word. It means nothing actual, tangible, real. Its meaning is an unreal vapor. So in the end Nietzsche is entirely right when he calls the "highest concepts" such as Being "the final wisp of evaporating reality" (*Twilight of the Idols* VIII, 78).[26] Who would want to chase after such a vapor, the term for which is just the name for a huge error! "In fact, nothing up to now has been more naively persuasive than the error of Being . . ." (VIII, 80).[27]

"Being" — a vapor and an error? What Nietzsche says here about Being is no casual remark, jotted down during the frenzy of labor in preparation for his authentic and never completed work. Instead, it is his guiding conception of Being since the earliest days of his philosophical labor. It supports and determines his philosophy from the ground up. But this philosophy remains, even now, well [28] guarded against all the clumsy and trifling importunities of the horde of scribblers that is becoming ever more numerous around

26. §4 of " 'Reason' in Philosophy," in *Twilight of the Idols*.
27. *Ibid.*, §5.

him today. It seems that his work hardly has the worst of this misuse behind it. In speaking of Nietzsche here, we want nothing to do with all this—nor with a blind hero worship. The task is much too decisive and, at the same time, too sober for such worship. It consists first and foremost in fully unfolding that which was realized through Nietzsche by means of a truly engaged attack on him. Being—a vapor, an error! If this is so, then the only possible conclusion is that we should also give up the question, "Why are there beings as such and as a whole instead of nothing?" For what is the point of the question anymore, if what it puts into question is just a vapor and an error?

Does Nietzsche speak the truth? Or is he himself only the final victim of a long-standing errancy and neglect, but *as* this victim the unrecognized witness to a new necessity?

Is it Being's fault that Being is so confused, and is it the fault of the word that it remains so empty, or is it our fault, because in all our bustling and chasing after beings, we have nevertheless fallen out of Being? What if the fault is not our own, we of today, nor that of our immediate or most distant forebears, but rather is based in a happening that runs through Western history from the inception onward, a happening that the eyes of all historians will never reach, but which nevertheless happens—formerly, today, and in the future? What if it were possible that human beings, that peoples in their greatest machinations and exploits, have a relation to beings but have long since fallen out of Being, without knowing it, and what if this were the innermost and most powerful ground of their decline? [Cf. *Being and Time*, §38, especially pp. 179 f.][28]

These are not questions that we pose here casually, nor do we pose them on account of some predisposition or worldview. Instead, they are questions to which we are forced by that prior ques-

28. In parentheses in the 1953 edition.

tion, which springs necessarily from the main question: "How does it stand with Being?"—a sober question perhaps, but certainly a very useless question, too. And yet a *question, the question:* "Is 'Being' a mere word and its meaning a vapor, or is it the spiritual fate of the West?"

This Europe, in its unholy blindness always on the point of cutting its own throat, lies today in the great pincers between Russia on the one side and America on the other. Russia and America, seen metaphysically, are both the same: the same hopeless frenzy of unchained technology and of the rootless organization of the average man. When the farthest corner of the globe has been conquered technologically and can be exploited economically; when any incident you like, in any place you like, at any time you like, becomes accessible as fast as you like; when you can simultaneously "experience" an assassination attempt against a king in France and a symphony concert in Tokyo; when time is nothing but speed, instantaneity, and simultaneity, and time as history has vanished from all Dasein of all peoples; when a boxer counts as the great man of a people; when the tallies of millions at mass meetings are a triumph; then, yes then, there still looms like a specter over all this uproar the question: what for? — where to? — and what then?

The spiritual decline of the earth has progressed so far that peoples are in danger of losing their last spiritual strength, the strength that makes it possible even to see the decline [which is meant in relation to the fate of "Being"][29] and to appraise it as such. This simple observation has nothing to do with cultural pessimism — nor with any optimism either, of course; for the darkening of the world, the flight of the gods, the destruction of the earth, the reduction of human beings to a mass, the hatred and mistrust of everything creative and free has already reached such proportions throughout

29. In parentheses in the 1953 edition.

the whole earth that such childish categories as pessimism and optimism have long become laughable.

We lie in the pincers. Our people, as standing in the center, suffers the most intense pressure — our people, the people richest in neighbors and hence the most endangered people, and for all that, the metaphysical people. We are sure of this vocation; but this people will gain a fate from its vocation only when it creates *in itself* a resonance, a possibility of resonance for this vocation, and grasps its tradition creatively. All this implies that this people, as a historical people, must transpose itself — and with it the history of the West — from the center of their future happening into the originary realm of the powers of Being. Precisely if the great decision regarding Europe is not to go down the path of annihilation — precisely then can this decision come about only through the development of new, historically *spiritual* forces from the center.

To ask: how does it stand with Being? — this means nothing less than to *repeat and retrieve* (*wieder-holen*) the inception of our historical-spiritual Dasein, in order to transform it into the other inception. Such a thing is possible. It is in fact the definitive form of history, because it has its onset in a happening that grounds history. But an inception is not repeated when one shrinks back to it as something that once was, something that by now is familiar and is simply to be imitated, but rather when the inception is begun again *more originally,* and with all the strangeness, darkness, insecurity that a genuine inception brings with it. Repetition as we understand it is anything but the ameliorating continuation of what has been, by means of what has been. [30]

The question "How does it stand with Being?" is included as a prior question in our guiding question: "Why are there beings at all instead of nothing?" If we now set out to pursue what stands in question in the prior question, namely Being, then Nietzsche's saying at once proves to be completely true after all. For if we look closely, what more is "Being" to us than a mere locution, an indeterminate meaning, intangible as a vapor? Nietzsche's judgment, of course, is meant in a purely dismissive sense. For him, "Being" is a deception that never should have happened. "Being"—indeterminate, evanescent as a vapor? It is in fact so. But we don't want to evade this fact. To the contrary, we must try to get clear about its factuality in order to survey its full scope.

Through our questioning, we are entering a landscape; to be in this landscape is the fundamental prerequisite for restoring rootedness to historical Dasein. We will have to ask why this fact, the fact that "Being" remains a vaporous word for us, stands out precisely today; we will have to ask whether and why it has persisted for a long time. We should learn to know that this fact is not as innocuous as it seems at first sight. For ultimately what matters is not that the word "Being" remains just a noise for us and its meaning just a vapor, but that we have fallen out of what this word is saying, and for now cannot find our way back; it is on *these* grounds and on no others that the word "Being" no longer applies to anything, that everything, if we merely want to take hold of it, dissolves like a shred of cloud in the sun. Because this is so, we *ask* about Being. And we *ask* because we know that truths have never yet fallen into a people's lap. The fact that even now one still cannot understand this question, and does not want to understand it, even if it is asked in a still *more* originary way, takes from this question none of its inevitability.

Of course, one can show oneself to be very clever and superior, and once again trot out the well-known reflection: "Being" is simply the most universal concept. Its range extends to any and every thing, even to Nothing, which, as something thought and said, "is" also something. So there is, in the strict sense of the word, nothing [31] above and beyond the range of this most universal concept "Being" in terms of which it could be further defined. One must be satisfied with this highest generality. The concept of Being is an ultimate. And it also corresponds to a law of logic that says: the more comprehensive a concept is in its scope — and what could be more comprehensive than the concept "Being"? — the more indeterminate and empty is its content.

For every normally thinking human being — and we all want to be normal — such trains of thought are immediately and entirely convincing. But now the question is whether the assessment of Being as the most universal concept reaches the essence of Being, or whether it so misinterprets Being from the start that questioning becomes hopeless. The question is whether Being can count only as the most universal concept that unavoidably presents itself in all particular concepts or whether Being has a completely different essence, and thus is anything but the object of an "ontology," if one takes this word in its established meaning.

The term "ontology" was first coined in the seventeenth century. It designates the development of the traditional doctrine of beings into a philosophical discipline and a branch of the philosophical system. But the traditional doctrine is the academic analysis and ordering of what for Plato and Aristotle, and again for Kant, was a *question,* though to be sure a question that was no longer originary. The word "ontology" is still used this way even today. Under this title, philosophy busies itself with the composition and exposition of a branch within its system. But one can also take the word "ontology" "in the broadest sense," "without reference to ontological directions and tendencies" (cf. *Being and Time,* 1927, p. 11, top). In this case "ontology" means the effort to put Being into words, and to do so by passing through the question of how it stands with Being [not just with beings as such].[30] But because until now this question has found neither an accord nor even a resonance, but

30. In parentheses in the 1953 edition.

instead it is explicitly rejected by the various circles of academic philosophical scholarship, which pursues an "ontology" in the traditional sense, it may be good in the future to forgo the use of the terms "ontology" and "ontological." Two modes of questioning which, as is only now becoming clearer, are worlds apart should not bear the same name.

[32]   We *ask* the question — How does it stand with Being? What is the meaning of Being? — *not* in order to compose an ontology in the traditional style, much less to reckon up critically the mistakes of earlier attempts at ontology. We are concerned with something completely different. The point is to restore the historical Dasein of human beings — and this also always means our ownmost future Dasein, in the whole of the history that is allotted to us — back to the power of Being that is to be opened up originally; all this, to be sure, only within the limits of philosophy's capability.

From the fundamental question of metaphysics, "Why are there beings at all instead of nothing?" we have extracted the *prior question* ⟨Vor-frage⟩: How does it stand with Being? The relation between these questions needs to be elucidated, for it is in a class of its own. Usually, a preliminary question ⟨Vorfrage⟩ is settled in advance and outside the main question, although with a view to it. But philosophical questions are in principle never settled as if some day one could set them aside. Here the preliminary question does not stand outside the fundamental question at all but is, as it were, the hearth-fire that glows in the asking of the fundamental question, the hearth at the heart of all questioning. That is to say: when we first ask the fundamental question, everything depends on our taking up the decisive fundamental position in asking its *prior question*, and winning and securing the bearing that is essential here. This is why we brought the question about Being into connection with the fate of Europe, where the fate of the earth is being decided, while for Europe itself our historical Dasein proves to be the center.

The question ran:

Is Being a mere word and its meaning a vapor, or does what is named with the word "Being" hold within it the spiritual fate of the West?

To many ears the question may sound forced and exaggerated. For if pressed, one could indeed imagine that discussing the question of Being might ultimately, at a very great remove and in a very indirect manner, have some relation to the decisive historical question of the earth, but by no means in such a way that from out of the history of the earth's spirit, the fundamental position and bearing of our questioning could directly be determined. And yet there is such a connection. Because our aim is to get the asking of the prior question going, we now must show how, and to what extent, the asking of this prior question moves directly, and from the ground up, along with the decisive historical question. To demonstrate this, it is necessary at first to anticipate an essential insight in the form of an assertion.

We assert that the asking of this prior question, and thereby the [33] asking of the fundamental question of metaphysics, is a historical questioning through and through. But does not metaphysics, and philosophy in general, thereby become a historical science? After all, historical science investigates the temporal, while philosophy, in contrast, investigates the supratemporal. Philosophy is historical only insofar as it, like every work of the spirit, realizes itself in the course of time. But in this sense, the designation of metaphysical questioning as historical cannot characterize metaphysics but can only propose something obvious. Thus either the assertion says nothing and is superfluous, or it is impossible, because it mixes up fundamentally different kinds of science: philosophy and the science of history.

In reply to this it must be said:

1. Metaphysics and philosophy are not science at all, and further-

more, the fact that their questioning is at bottom historical cannot make them so.

2. For its part, the science of history does not at all determine, as science, the originary relation to history; instead, it always already presupposes such a relation. This is why the science of history can either deform the relation to history—a relation that is itself always historical—misinterpret it and reduce it to mere antiquarian expertise, or else prepare essential domains of vision for the already grounded relation to history and let history be experienced in its bindingness. A historical relation of our historical Dasein to history can become an object of knowledge and a developed state of knowledge; but it need not. Besides, not all relations to history can be scientifically objectified and become scientific, and in fact it is precisely the essential relations that cannot. The science of history can *never institute* the historical relation to history. It can only illuminate a relation once it is instituted, ground it informatively, which to be sure is an essential necessity for the historical Dasein of a knowing people, and thus neither merely an "advantage" nor a "disadvantage."[31] It is only in philosophy—*in distinction from every science*—that essential relations to beings always take shape; and therefore this relation *can,* indeed *must,* be an originally historical one for us today.

But in order to understand our assertion that the "metaphysical" asking of the prior question is historical through and through, one must consider one thing above all: in this assertion, history is not [34] equivalent to what is past; for this is precisely what is no longer happening.[32] But much less is history what is merely contemporary,

31. With the terms "antiquarian," "advantage," and "disadvantage," Heidegger alludes to Nietzsche's "On the Advantage and Disadvantage of History for Life." Cf. *Being and Time,* §76. In the winter semester of 1938–1939 Heidegger gave a lecture course on this essay by Nietzsche.

32. Throughout this passage and elsewhere, Heidegger plays on *Geschichte* and *geschehen* ("history" and "happen").

which also never happens, but always just "passes," makes its entrance and goes by. History as happening is determined from the future, takes over what has been, and acts and endures its way through the *present*. It is precisely the present that vanishes in the happening.

Our asking of the fundamental metaphysical question is historical because it opens up the happening of human Dasein in its essential relations—that is, its relations to beings as such and as a whole—opens it up to possibilities not yet asked about, futures to come ⟨Zu-künften⟩, and thereby also binds it back to its inception that has been, and thus sharpens and burdens it in its present. In this questioning, our Dasein is summoned to its history in the full sense of the word and is called to make a decision in it—and this is not a derivative, useful application of this questioning in terms of morality and worldviews. Instead, the fundamental position and bearing of the questioning is in itself historical, stands and holds itself in the happening, and questions on the ground of this happening and for this happening.

But we still lack the essential insight into how far this asking of the question of Being, an asking which is in itself historical, intrinsically belongs to the world history of the earth. We said: on the earth, all over it, a darkening of the world is happening. The essential happenings in this darkening are: the flight of the gods, the destruction of the earth, the reduction of human beings to a mass, the preeminence of the mediocre.

What does "world" mean, when we speak of the darkening of the world? World is always *spiritual* world. The animal has no world ⟨Welt⟩, nor any environment ⟨Umwelt⟩. The darkening of the world contains within itself a *disempowering of the spirit,* its dissolution, diminution, suppression, and misinterpretation. We will try to elucidate this disempowering of the spirit in *one* respect, namely, the misinterpretation of the spirit. We said: Europe lies in the pincers between Russia and America, which are metaphysically the same, namely in regard to their world-character and their relation to the spirit. The situation of Europe is all the more dire because the disempowering of the spirit comes from Europe itself and—though prepared by earlier factors—is determined at last by its own spiritual situation in the first half of the nineteenth century. Among us at that time something happened that is all too readily and swiftly characterized as the "collapse of German idealism." This formula is like a shield behind which the already dawning spiritlessness, the dissolution of spiritual powers, the deflection of all originary questioning about grounds and the bonding to such grounds, are hidden and obscured. For it was not German idealism that collapsed, but it was the age that was no longer strong enough to stand up to the greatness, breadth, and originality of that spiritual world—that is, truly to realize it, which always means something other than merely applying propositions and insights. Dasein began to slide into a world that lacked that depth from which the essential always comes and returns to human beings, thereby forcing them to superiority and allowing them to act on the basis of rank. All things sank to the same level, to a surface resembling a blind mirror that no longer mirrors, that casts nothing back. The prevailing dimension became that of extension and number. *To be able*—this no longer means to spend and to lavish, thanks to lofty overabundance and the mastery of energies; instead, it means only practicing a routine in which anyone can be trained, always combined with a certain amount of sweat and display. In America and Russia, then, this all intensified until it turned into the measureless so-on-and-so-forth of the ever-identical and the indifferent, until finally this quantitative temper became a quality of its own. By now in those countries the predominance of a cross-section of the indifferent is no longer something inconsequential and merely barren but is the onslaught of that which aggressively destroys all rank and all that is world-

[35]

spiritual, and portrays these as a lie. This is the onslaught of what we call the demonic [in the sense of the destructively evil].[33] There are many omens of the arising of this demonism, in unison with the growing perplexity and uncertainty of Europe against it and within itself. One such omen is the disempowering of the spirit in the sense of its misinterpretation—a happening in the middle of which we still stand today. Let us briefly describe four aspects of this misinterpretation of the spirit.

1. One decisive aspect is the reinterpretation of the spirit as *intelligence,* and this as mere astuteness in the examination, calculation and observation of given things, their possible modification, and their additional elaboration. This astuteness is a matter of mere talent and practice and mass distribution. This astuteness is itself subject to the possibility of organization, none of which ever applies to the spirit. The whole phenomenon of literati and aesthetes is just a late consequence and mutation of the spirit falsified as intelligence. *Mere* ingenuity is the semblance of spirit and veils its absence.

2. Spirit, thus falsified as intelligence, is thereby reduced to the role of a tool in the service of something else, a tool whose handling can be taught and learned. Whether this service of intelligence now [36] relates to the regulation and mastery of the material relations of production (as in Marxism) or in general to the clever ordering and clarification of everything that lies before us and is already posited (as in positivism), or whether it fulfills itself in organizing and directing the vital resources and race of a people—be this as it may, the spirit as intelligence becomes the powerless superstructure to something else, which, because it is spirit-less or even hostile to spirit, counts as authentic reality. If one understands spirit as intelligence, as Marxism in its most extreme form has done, then it is

33. In parentheses in the 1953 edition.

completely correct to say in response that the spirit — that is, intelligence, in the ordering of the effective energies of human Dasein — must always be subordinated to healthy bodily fitness and to character. But this ordering becomes untrue as soon as one grasps the essence of spirit in its truth. For all true energy and beauty of the body, all sureness and boldness of the sword, but also all genuineness and ingenuity of the understanding, are grounded in the spirit, and they rise or fall only according to the current power or powerlessness of the spirit. Spirit is what sustains and rules, the first and the last, not a merely indispensable third element.

3. As soon as this instrumental misinterpretation of the spirit sets in, the powers of spiritual happening — poetry and fine arts, statescraft and religion — shift to a sphere where they can be *consciously* cultivated and planned. At the same time, they get divided up into regions. The spiritual world becomes culture, and in the creation and conservation of culture the individual seeks to fulfill himself. These regions become fields of a free endeavor that sets its own standards for itself, according to the meaning of "standards" that it can still attain. These standards of validity for production and use are called values. Cultural values secure meaning for themselves in the whole of a culture only by restricting themselves to their self-validity: poetry for poetry's sake, art for art's sake, science for science's sake.

In respect to science, which concerns us especially here in the university, the situation of the last few decades, a situation which remains unchanged today despite some cleansing, is easy to see. Although two seemingly different conceptions of science are now seemingly struggling against each other — science as technical and practical professional knowledge and science as a cultural value in itself — nevertheless *both* are moving along *the same* decadent path of a misinterpretation and disempowering of the spirit. They are distinct only in that the technical and practical conception of science as specialized science may still lay claim to the merit of open and clear consistency within today's situation, whereas the reactionary interpretation of science as a cultural value, which is now again appearing, tries to hide the powerlessness of the spirit through an unconscious mendacity. The confusion of spiritlessness can even go so far that the practical, technical explanation of science confesses itself at the same time to be science as cultural value, so that both understand each other very well in the same dearth of spirit. One may wish to call the arrangement of the amalgam of the specialized sciences for purposes of teaching and research a university, but this is now just a name and no longer an originally unifying spiritual power that imposes duties. What I said here in my inaugural address in 1929 about the German university still applies today: "The regions of science lie far asunder. Their ways of handling their subject matters are fundamentally different. This disintegrated multiplicity of disciplines is still meaningfully maintained[34] today only through the technical organization of universities and faculties and through the practical aims of the disciplines. Yet the rootedness of the sciences in their essential ground has atrophied" (*What is Metaphysics?* 1929, p. 8).[35] In all its areas, science today is a technical, practical matter of gaining information and communicating it. No awakening of the spirit at all can proceed from it as science. Science itself needs such an awakening.

4. The last misinterpretation of the spirit rests on the formerly mentioned falsifications that represent the spirit as intelligence, this intelligence as a tool serviceable for goals, and this tool, together

34. Heidegger misquotes himself slightly. The original *gehalten* appears here as *erhalten,* with little change in meaning.
35. "Was ist Metaphysik?" in *Wegmarken* (Frankfurt: Vittorio Klostermann, 1978), 104. Cf. "What is Metaphysics?" in *Pathmarks,* 82–83.

with what can be produced, as the realm of culture. The spirit as intelligence in the service of goals and the spirit as culture finally become showpieces and spectacles that one takes into account along with many others, that one publicly trots out and exhibits as proof that one does *not* want to deny culture in favor of barbarism. Russian Communism, after an initially purely negative attitude, went directly over to such propagandistic tactics.

Against these multiple misinterpretations of the spirit, we determine the essence of the spirit briefly in this way (I choose the formulation from my Rectoral Address, because there everything is succinctly brought together in accordance with the occasion): "Spirit is neither empty acuity, nor the noncommittal play of wit, nor the understanding's boundless pursuit of analysis, nor even world reason, but rather spirit is originally attuned, knowing reso-

[38] lution to the essence of Being" (*Rectoral Address,* p. 13).[36] Spirit is the empowering of the powers of beings as such and as a whole. Where spirit rules, beings as such always and in each case come more into being ⟨*wird . . . seiender*⟩. Asking about beings as such and as a whole, asking the question of Being, is then one of the essential fundamental conditions for awakening the spirit, and thus for an originary world of historical Dasein, and thus for subduing the danger of the darkening of the world, and thus for taking over the historical mission of our people, the people of the center of the West. Only in these broad strokes can we make plain here to what ex-

36. Cf. *Die Selbstbehauptung der deutschen Universität; Das Rektorat 1933/34* (Frankfurt: Vittorio Klostermann, 1983), 14; in the original Rectoral Address, the first occurrence of the word *Geist* at the beginning of this passage is printed in quotation marks. For another English translation, see "The Self-Assertion of the German University," trans. Lisa Harries, in *Martin Heidegger and National Socialism: Questions and Answers,* ed. Günther Neske and Emil Kettering (New York: Paragon, 1990), 9.

tent asking the question of Being is in itself historical through and through, and that accordingly our question, whether Being is to remain a mere vapor for us or whether it is to become the fate of the West, is anything but an exaggeration and a figure of speech.

But if our question about Being has this essential character of decision, then we must above all proceed in full seriousness with the *fact* that gives the question its immediate necessity: the fact that Being is in fact almost nothing more than a word now, and its meaning is an evanescent vapor. We do not just stand before this fact as something alien and other, which we may simply ascertain as an occurrence in its Being-present-at-hand. The fact is such that we stand within it. It is a state of our Dasein, though certainly not in the sense of a property that we could simply exhibit psychologically. "State" here means our whole constitution, the way in which we ourselves are constituted in relation to Being. This is not a matter of psychology; instead, it concerns our history in an essential respect. If we call it a "fact" that Being for us is a mere word and a vapor, this is a very provisional formulation. With it, we are for once simply establishing and coming to grips with something that has still not been thought through at all, something that we still have no place for, even if it seems as if it were an occurrence among us, we human beings, "in" us, as one likes to say.

One would like to treat the particular fact that Being for us is now just an empty word and an evanescent vapor as a case of the more general fact that many words — indeed, the essential words — are in the same situation, that language in general is used up and abused, that language is an indispensable but masterless, arbitrarily applicable means of communication, as indifferent as a means of public transportation, such as a streetcar, which everyone gets on and off. Thus everyone talks and writes unhindered and above all [39] *unendangered* in language. That is certainly correct. Moreover, only a very few are still in a position to think through in its full scope this misrelation and unrelation of today's Dasein to language.

But the emptiness of the word "Being," the complete withering of its naming force, is not just a particular case of the general abuse of language — instead, the destroyed relation to Being as such is the real ground for our whole misrelation to language.

The organizations for the purification of language and for defense against its progressive mutilation deserve respect. Nevertheless, through such institutions one finally demonstrates only more clearly that one no longer knows what language is all about. Because the fate of language is grounded in the particular *relation* of a people to *Being*, the question about *Being* will be most intimately intertwined with the question about *language* for us. It is more than a superficial accident that now, as we make a start in laying out the above mentioned fact of the vaporization of Being in all its scope, we find ourselves forced to proceed from linguistic considerations.

CHAPTER TWO

On the Grammar and Etymology
of the Word "Being"

IF FOR US Being is just an empty word and an evanescent meaning, then we must at least try to grasp fully this last remnant of a connection. So we ask, to begin with:

1. What sort of word is this anyway—"Being"—as regards its formal character as a word?

2. What does linguistics tell us about the originary meaning of this word?

To put this in scholarly terms, we are asking 1) about the grammar and 2) about the etymology of the word "Being."[1]

The grammatical analysis of words is neither exclusively nor primarily concerned with their written or spoken form. It takes these formal elements as clues to definite directions and differences in direction in the possible meanings of words; these directions

1. In regard to this section, see now Ernst Fraenkel, "Das Sein und seine Modalitäten," in *Lexis (Studien zur Sprachphilosophie, Sprachgeschichte und Begriffsforschung)*, ed. Johannes Lohmann, vol. II (1949), 149 ff. (Heidegger's note in the 1953 edition.)

dictate how the words can be used within a sentence or within a larger discursive structure. The words: he goes, we went, they have gone, go!, going, to go—these are inflections of the same word according to definite directions of meaning. We are familiar with these from the terminology of linguistics: present indicative, imperfect, perfect, imperative, participle, infinitive. But for a long time these terms have just been technical instruments that we use mechanically to dissect language and establish rules. Wherever a more originary relation to language still stirs, one feels how dead these grammatical forms are as mere mechanisms. Language and the study of language have gotten stuck in these rigid forms as if in a net of steel. Beginning with the spiritless and barren language instruction in the schoolroom, these formal concepts and grammarbook labels become empty shells for us, understood and understandable by no one.

[41]

It is certainly correct that instead of this, students should learn something from their teachers about the prehistory and early history of the Germans. But all of this will just as quickly deteriorate into the same barren wasteland if we do not succeed in reconstructing the spiritual world of the school from within and from the ground up, which means furnishing the school with a spiritual, not a scientific, atmosphere. And for this, the first thing we need is a real revolution in our relation to language. But for this we have to revolutionize the teachers, and for this the university first has to transform itself and come to grips with its task, instead of puffing itself up with irrelevancies. It simply no longer occurs to us that everything that we have all known for so long, and all too well, could be otherwise—that these grammatical forms have not dissected and regulated language as such since eternity like an absolute, that instead, they grew out of a very definite interpretation of the Greek and Latin languages. This was all based on the assumption that language, too, is something in being, something that, like other beings, can be made accessible and circumscribed in a definite manner. How such an undertaking gets carried out and to what extent it is valid clearly depends on the fundamental conception of Being that guides it.

The determination of the essence of language, and even the act of asking about it, regulates itself in each case according to what has become the prevailing preconception about the essence of beings and about how we comprehend essence. But essence and Being speak in language. The reference to this connection is important here, because we are asking about the word "Being." If we make use of the traditional grammar and its forms in this grammatical designation of the word, as is at first unavoidable, then in this particular case, we must do so with the fundamental reservation that these grammatical forms are insufficient for what we are striving toward. In the course of our study we will show that this is so in regard to one essential grammatical form.

But this demonstration will soon dispel the impression that what is at issue is just an improvement in grammar. What is really at issue is an essential clarification of the essence of Being as regards its essential involvement with the essence of language. We should keep this in mind in what follows, so that we do not mistake the linguistic and grammatical investigations for a barren and irrelevant game. We will ask 1) about the grammar and 2) about the etymology of the word "Being."

1. The Grammar of the Word "Being" [42]

What sort of word is this, "Being," as regards its form as a word? "Being" ⟨*das Sein*⟩ corresponds to "going," "falling," "dreaming" ⟨*das Gehen, das Fallen, das Träumen*⟩, etc. These linguistic forms behave like the words "bread," "house," "grass," "thing." But we immediately notice the difference from the first set of words: we can easily trace the first set back to the temporal words (verbs) "to go," "to fall" ⟨*gehen, fallen*⟩, etc., which does not seem possible with the second set. It is true that for "house" there is the form "to house": "he is housed in the forest." But the grammatical relation, in terms of meaning, between "the going" ⟨*das Gehen*⟩ and "to go" ⟨*gehen*⟩ is different from the relation between "the house" ⟨*das Haus*⟩ and "the housing" ⟨*das Hausen*⟩. On the other hand, there are word forms that correspond exactly to the first group ("the going," "the flying") but resemble "the bread" and "the house" in their character and meaning. For example, "The ambassador gave a dinner ⟨*Essen:* verbal substantive of *essen,* to eat)"; "he died of an incurable illness ⟨*Leiden:* verbal substantive of *leiden,* to suffer)."[2] Here we no longer notice the relation to a verb. From this verb has come a substantive, a name, and this by way of a definite form of the verb (the temporal word) that in Latin is called the *modus infinitivus*.

We also find the same relations in our word "Being" ⟨*das Sein*⟩. This substantive derives from the infinitive "to be" ⟨*sein*⟩, which belongs with the forms "you are," "he is," "we were," "you have been." "Being" as a substantive came from the verb. We thus call the word "Being" a "verbal substantive." Once we have cited this grammatical form, the linguistic characterization of the word "Being" is complete. We are talking here at length about well-known and self-evident things. But let us speak better and more carefully: these linguistic, grammatical distinctions are worn out and commonplace; they are by no means "self-evident." So we must turn an eye to the grammatical forms in question (verb, substantive, substantivization of the verb, infinitive, participle).

We can easily see that in the formation of the word "Being," the

---

2. Heidegger's examples are impossible to translate into idiomatic English here. An English sentence of the type he is discussing would be: "There was quite a *to-do* at the embassy last night."

decisive precursor is the infinitive "to be." This form of the verb is tranformed into a substantive. The character of our word "Being," as a word, is determined, accordingly, by three grammatical forms: verb, infinitive, and substantive. Thus our first task is to understand the meaning of these grammatical forms. Of the three we have named, verb and substantive are among those that were first recognized at the start of Western grammar and that even today are taken as the fundamental forms of words and of language in general. And so, with the question about the essence of the substantive and of the verb, we find ourselves in the midst of the question about the essence of language. For the question of whether the primordial form of the word is the noun (substantive) or the verb coincides with the question of the originary character of speech and speaking. In turn, this question entails the question of the origin of language. We cannot start by immediately going into this question. We are forced onto a detour. We will restrict ourselves in what follows to that grammatical form which provides the transitional phase in the development of the verbal substantive: the infinitive (to go, to come, to fall, to sing, to hope, to be, etc.).

[43]

What does "infinitive" mean? This term is an abbreviation of the complete one: *modus infinitivus,* the mode of unboundedness, of indeterminateness, regarding the manner in which a verb exercises and indicates the function and direction of its meaning.

This Latin term, like all other grammatical terms, stems from the work of the Greek grammarians. Here again we run up against the process of translation that we mentioned in the course of our discussion of the word *phusis*. We need not go into the details of how grammar was inaugurated with the Greeks, was taken over by the Romans, and was passed on to the Middle Ages and modernity. We are acquainted with many details of this process. So far, there has been no really thoroughgoing investigation of this happening that has been so fundamental for the establishment and formation of the whole Western spirit. We even lack an adequate way of posing the questions in such a meditation, which one day we will no longer be able to avoid, as irrelevant as this whole process may seem to the preoccupations of today.

The fact that the development of Western grammar began with Greek meditation on the *Greek* language gives this process its whole meaning. For along with the German language, Greek (in regard to the possibilities of thinking) is at once the most powerful and the most spiritual of languages.

Above all we must consider the fact that the definitive differentiation of the fundamental forms of words (noun and verb) in the Greek form of *onoma* and *rhēma* was worked out and first established in the most immediate and intimate connection with the conception and interpretation of Being that has been definitive for the entire West. This inner bond between these two happenings is accessible to us unimpaired and is carried out in full clarity in Plato's *Sophist*. The terms *onoma* and *rhēma* were already known before Plato, of course. But at that time, and still in Plato, they were understood as terms denoting the use of words as a whole. *Onoma* means the linguistic name as distinguished from the named person or thing, and it also means the speaking of a word, which was later conceived grammatically as *rhēma*. And *rhēma* in turn means the spoken word, speech; the *rhētōr* is the speaker, the orator, who uses not only verbs but also *onomata* in the narrower meaning of the substantive.

The fact that both terms originally governed an equally wide domain is important for our later point that the much-discussed question in linguistics of whether the noun or the verb represents the primordial form of the word is not a genuine question. This pseudoquestion first arose in the context of a developed grammar rather than from a vision of the essence of language, an essence not yet dissected by grammar.

[44]

Thus the two terms *onoma* and *rhēma,* which at first indicated all speaking, narrowed their meaning and became terms for the two main classes of words. In the dialogue cited (261e ff.), Plato provides the first interpretation and foundation of this distinction. Plato here proceeds from a general characterization of the function of words. *Onoma* in the wider sense is *dēloma tēi phōnēi peri tēn ousian:* a revelation by means of sound in relation to and in the sphere of the Being of beings.

In the sphere of beings we may distinguish between *pragma* and *praxis.* The former are the things we have something to do with, the things with which we are always concerned. The latter is doing and acting in the broadest sense, which also includes *poiēsis.* Words are of two kinds. They are *dēlōma pragmatos (onoma),* a manifestation of things, and *dēlōma praxeōs (rhēma),* a manifestation of a doing. Wherever a *plegma,* a *sumplokē* (a construction that weaves both together), happens, there is the *logos elachistos te kai prōtos,* the shortest and (at the same time) the first (real) discourse. But Aristotle is the first to give the clearer metaphysical interpretation of the *logos* in the sense of the propositional statement. He distinguishes *onoma* as *sēmantikon aneu chronou* ⟨signifying without reference to time⟩ and *rhēma* as *prossēmmainon chronon* ⟨indicating time⟩ (*De Interpretatione,* chapters 2–4). This elucidation of the essence of the *logos* became the model and measure for the later development of logic and grammar. And even though this development deteriorated into [45] an academic matter right away, the topic itself always managed to remain crucially significant. The textbooks of the Greek and Latin grammarians were schoolbooks in the West for over a thousand years. We know that these were anything but weak and petty times.

We are asking about the word form that the Latins call the *infinitivus.* The negative expression, *modus* infinitivus *verbi,* already points to a *modus finitus,* a mode of limitedness and definiteness in verbal meaning. Now what is the Greek prototype for this distinction?

What the Roman grammarians designate with the bland expression *modus* the Greeks call *enklisis,* an inclining to the side. This word moves in the same direction of meaning as another Greek word indicating grammatical form. We know this word, *ptōsis,* better in its Latin translation: *casus,* case, in the sense of the inflection of the noun. But to begin with, *ptōsis* designates any kind of inflection of the fundamental form (deviation, declension), not only in substantives but also in verbs. Only after the difference between these word forms had been more clearly worked out were the inflections that belong to them also designated with separate terms. The inflection of the noun is called *ptōsis (casus);* that of the verb is called *enklisis (declinatio).*

Now how do these two terms *ptōsis* and *enklisis* come into use in the examination of language and its inflections? Language is obviously taken as another thing that is, as a *being* among others. The way in which the Greeks generally understood beings in their Being must have made itself felt in the conception and definition of language. Only on this basis can we grasp these terms, which, as *modus* and *casus,* have long since become hackneyed labels that tell us nothing.

In these lectures, we constantly return to the Greek conception of Being because this conception, though entirely flattened out and rendered unrecognizable, is the conception that still rules even today in the West — not only in the doctrines of philosophy but in the most everyday routines. Because of this, we want to characterize the Greek conception of Being in its first fundamental traits as we follow the Greek treatment of language.

This approach has been chosen intentionally in order to show, through an example from grammar, how the experience, conception, and interpretation of language that set the standard for the West grew out of a very definite understanding of Being.

[46]   The terms *ptōsis* and *enklisis* mean a falling, tipping, or inclining.

This implies a dropping-off from an upright, straight stance. But this standing-there, this taking and maintaining a *stand* that stands erected high in itself, is what the Greeks understood as Being. Whatever takes such a stand becomes *constant* in itself and thereby freely and on its own runs up against the necessity of its limit, *peras*. This *peras* is not something that first accrues to a being from outside. Much less is it some deficiency in the sense of a detrimental restriction. Instead, the self-restraining hold that comes from a limit, the having-of-itself wherein the constant holds itself, is the Being of beings; it is what first makes a being be a being as opposed to a nonbeing. For something to take such a stand therefore means for it to attain its limit, to de-limit itself. Thus a basic characteristic of a being is its *telos*, which does not mean goal or purpose, but end. Here "end" does not have any negative sense, as if "end" meant that something can go no further, that it breaks down and gives out. Instead, "end" means completion in the sense of coming to fulfillment ⟨*Vollendung*⟩. Limit and end are that whereby beings first begin to *be*. This is the key to understanding the highest term that Aristotle used for Being: *entelecheia,* something's holding-(or maintaining)-itself-in-its-completion-(or limit). What was done with the term "entelechy" by later philosophy (cf. Leibniz), not to mention biology, demonstrates the full extent of the decline from what is Greek. Whatever places itself into and thereby enacts its limit,[3] and thus stands, has form, *morphē*. The essence of form, as understood by the Greeks, comes from the emergent placing-itself-forth-into-the-limit.

But from an observer's point of view, what stands-there-in-itself becomes what puts itself forth, what offers itself in how it looks. The Greeks call the look of a thing its *eidos* or *idea*. Initially, *eidos*

3. Here we translate the *ergrenzend* of the later German editions; the earlier editions have *ergänzend* (completes its limit).

resonates with what we mean when we say that a thing has a face, a visage, that it has the right look, that it stands. The thing "fits." It rests in its appearing, that is, in the coming-forth of its essence. What grounds and holds together all the determinations of Being we have listed is what the Greeks experienced without question as the meaning of Being, which they called *ousia,* or more fully *parousia.* The usual thoughtlessness translates *ousia* as "substance" and thereby misses its sense entirely. In German, we have an appropriate expression for *parousia* in our word *An-wesen* (coming-to-presence). We use *Anwesen* as a name for a self-contained farm or homestead. In Aristotle's times, too, *ousia* was still used in this sense *as well as* in its meaning as a basic philosophical word. Something comes to presence. It stands in itself and thus puts itself forth. It is. For the Greeks, "Being" fundamentally means presence.

[47]   But Greek philosophy never returned to this ground of Being, to what it contains. It remained in the foreground of that which comes to presence and tried to examine it through the determinations discussed above.

What we have said helps us to understand the Greek interpretation of Being that we mentioned at the beginning, in our explication of the term "metaphysics" — that is, the apprehension of Being as *phusis.* The later concepts of "nature," we said, must be held at a distance from this: *phusis* means the emergent self-upraising, the self-unfolding that abides in itself. In this sway, rest and movement are closed and opened up from an originary unity. This sway is the overwhelming coming-to-presence that has not yet been surmounted in thinking, and within which *that which* comes to presence essentially unfolds as beings. But this sway first steps forth from concealment — that is, in Greek, *alētheia* (unconcealment) happens — insofar as the sway struggles itself forth as a world. Through world, beings first come into being.

Heraclitus says (fragment 53): πόλεμος πάντων μὲν πατήρ ἐστι,

πάντων δὲ βασιλεύς, καὶ τοὺς μὲν θεοὺς ἔδειξε τοὺς δὲ ἀνθρώπους,
τοὺς μὲν δούλους ἐποίησε τοὺς δὲ ἐλευθέρους.

Confrontation is indeed for all (that comes to presence) the sire
(who lets emerge), but (also) for all the preserver that holds sway.
For it lets some appear as gods, others as human beings, some it
produces (sets forth) as slaves, but others as the free.[4]

The *polemos* named here is a strife that holds sway before everything divine and human, not war in the human sense. As Heraclitus
thinks it, struggle first and foremost allows what essentially unfolds
to step apart in opposition, first allows position and status and rank
to establish themselves in coming to presence. In such a stepping
apart, clefts, intervals, distances, and joints open themselves up. In
con-frontation, world comes to be. [Confrontation does not divide
unity, much less destroy it. It builds unity; it is the gathering *(logos)*.
Polemos and *logos* are the same.][5]

The struggle meant here is originary struggle, for it allows those
that struggle to originate as such in the first place; it is not a mere assault on the present-at-hand. Struggle first projects and develops the
un-heard, the hitherto un-said and un-thought. This struggle is then
sustained by the creators, by the poets, thinkers, and statesmen.
Against the overwhelming sway, they throw the counterweight
of their work and capture in this work the world that is thereby
opened up. With these works, the sway, *phusis,* first comes to a stand
in what comes to presence. Beings as such now first come into
being. This becoming-a-world is authentic history. Struggle as such   [48]
not only allows for arising and standing-forth; it alone also preserves beings in their constancy. Where struggle ceases, beings indeed do not disappear, but world turns away. Beings are no longer

4. A more conventional translation of the fragment might be: "War is the
father of all and the king of all, and it has shown some as gods and others as
human beings, made some slaves and others free."
5. In parentheses in the 1953 edition.

asserted [that is, preserved as such].[6] Beings now become just something one comes across; they are findings. What is completed is no longer that which is pressed into limits [that is, set into its form][7] but is now merely what is finished and as such is at the disposal of just anybody, the present-at-hand, within which no world is worlding any more — instead, human beings now steer and hold sway with whatever is at their disposal. Beings become objects, whether for observing (view, picture) or for making, as the fabricated, the object of calculation. That which originarily holds sway,[8] *phusis,* now degenerates into a prototype for reproduction and copying. Nature now becomes a special domain, as distinguished from art and from everything that can be produced and regulated according to a plan. The originarily emergent self-upraising of the violent forces of what holds sway, the *phainesthai* as appearing in the broad sense of the epiphany of a world, now becomes reduced to the demonstrable visibility of present-at-hand things. The eye, the seeing, which first viewed the project *into* the sway in an originary viewing, and pro-duced the work while seeing into the sway, has now been reduced to mere observing and inspecting and staring. The view is now only the optical. (Schopenhauer's "world eye" — pure cognition. . . .)[9]

To be sure, beings are still given. The motley mass of beings is more noisily and more widely given than ever before; but Being has deserted them. Because of this, beings are maintained in a seeming

6. In parentheses in the 1953 edition.
7. In parentheses in the 1953 edition.
8. Here we translate *das ursprünglich Waltende* of the later German editions; the earlier editions have *das ursprünglich Weltende* (that which originarily worlds).
9. See, e.g., Arthur Schopenhauer, *The World as Will and Representation,* trans. E. F. J. Payne (New York: Dover, 1966), vol. 1, 186, 198, 282.

constancy ⟨*Ständigkeit*⟩ only when they are made into the "object" ⟨"*Gegenstand*"⟩ of endless and ever-changing busy-ness.

When the creators have disappeared from the people, when they are barely tolerated as irrelevant curiosities, as ornaments, as eccentrics alien to life, when authentic struggle ceases and shifts into the merely polemical, into the intrigues and machinations of human beings within the present-at-hand, then the decline has already begun. For even when an age still makes an effort just to uphold the inherited level and dignity of its Dasein, the level already sinks. It can be upheld only insofar as at all times it is creatively transcended.

For the Greeks "Being" says *constancy* in a twofold sense:

1. standing-in-itself as arising and standing forth *(phusis),*

2. but, as such, "constantly," that is, enduringly, abiding *(ousia).*

Not-to-be accordingly means to step out of such constancy that [49] has stood-forth in itself: *existasthai* — "existence," "to exist" means, for the Greeks, precisely not-to-be. The thoughtlessness and vapidity with which one uses the words "existence" and "to exist" as designations for Being offer fresh evidence of our alienation from Being and from an originally powerful and definite interpretation of it.

Ptōsis and *enklisis* mean to fall, to incline, that is, nothing other than to depart from the constancy of the stand and thus to deviate from it. We are posing the question of why these two particular terms came into use in the study of language. The meaning of the words *ptōsis* and *enklisis* presupposes the notion of an upright stand. We said that language, too, is conceived by the Greeks as something in being and thereby as something in keeping with the sense of their understanding of Being. What is in being is what is constant and as such, something that exhibits itself, something that appears. This shows itself primarily to seeing. The Greeks examine language optically in a certain broad sense—namely, from the point of view of the written word. In writing, what is spoken comes to a stand. Language *is*—that is, it stands in the written image of the word, in the written signs, in the letters, *grammata*. This is why it is grammar that represents language as something in being, whereas through the flow of talk, language drains away into the impermanent. And so the theory of language has been interpreted grammatically up to our time. The Greeks, however, also knew about the oral character of language, the *phōnē*. They founded rhetoric and poetics. [Yet all of this did not in itself lead to an adequate definition of the essence of language.][10]

The standard way of examining language is still the grammatical way. Among words and their forms, it finds some that are deviations, inflections of the basic forms. The basic position of the noun (the substantive) is the nominative singular: for example, *ho kuklos*, the circle. The basic position of the verb is the first person singular present indicative: for example, *legō*, I say. The *infinitive*, in contrast, is a particular *modus verbi*, an *enklisis*. Of what sort? This is what we must now determine. It is best to do so with an example. One form of *legō* is *lexainto*, "they (the men, in this case) could be called and addressed"—as traitors, for example. This inflection consists more precisely in the form's making manifest another person (the third), another number (not the singular, but the plural), another voice (passive instead of active), another tense (aorist instead of present), another mood (not indicative but optative). What is named [50] in the word *lexainto* is not addressed as actually present at hand but rather represented as only possibly in being.

The inflected form of the word makes all of this manifest in addition and lets it be understood immediately. To make something else manifest in addition, to allow it to arise and be seen in addition—

10. In parentheses in the 1953 edition.

this is the function of the *enklisis,* in which the word that stands straight inclines to the side. This is why it is called *enklisis paremphatikos*. The descriptive word *paremphainō* is used genuinely according to the fundamental relation of the Greeks to beings as what is constant.

This word is found, for example, in Plato (*Timaeus* 50e), in an important context. The question here is the essence of the becoming of what becomes. Becoming means: coming to Being. Plato distinguishes three things: 1) *to gignomenon,* that which becomes; 2) *to en hōi gignetai,* that *within which* it becomes, the medium in which something builds itself up while it is becoming and from which it then stands forth once it has become; 3) *to hothen aphomoioumenon,* the source from which what becomes takes the standard of resemblance; for everything that becomes, everything that becomes something, takes what it becomes in advance as prototype.

To elucidate the meaning of *paremphainō,* we pay attention to what we mentioned under (2) above. That within which something becomes is what we call "space." The Greeks have no word for "space." This is no accident, for they do not experience the spatial according to *extensio* but instead according to place *(topos)* as *chōra,* which means neither place nor space but what is taken up and occupied by what stands there. The place belongs to the thing itself. The various things each have their place. That which becomes is set into this placelike "space" and is set forth from it.[11] But in order for this to be possible, "space" must be bare of all the modes of appearance,[12] any modes that it may receive from anywhere. For if it were like any one of the modes of appearance that enter into it,

11. In the next two sentences Heidegger paraphrases *Timaeus* 50d–e, which he then proceeds to quote. His main departure from conventional renderings is his translation of *idea* as "mode of appearance" rather than "form."

12. In general, we have reserved "appearance" as the translation for *Erscheinung,* but in this passage, it seems to be the best rendering for *Aussehen.*

then in receiving forms, some opposed in essence to it, some of an entirely other essence, it would allow a bad actualization of the prototype to come to stand, for it would make manifest its own appearance in addition. ἄμορφον ὂν ἐκείνων ἁπασῶν τῶν ἰδεῶν ὅσας μέλλοι δέχεσθαί ποθεν. ὅμοιον γὰρ ὂν τῶν ἐπεισιόντων τινὶ τὰ τῆς ἐναντίας τά τε τῆς παράπαν ἄλλης φύσεως ὁπότ' ἔλθοι δεχόμενον κακῶς ἂν ἀφομοιοῖ τὴν αὐτοῦ παρεμφαῖνον ὄψιν. That wherein the things that are becoming are set must precisely not proffer its own look and its own appearance. [The reference to the *Timaeus* passage not only intends to clarify the correlation of *paremphainon* and *on*, of appearing-with and of Being as constancy, but also tries to inti-

[51] mate that Platonic philosophy — that is, the interpretation of Being as *idea* — prepared the transfiguration of place *(topos)* and of *chōra,* the essence of which we have barely grasped, into "space" as defined by extension. Might not *chōra* mean: that which separates itself from every particular, that which withdraws, and in this way admits and "makes room" precisely for something else?][13] Let us return to the word form *lexainto* that we mentioned above. What it does is make manifest a *poikilia* ⟨diversity: *Timaeus* 50d⟩ of directions of meaning. This is why it is called an *enklisis paremphatikos,* a deviation that *is* capable of making manifest *in addition* person, number, tense, voice, and mood. This is because a word as such *is* a word to the extent that it lets shine forth *(dēloun).* If we place the form *legein,* the infinitive, next to *lexainto,* then we also find here an inflection, *enklisis,* in respect to the fundamental form *legō,* but one in which person, number, and mood do *not* manifest themselves. Here the *enklisis* and its significant making-manifest show a deficiency, and so this word form is called *enklisis a-paremphatikos.* In Latin, the term *modus* in-*finitivus* corresponds to this negative term. The meaning of the infinitive form is limited and cut to shape in the

13. In parentheses in the 1953 edition.

respects mentioned above, according to person, number, etc. The Latin translation of *a-paremphatikos* by *infinitivus* deserves attention. The original Greek, which refers to the look of a thing and the self-manifestation of what stands in itself or inclines itself, has vanished. Now the determining factor is the merely formal notion of limitation.

Now of course, and particularly in Greek, there is also the infinitive in the passive and middle voice, and one in the present, perfect, and future, so that the infinitive at least makes manifest voice and tense. This has led to various disputed questions concerning the infinitive, which we will not pursue here. We will clarify only one point in what follows. The infinitive form *legein,* to say, can be understood in such a way that one no longer even thinks about voice and tense but only about what the verb in general means and makes manifest. In this respect the original Greek designation hits the mark especially well. In the sense of the Latin term, the infinitive is a word form that, as it were, cuts off what it means from all definite relations of meaning. The meaning is pulled away (abstracted) from all particular relations. In this abstraction, the infinitive offers only what one represents to oneself with the word in general. This is why today's grammarians say that the infinitive is the "abstract verbal concept." It conceives and grasps what is meant only overall and in general. It names only this general meaning. In our language the infinitive is the form with which one names the verb. There is a deficiency, a lack, in the infinitive, in its word form and its manner of meaning. The infinitive *no longer* makes manifest what the verb otherwise reveals. [52]

Furthermore, the infinitive is a later, if not the latest, result in the chronological development of the word forms of language. This can be shown with the infinitive of that Greek word whose questionableness is the occasion for our discussion. "To be" is *einai* in Greek. We know that a standardized language unfolds from the speech of dialects that originally stand rooted in soil and history. Thus Homer's language is a mixture of various dialects that preserve the earlier form of the language. It is in the formation of the infinitive that the Greek dialects diverge from each other the most, and so linguistic scholarship has made the differences among infinitives into a principal criterion "for separating and grouping the dialects" (see Wackernagel, *Vorlesungen über Syntax,* vol. I, pp. 257 ff.).[14]

To be is *einai* in Attic, *ēnai* in Arcadian, *emmenai* in Lesbian, *ēmen* in Doric. To be is *esse* in Latin, *ezum* in Oscan, *erom* in Umbrian. In both ⟨the Greek and Latinate⟩ languages the *modi finiti* were already fixed and were common property, while the *enklisis aparemphatikos* still retained its varying peculiarities of dialect. We consider this state of affairs an indication that the infinitive has a preeminent significance in language as a whole. The question remains whether this persistence of the infinitive forms stems from the fact that the infinitive represents an abstract and late verbal form, or whether it names something that lies at the foundation of all inflections of the verb. On the other hand, it is right to warn us to be on our guard against the infinitive word form, for precisely this form, seen grammatically, communicates the least of the verb's meaning.

But we are still far from having fully clarified the word form that we are discussing, at least if we pay attention to the form in which we ordinarily go about saying "to be." We say *das Sein.* Such a manner of speaking results when we transform the abstract infinitive form into a substantive by placing the article in front of it: *to*

14. Jacob Wackernagel, *Vorlesungen über Syntax, mit besonderer Berücksichtigung von Griechisch, Lateinisch und Deutsch,* vol. I (Basel: Emil Birkhäuser, 1920). Wackernagel discusses the infinitive in general on 257–265. See 257 for his explanation of *paremphainō,* 257–258 for the various forms of the infinitive of "be" in Greek and Latinate languages, and 258 for the phrase that Heidegger quotes.

einai. The article is originally a demonstrative pronoun. It means that what is indicated stands and is for itself, as it were. This naming that demonstrates and indicates always has a preeminent function in language. If we just say *sein,* then what we have named is already indefinite enough. But through the linguistic transformation of the [53] infinitive into the verbal substantive, the emptiness that already lies in the infinitive is, as it were, further fixed; *sein* is posed like a fixed, standing object *(feststehender Gegenstand).* The substantive *das Sein* implies that what is so named, itself "is." Being now itself becomes something that "is," whereas obviously only beings are, and it is not the case that Being also is. If Being itself were something in being about beings, then it would have to be something that we find before us, all the more so because we encounter the Being-in-being *(Seiendsein)* of beings, even if we do not definitely grasp its particular characteristics in detail.

Can it still be any wonder to us now that "Being" is so empty a word when the word form itself is based on an emptying ⟨of meaning⟩ and the apparent fixation of this emptiness? This word "Being" serves as a warning to us. Let us not be lured away into the emptiest of forms, the verbal substantive. And let us not entangle ourselves in the abstraction of the infinitive "to be." If we really want to arrive at the "to be" along the path of language, let us keep to forms like these: I am, you are, he, she, it is, we are, and so forth; I was, we were, they have been, and so forth. But then we gain no clearer understanding of what "to be" means here, or what its essence consists in. On the contrary! Let us simply make the attempt!

We say: "I am." One can speak of this sort of Being only in reference to oneself: my Being. What does it consist of, and where is it situated? It would seem that this should be what we can most easily bring to light, for there is no being to which we are closer than the one that we ourselves are. All other beings we ourselves are not. All other beings still "are" even when we ourselves are not. It seems we cannot be as close to any other being as we are to the being that we ourselves are. Actually, we cannot even say that we are close to the being that we ourselves in each case are, since after all we ourselves are this being. Here we must admit that everyone is the furthest from himself, as far as the I from the you in "you are."

But today the We is what counts. Now it is the "time of the We" instead of the I. We are. What Being do we name in this sentence? We also say: the windows are, the rocks are. We—are. Does this statement ascertain the Being-present-at-hand of a plurality of I's? And how does it stand with the "I was" and "we were," with Being in the past? Is it something by-gone for us? Or *are* we precisely that which we were? Are we not becoming precisely just what we *are*?

The examination of the *definite* verbal forms of "to be" yields the opposite of an elucidation of Being. What is more, it leads to a new difficulty. Let us compare the infinitive "to say" and the basic form [54] "I say" with the infinitive "to be" and the basic form "I am." In this comparison, "be" and "am" (*"sein" und "bin"*) show that they have different stems. Furthermore, "was" and "been" (*"war" und "gewesen"*) in the past form are different from both of these. We stand before the question of the different stems of the word "to be."

B. The Etymology of the Word "Being"

First, we should briefly report on what linguistics knows about the word stems that are found in the inflections of the verb *sein*. Current information about this is hardly definitive—not so much because new facts may turn up but because it is to be expected that what has been known up to this point will be reviewed with new eyes and more genuine questions. The full variety of the inflections of the verb "to be" is determined by three different stems.

The first two stems we should mention are Indo-Germanic and are also found in the Greek and Latin words for "to be."

1. The oldest and authentic stem word is *es*, Sanskrit *asus*, life, the living, that which from out of itself and in itself stands and goes and reposes: the self-standing. To this stem belong the Sanskrit verb forms *esmi, esi, esti, asmi*. To these correspond the Greek *eimi* and *einai* and the Latin *esum* and *esse*. *Sunt, sind* and *sein* belong together. It is worth noticing that the *ist* (*estin, est*, ⟨is⟩. . .) persists throughout the Indo-Germanic languages from the very start.

2. The other Indo-Germanic root is *bhū, bheu*. To this belongs the Greek *phuō*, to emerge, to hold sway, to come to a stand from out of itself and to remain standing. Until now, *bhū* has been interpreted according to the usual superficial conception of *phusis* and *phuein* as nature and as "growing." According to the more originary interpretation, which stems from the confrontation with the inception of Greek philosophy, this "growing" proves to be an emerging which in turn is determined by coming to presence and appearing. Recently, the radical *phu-* has been connected with *pha-, phainesthai* (to show itself). *Phusis* would then be that which emerges into the light, *phuein*, to illuminate, to shine forth and therefore to appear. (See *Zeitschrift für vergleichende Sprachforschung*, vol. 59.)[15]

From this same stem comes the Latin perfect *fui, fuo*, as well as our German *bin, bist, wir "birn," ihr "birt"* (forms that died out in the fourteenth century). The imperative *bis* (*bis mein Weib* ⟨be my wife⟩) has held out longer next to *bin* and *bist*, which have survived.   [55]

3. The third stem appears only in the inflection of the German verb *sein: wes;* Sanskrit: *vasami;* Germanic: *wesan*, to dwell, to abide, to sojourn; to *ves* belong: *westia, wastu, Vesta, vestibulum*. From this we have the German form *gewesen* and additionally: *was, war, es west, wesen*. The participle *wesend* is still retained in *an-wesend*,

---

15. F. Specht, "Beiträge zur griechischen Grammatik," in *Zeitschrift für vergleichende Sprachforschung*, vol. 59 (1932): 31–131. For the connections among *bhū, pha-*, and *phu-*, see 60–62.

ab-wesend ⟨pre-sent, ab-sent⟩. The substantive *Wesen* does not originally mean what-ness ⟨*Was-sein*⟩, *quidditas,* but rather enduring as
present ⟨*Gegenwart*⟩, pre-sencing and ab-sencing. The *sens* in the
Latin *prae-sens* and *ab-sens* has been lost. Does *Dii con-sentes* ⟨usually
translated "the gods willing"⟩ mean the gods who together are
pre-sencing?

From the three stems we derive three initial and vividly definite
meanings: living, emerging, abiding. Linguistics establishes them.
Linguistics also establishes that today these initial meanings have
died out, that only an "abstract" meaning, "to be," has survived. But
here a decisive question announces itself: how are the three stems
above unified? What carries and leads the saga ⟨*Sage*⟩ of Being?
What is our speaking ⟨*Sagen*⟩ of Being based on — after all its linguistic inflections? This speaking and the understanding of Being,
are they the same, or not? How does the distinction between Being
and beings essentially unfold in the saga of Being? As valuable as
these conclusions of linguistics are, we cannot be satisfied with
them. For after these conclusions, the *questioning* must first begin.

We have a chain of questions to pose:

1. What kind of "abstraction" came into play in the formation of
the word *sein*?

2. May we even speak of abstraction here?

3. What is the abstract meaning that is left over, then?

4. Can one explain the happening that opens itself up here — the
fact that different meanings, which also imply experiences, grow
together into the inflections of *one* verb, and not just any verb —
simply by saying that something has been lost in the process? Nothing arises merely through loss, and least of all that which unifies and
blends, in the unity of its meaning, what is originally different.

5. What leading, fundamental meaning can have guided the
blending that happened here?

6. What dominant meaning persists through all the blurring of this blending?

7. Must not the inner history of precisely this word *sein* be ex- [56] cepted from the usual equivalence with any other arbitrary word whose etymology can be studied, especially when we consider that even the root meanings (living, emerging, dwelling), in their addressing and naming and saying, do not unveil arbitrary details in the sphere of the sayable?

8. Can the meaning of Being, which presents itself to us as "abstract" and therefore derivative in the merely logical, grammatical interpretation, be whole and originary in itself?

9. Can this be shown from the essence of language, if this essence has been grasped sufficiently and originally?

As the fundamental question of metaphysics, we ask: "Why are there beings at all instead of nothing?" In this fundamental question there already resonates the prior question: how does it stand with Being?

What do we mean by the words "to be," "Being"? In our attempt to answer, we run into difficulties. We grasp at the un-graspable. Yet we are incessantly engaged by beings, related to beings, and we know about ourselves "as beings."

"Being" now just counts as the sound of a word for us, a used-up term. If this is all we have left, then we must at least attempt to grasp this last remnant of a possession. This is why we asked: how does it stand with the *word* "Being"?

We answered this question in two ways, which led into the grammar and etymology of the word. Let us sum up the results of the twofold discussion of the word "Being."

1. The grammatical examination of the form of the word had this result: in the infinitive, the word's definite modes of meaning

are no longer in effect; they are blurred. The substantivization completely fixes and objectifies this blurring. The word becomes a name for something indefinite.

2. The etymological examination of the meaning of the word had this result: what we today, and for a long time previously, have called by the name "Being" is, as regards its meaning, a blending that levels off three different stem meanings. None of these is evident definitively and on its own within the meaning of the word anymore. This blurring and blending go hand in hand. The combination of these two processes provides a sufficient explanation for the fact from which we set out: that the word "to be" is empty and its meaning is evanescent.

The Question of the Essence of Being

WE HAVE UNDERTAKEN a study of the expression "to be" in order to penetrate the fact under discussion, and so to put it in the place where it belongs. We do not want to accept this fact blindly, as if it were the fact that there are dogs and cats. We want to establish a position regarding this fact itself. We want this, even at the risk that our "will" to do so may create the appearance of stubbornness and may seem to be an unworldly befuddlement that mistakes what is peripheral and unreal for something real, and gets obsessed with dissecting mere words. We want to illuminate the fact thoroughly. Our investigation has determined that in the course of its development, language forms "infinitives" — for instance, "to be" — and that with time, language has brought about a worn-down, indefinite meaning of this word. This simply *is* so. Instead of thoroughly illuminating the fact, we have just set another fact of linguistic history next to it or behind it.

If we now begin again with these facts of linguistic history and ask why they are as they are, then perhaps what we can still offer as an explanation becomes not clearer but only more obscure. The fact that matters stand as they do with the word "Being" really hardens now in its indisputable factuality. But we reached this state of affairs long ago. After all, this is what the usual procedure in philosophy appeals to, when it explains in advance that the meaning of the word "Being" is the emptiest and thus embraces everything. What is thought with this word, the concept, is thus the highest generic concept, the genus. It is true that one can still point to the *ens in genere* ⟨the being as genus⟩, as the old ontology says, but it is just as certain that there is nothing further to be sought there. To want to go so far as to attach the decisive question of metaphysics to this empty word "Being" means to bring everything into confusion. There is only one possibility left here: to acknowledge the afore-mentioned fact of the emptiness of the word and to leave this fact in peace. It appears that we may do so with a clear conscience, all the more so now that the fact has been explained historically by the history of language.

[58]

So: away from the empty schema of this word "Being"! But where to? The answer cannot be difficult. At most we can wonder why we have persisted in such a long and minute examination of the word "Being." Away from the empty, universal word "Being," toward the special characteristics of the particular domains of be-ings themselves! For this project, we have all sorts of things imme-diately at our disposal: the things that we can grasp with our hands right away, all the equipment that is at hand for us all the time — tools, vehicles, etc. If these particular beings strike us as too ordi-nary, not refined and soulful enough for "metaphysics," then we can stick to the nature that surrounds us — land, sea, mountains, rivers, forests, and the individual things in them: trees, birds and insects, grasses and stones. If we are looking for a mighty being, then the earth is nearby. The moon that is rising back there is in being ⟨*seiend*⟩ in the same way as the nearest mountaintop — and so is a planet. In being is the surging swarm of people on an animated street. In being are we ourselves. In being are the Japanese. In being are Bach's fugues. In being is the cathedral of Strasbourg. In being are Hölderlin's hymns. In being are criminals. In being are the madmen in a madhouse.

Beings everywhere and anytime you like. Certainly. But how is it, then, that we know that each of these things that we so confidently list and count up is a *being*? The question sounds foolish; for after all, we can determine, in a way that any normal human being would find undeniable, that this being *is*. Granted. [Furthermore, there is no need here for us to use the words "beings" and "what is," which are alien to ordinary language.] And we are not now contemplating casting any doubt on *whether* all these beings *are* in the first place — basing such a doubt on the supposedly scientific observation that what we are experiencing here is just our own sensations, and that we cannot get out of our own body, a body to which everything we have mentioned remains related. In fact, we would like to remark in advance that such considerations, which so easily and cheaply give themselves airs of being supremely critical and superior, are thoroughly uncritical.

Meanwhile, we *let* beings be, just as they swarm around us and assail us, elate us and depress us, in everyday life as well as in hours and moments of greatness. We let all beings *be* as they are. But if we behave in this way in the course of our historical Being-here, spontaneously as it were and without ruminating over it, if we let each being be the being that it *is*, then in all this we must know what that means: "is" and "to be."

And how are we to determine that something that is presumed to be, at some place and time, is not — unless we can clearly distinguish in advance between Being and not-Being? How are we to make this decisive distinction unless we know just as decisively and definitely what is meant by that which is distinguished here: not-

[59]

Being and Being? How can beings always and in each case be beings for us unless we already understand "Being" and "not-Being"?

But we are constantly faced with beings. We distinguish between their Being-thus and Being-otherwise, we judge about Being and not-Being. We therefore know unambiguously what "Being" means. The claim that this word is empty and indefinite would then just be a superficial way of speaking and an error.

Such reflections put us in a supremely ambivalent position. We first determined that the word "Being" tells us nothing definite. We did not just talk ourselves into this; instead, we found out, and we still find now that "Being" has an evanescent, indefinite meaning. But on the other hand, our latest considerations convince us that we clearly and surely distinguish "Being" from not-Being.

In order to get our bearings here, we must pay attention to the following. Surely it can come into doubt whether at some place and time an individual being is or is not. We can deceive ourselves about whether, for example, the window over there, which is of course a being, *is* closed or *is not*. However, merely in order for such a thing to come into doubt in the first place, we must presume the definite distinction between Being and not-Being. Whether Being is distinct from not-Being is not something we doubt in this case.

The word "Being" is thus indefinite in its meaning, and nevertheless we understand it definitely. "Being" proves to be extremely definite and completely indefinite. According to the usual logic, we have here an obvious contradiction. But something contradictory cannot be. There is no square circle. And yet, there is this contradiction: Being as definite and completely indefinite. We see, if we do not deceive ourselves, and if for a moment amid all the day's hustle and bustle we have time to see, that we are standing in the midst of this contradiction. This standing of ours is more actual than just [60] about anything else that we call actual — more actual than dogs and cats, automobiles and newspapers.

The fact that Being is an empty word for us suddenly takes on a completely different aspect. In the end, we become suspicious of the supposed emptiness of the word. If we meditate more closely on the word, then finally it becomes apparent that with all the blurred, blended universality of its meaning, we still mean something definite by it. This definite meaning is so definite and so unique in its own way that we must even say:

Being, that which pertains to every being whatsoever and thus disperses itself into what is most commonplace, is the most unique of all.

Everything else besides Being, each and every being, even if it is unique, can still be compared with another being. These possibilities of comparison increase every being's determinability. Because of this, every being is multiply indeterminate. But Being, in contrast, can be compared to nothing else. Its only other is Nothing. And here there is nothing to be compared. If Being is thus what is most unique and most determinate, then the expression "to be" cannot remain empty either. And in truth, it is never empty. We can easily convince ourselves of this by a comparison. When we perceive the expression "to be," either by hearing it as a sound or seeing it in its written form, then it does present itself differently from the sequence of sounds and letters "abracadabra." Of course, this too is a sequence of sounds, but, as we say at once, it is meaningless, even if it has some sense as a magical formula. In contrast, "to be" is not senseless in this way. Likewise, "to be," when written and seen, is different at once from "kzomil." This written mark is also a sequence of letters, of course, but one by which we are unable to think anything. There is no such thing as an empty word — only one that is worn out, yet remains full. The word "Being" retains its naming force. The slogan, "Away from this empty word 'Being,' towards the particular beings!" is not only an overhasty but a highly questionable slogan. Let us reflect on all this once again by means of an example, which, however, like every example that we can adduce in the field of our question, can never clarify the entire state of affairs in all its scope, and thus remains subject to some reservations.

Instead of the universal concept "Being," we will consider, as an example, the universal representation "tree." If we are now to say and define what the essence of a tree is, we turn away from the universal representation, to the various species of trees and individual examples of these species. This procedure is so self-evident that we are almost embarrassed to make special mention of it. However, the matter is not quite *that* simple. How are we supposed to discover the much-invoked particular, the individual trees as *such, as* trees — how are we supposed to be able even to *look for* such things as trees, unless the representation of what a tree is in general is already lighting our way in advance? If this universal representation "tree" were so completely indefinite and confused, if it gave us no sure directive in our searching and finding, it could happen that instead of trees, we took cars or rabbits as the determinate particulars, as examples of a tree. Even though it may be correct that in order to determine more precisely the essential multiplicity of the essence "tree," we must go through the particular, it remains at least equally correct that the illumination of the essential multiplicity and of the essence takes hold and progresses only when we conceive and know more originally the universal essence "tree," and this then means the essence "plant," and this means the essence "living thing" and "life." We may seek out thousands and thousands of trees — but if the self-developing knowledge of the *tree as such* does not light our way in advance in this enterprise, and does not clearly determine itself on the basis of itself and its essential ground, then all this will remain an idle enterprise in which we cannot see the tree for the trees.

Now one could object, precisely in regards to the universal meaning "Being," that our representing can no longer rise from it to

[61]

anything higher, since it is, after all, the most universal meaning. When it comes to the concept that is most universal and highest of all, reference to what stands "under" it not only is advisable, but is the only way out if we want to overcome the emptiness of the concept.

As convincing as this reflection may seem to be, it is nonetheless untrue. Let us mention two reasons:

1. It is questionable, to begin with, whether the generality of Being is that of a genus. Aristotle already suspected this.[1] Consequently, it remains questionable whether an individual being can ever count as an example of Being at all, as this oak does for "tree in general." It is questionable whether the ways of Being (Being as nature, Being as history) represent "species" of the genus "Being."

2. The word "Being" is a universal name, it is true, and seemingly one word among others. But this seeming is deceptive. The name and what it names are one of a kind. Therefore, we distort it fundamentally if we try to illustrate it by examples — precisely because every example in this case manifests not too much, as one might say, but always too little. Earlier we stressed that we must already know in advance what "tree" means in order to be able to seek and find what is particular, the species of trees and individual trees as such. This is all the more decisively true of Being. The necessity for us already to understand the word "Being" is the highest and is incomparable. So the "universality" of "Being" in regard to all beings does not imply that we should turn away from this universality as fast as possible and turn to the particular; instead, it implies the opposite, that we should remain there, and raise the uniqueness of this name and its naming to the level of knowledge.

The fact that for us the meaning of the word "Being" remains an indeterminate vapor is counterbalanced by the fact that we

[62]

1. Cf. Aristotle, *Metaphysics* Γ, 1, and K, 3.

still understand Being, and distinguish it with certainty from not-Being—and this is not just another, second fact, but both belong together as one. In the meantime, this One has completely lost the character of a fact for us. By no means do we find it among many other present-at-hand things, as something that is *also* present at hand. Instead, we suspect that in what we have taken up to now merely as a fact, there is something going on. It is happening in a way that does not fit into the series of other "incidents."

But before we concern ourselves any further with grasping in its truth what is going on in this fact, let us once again and for the last time attempt to take it as something familiar and indifferent. Let us assume that there is no such fact at all. Suppose that there were no indeterminate meaning of Being, and that we did not understand what this meaning signifies. Then what? Would there just be one noun and one verb less in our language? No. *Then there would be no language at all*. Beings *as such* would no longer open themselves up in words at all; they could no longer be addressed and discussed. For saying beings as such involves understanding beings as beings—that is, their Being—in advance. Presuming that we did not understand Being at all, presuming that the word "Being" did not even have that evanescent meaning, then there would not be any single word at all. We ourselves could never be those who *say*. We would never be able to be those who we are. For to be human means to be a sayer. Human beings are yes- and no-sayers only because they are, in the ground of their essence, sayers, *the* sayers. That is their distinction and also their predicament. It distinguishes them from stone, plant, and animal, but also from the gods. Even if we had a thousand eyes and a thousand ears, a thousand hands and many other senses and organs, if our essence did not stand within the power of language, then all beings would remain closed off to us—the beings that we ourselves are, no less than the beings that we are not.

[63]

Thus, as we review our discussion up to this point, the following state of affairs becomes apparent. When we set out by proposing this as a *fact* — *this* [which shall for now remain nameless],[2] that for us Being is only an empty word with an evanescent meaning — then we deposed it and thus demoted it from its authentic rank. In contrast, for our Dasein, *this* — that we understand Being, if only in an indefinite way — has the highest rank, insofar as in *this*, a power announces itself in which the very possibility of the essence of our Dasein is grounded. It is not one fact among others, but that which merits the highest worth according to its rank, provided that our Dasein, which is always a historical Dasein, does not remain a matter of indifference to us. Yet even in order for Dasein to remain an indifferent being for us, we must understand Being. Without this understanding, we could not even say no to our Dasein.

Only insofar as we deem this preeminence ⟨*Vorrang*⟩ of the understanding of Being worthy in its own rank ⟨*Rang*⟩ do we preserve this preeminence as rank. In what way can we deem this rank worthy, preserve it in its worth? This we cannot decide arbitrarily.

Because the understanding of Being fades away, at first and for the most part, in an indefinite meaning, and nonetheless remains certain and definite in this knowledge — because consequently the understanding of Being, despite all its rank, is dark, confused, covered over and concealed — it must be illuminated, disentangled, and ripped away from concealment. That can happen only insofar as we *inquire about* this understanding of Being — which at first we simply treated as a fact — in order to put it into question.

Questioning is the genuine and the right and the only way of deeming worthy that which, by its highest rank, holds our Dasein in its power. This understanding of Being of ours, and Being itself altogether, is therefore what is most worthy of questioning in all

2. In parentheses in the 1953 edition.

questioning. We question all the more genuinely the more immediately and directly we hold on to what is most worthy of questioning, namely, that for us Being is what we understand in a completely indefinite and yet supremely definite way.

We understand the word "Being," and hence all its inflections,
even though it looks as if this understanding were indefinite. We
say of what we thus understand, of whatever *opens itself up* to us
[64] somehow in understanding, that it has meaning ⟨*Sinn*⟩. Being, insofar as it is understood at all, has a meaning. To experience and
conceive of Being as what is most worthy of questioning, to inquire
especially about Being, then means nothing other than asking
about the meaning of Being.

In the treatise *Being and Time* the question of the meaning of
Being is first posed and developed especially *as a question*. The treatise also contains an explicit statement and grounding of what is
meant by meaning [namely, the openness of Being, not only of
beings as such — see *Being and Time*, §§32, 44, 65].[3]

Why may we no longer call what we have just mentioned a fact?
Why was this designation misleading from the start? Because *this*,
that we understand Being, does not just occur in our Dasein like the
fact, say, that we possess earlobes of such and such a sort. Instead of
earlobes, some other structure could form part of our hearing or-
gan. That we understand Being is not just actual; it is also necessary.
Without such an opening up of Being, we could not be "human" in
the first place. Of course, it is not unconditionally necessary that we
should be. There is always the possibility that there could be no
human beings at all. After all, there was a time when there were no
human beings. But strictly speaking, we cannot say there was a time
when there were no human beings. At every *time*, there were and

3. In parentheses in the 1953 edition.

are and will be human beings, because time temporalizes itself[4] only as long as there are human beings. There is no time in which there were no human beings, not because there are human beings from all eternity and for all eternity, but because time is not eternity, and time always temporalizes itself only at one time, as human, historical Dasein. But if human beings stand in Dasein, then one necessary condition for our ability to be here ⟨da-sein⟩ is this: that we understand Being. Insofar as this is necessary, human beings are also historically actual. For this reason we understand Being—and not only, as it might seem at first, as an evanescent meaning of a word. Rather, the definiteness with which we understand the indefinite meaning can be delimited unambiguously, and not as a subsequent addition, but as a definiteness that, unbeknownst to us, rules us from the ground up. In order to show this, we will once again take the word "Being" as our point of departure. But here one must remember that we use the word, in accordance with the guiding metaphysical question that we posed at the start, so broadly that it finds its limit only at Nothing. Everything that is not simply nothing, *is*—and for us, even Nothing "belongs" to "Being."

In our preceding discussion, we have taken a decisive step. In a lecture course, everything depends on such steps. Occasional questions that have been submitted to me regarding the lectures have betrayed over and over again that most of the listeners are listening in the wrong direction and getting stuck in the details. Of course, the overall context is important even in lectures on the special sciences. But for the sciences the overall context is immediately determined by the object, which for the sciences is always given in

[65]

4. *Zeit sich . . . zeitigt: zeitigen,* which ordinarily means "bring to fruition," is introduced as a technical term in *Being and Time,* §61, where it refers to the manner in which time *(Zeit)* itself occurs.

advance in some way. In contrast, it is not just that the object of philosophy does not lie at hand, but philosophy has no object at all. Philosophy is a happening that must at all times work out Being for itself anew [that is, Being in its openness that belongs to it].[5] Only in this happening does philosophical truth open up. So it is of decisive importance here that one follow the individual steps in the happening, and share in taking these steps.

What step have we taken? What step must we take again and again?

At first, we examined this as a fact: the expression "to be" has an evanescent meaning, it is almost like an empty word. The result of the more precise explication of this fact was that the evanescence of the meaning of the word is to be explained 1) by the blurring typical of the infinitive and 2) by the blending to which all three of the original root meanings have been subjected.

Once we had explained the fact in this way, we characterized it as the unshaken point of departure for all the traditional metaphysical questioning about "Being." It begins with *beings* and is directed toward them. It does *not* begin with *Being* in the questionworthiness of *its* openness. Because the meaning and concept "Being" have the highest universality, meta-physics, as "physics," cannot rise any higher to define them more precisely. Thus it has only one way left: away from the universal, to the particular beings. In this way, to be sure, the emptiness of the concept of Being is filled, namely by beings. But now the slogan "away from Being and toward the particular beings" has shown that it is mocking itself in some way it does not understand.

For the much-invoked particular beings can *open themselves up as such* to us only if and when we already understand Being in advance in *its* essence.

---

5. In parentheses in the 1953 edition.

This essence has already lit itself up. But it *still* remains in the realm of the unquestioned.

Now let us recall the question that was posed at the start. Is "Being" merely an empty word? Or are Being and the asking of the question of Being the fate of the spiritual history of the West?

Is Being just a last wisp of evaporating reality, and is the only [66] attitude left for us to let it evaporate completely into a matter of indifference? Or is Being what is most worthy of questioning?

By questioning in this way, we complete the decisive step from an indifferent fact and the supposed emptiness of the meaning of the word "Being" to the happening that is most worthy of questioning: that Being necessarily opens itself up in our understanding.

The sheer fact, apparently so unshakable, to which metaphysics blindly appeals, has now been shaken.

Up to now, in the question of Being, we have mainly tried to grasp the word according to its linguistic form and its meaning. It has now become clear that the question of Being is not a matter of grammar and etymology. If in spite of this we now begin once again with the word, then language must be at stake, here and in general, in a special way.

Language, the word, is ordinarily taken as a derivative and incidental expression of experiences. Insofar as things and processes are experienced in these experiences, language is also, indirectly, an expression and, as it were, a reproduction of the experienced being. The word "clock," for example, lends itself to the well-known three-fold distinction: 1) the audible and visible word form; 2) the meaning of what one generally represents to oneself with the word form; 3) the thing — a clock, this individual clock. Here (1) is the sign for (2), and (2) indicates (3). So presumably we can also distinguish in the word "Being" the word form, the meaning of the word, and the thing. And one can easily see that as long as we dwell solely on the word form and its meaning, our question of Being has not reached the thing, has not gotten to the point.[6] If we were to go so far as to intend to grasp the thing and the essence of the thing, in this case Being, through mere explications of the word and its meaning, then this would be an obvious error. We are hardly likely to fall prey to it—for our procedure would be like going about determining and investigating the motions of the ether or of matter, or atomic processes, by giving grammatical explications of the words "atom" and "ether," instead of carrying out the necessary physical experiments.

So regardless of whether the word "Being" has an indefinite or a definite meaning, or, as has become apparent, both at once, the point is to get beyond the level of meanings and get at the thing. But is "Being" a thing like clocks, houses, or any being at all? We have run up against this already—we have run up against this quite enough: Being is not a being, nor any ingredient of beings that is itself in being. The Being of the building over there is not *another* thing of the *same* sort as the roof and the cellar. Thus no thing corresponds to the word and the meaning "Being."

But we cannot conclude from this that Being consists only in the word and its meaning. The meaning of the word does not, as a meaning, constitute the essence of Being. This would mean that the Being of beings—for instance, the Being of the building we mentioned—consisted in the meaning of a word. It would obviously be absurd to think so. Instead, in the word "Being," in its meaning and passing through this meaning, we mean Being itself—but it is simply not a thing, if by thing we understand any sort of being.

From this it follows that ultimately, in the word "Being" and its inflections, and in everything that lies in the domain of this word,

[67]

6. *Zur Sache kommen* means "to get to the point," but more literally "to come to the thing."

the word and its meaning are bound more originally to what is meant by them — but also vice versa. Being itself relies on the word in a totally different and more essential sense than any being does.

The word "Being," in every one of its inflections, relates to the Being itself that is said, in a way that is essentially different from the relation of all other nouns and verbs in language to the beings that are said in them.

This implies that our previous explanations of the word "Being" are of greater import than any other remarks about words and linguistic usage regarding just any item. But even though here in the word "Being" there is a quite distinctive connection between word, meaning, and Being itself, and the thing, so to speak, is lacking, we should not think that once we have characterized the meaning of the word, the essence of Being itself can just be picked out of it.

After this excursus on the peculiarity that the question of Being remains intimately linked to the question of the word, let us resume the course of our questioning. We must show that, and to what extent, our understanding of Being is distinctively definite in a manner arranged and enjoined by Being itself. If we now begin by considering one way of saying Being — for we are always and essentially forced to such saying in some manner — then what we are trying to do is pay attention to Being itself, which is said in this saying. We choose a simple and common and almost careless kind of saying, in which Being is said in a word form whose use is so frequent that we hardly even notice it.

We say, "God is." "The earth is." "The lecture is in the auditorium." "This man is from Swabia." "The cup is of silver." "The peasant is in the fields." "The book is mine." "He is dead." "Red is the port side." "In Russia there is famine." "The enemy is in retreat." "The vine disease is in the vineyards." "The dog is in the garden." "Over all the peaks / is peace." ⟨*Über allen Gipfeln / ist Ruh.*⟩ [68]

In each case, the "is" is meant differently. We can easily convince ourselves of this, as long as we take this saying of the "is" as it actually happens, that is, as spoken each time from out of a particular situation, task and mood, and not as mere sentences and stale examples in a grammar book.

"God is": that is, *actually present* ⟨gegenwärtig⟩. "The earth is": that is, we experience and believe it to be *constantly present at hand* ⟨vorhanden⟩. "The lecture is in the auditorium": that is, *it takes place*. "The man is from Swabia": that is, *he comes from there*. "The cup is of silver": that is, it *consists of* . . . "The peasant is in the fields": that is, *he has moved to the fields, he is staying there*. "The book is mine": that is, it *belongs* to me. "He is dead": that is, he has *succumbed* to death. "Red is the port side": that is, *it stands for*. "The dog is in the garden": that is, it *is running around there*. "Over all the peaks / is peace": that is — ??? Does the "is" in the verses mean that peace comes about, that it is present at hand, that it takes place, that it stays there? None of that will do here. And yet it is the same simple "is." Or does the verse mean: over all the peaks *peace prevails,* as in a classroom peace prevails? No, not that either! Or maybe: over all the peaks lies peace, or peace holds sway? That's closer, but this paraphrase is not right either.

"Over all the peaks / is peace": the "is" simply cannot be paraphrased, and yet it is merely this "is," as it was said in passing in those few verses that Goethe wrote in pencil on the windowframe of a hut on the Kickelhahn near Ilmenau (see the letter to Zelter of Sept. 4, 1831).[7] Strange how we waver here with our paraphrase, hesitate, and finally just let it go, not because this is too complicated and hard to understand, but because the verse is said so simply, even more simply and uniquely than any other, ordinary "is" that mixes itself inconspicuously and constantly into everyday saying and talking.

7. Johann Wolfgang von Goethe, *Goethe: Leben und Welt in Briefen* (Munich: Carl Hanser, 1978), 792.

However we may interpret the individual examples, this saying of the "is" shows us one thing clearly: in the "is," Being opens up to us in a manifold way. The assertion, at first so facile, that Being is an empty word, proves once again, and still more strikingly, to be untrue.

But—one could now object—the "is" is certainly meant in a manifold way. But that has nothing at all to do with the "is" itself; it simply depends on the manifold contents of the assertions, whose contents refer in each case to a different being: God, earth, cup, peasant, book, famine, peace over the peaks. It is only because the "is" in itself remains indeterminate and empty in its meaning that it can lie ready for such a manifold use, and can fill and determine itself "according to the situation." The manifoldness of determinate meanings we have cited thus proves the opposite of what we were trying to show. It just proves as clearly as possible that Being must be indeterminate in order to be susceptible to determination. [69]

What are we to say in reply? Here we are entering the domain of a decisive question: does the "is" become manifold on the basis of the content of the sentence that is attached to it in each case—i.e., on the basis of the domain of that about which the sentences are making assertions—or does the "is"—i.e., Being—contain in itself the manifoldness whose folding makes it possible for us to make manifold beings accessible to ourselves in the first place, each *as* it is? For now, let this question simply be posed. We are not yet sufficiently equipped to develop it further. What cannot be denied, and the only point we would like to make for now, is this: the "is" evinces, in its saying, a rich manifoldness of meanings. We always say the "is" in one of these meanings, although neither before nor after this saying do we carry out a special interpretation of the "is," much less meditate on Being. The "is," meant now this way and now that, simply wells up in our saying. And yet the manifoldness of its meanings is not arbitrary. We now want to convince ourselves of this.

Let us count up one by one the various meanings that we have interpreted by paraphrase. The "to be" said in the "is" signifies: "actually present," "constantly present at hand," "take place," "come from," "consist of," "stay," "belong," "succumb to," "stand for," "come about," "prevail," "have entered upon," "come forth." It is still difficult, and perhaps even impossible, because it goes against the essence of the matter, to extract a common meaning as a universal generic concept under which these modes of the "is" could be classified as species. However, a definite, unitary trait runs through all these meanings. It points our understanding of "to be" toward a definite horizon by which the understanding is fulfilled. The boundary drawn around the sense of "Being" stays within the sphere of presentness and presence ⟨*Gegenwärtigkeit und Anwesenheit*⟩, subsistence and substance ⟨*Bestehen und Bestand*⟩, staying and coming forth.

[70]   This all points in the direction of what we ran into when we first characterized the Greek experience and interpretation of Being. If we follow the usual explication of the infinitive, then the expression "to be" gets its sense from the unity and definiteness of the horizon that guides our understanding. In short, we thus understand the verbal noun "Being" on the basis of the infinitive, which in turn remains linked to the "is" and to the manifoldness we have pointed out in this "is." The definite and particular verb form "is," the *third person singular of the present indicative*, has a priority here. We do not understand "Being" with regard to the "thou art," "you are," "I am," or "they would be," although these all represent verbal inflections of "Being" that are just as good as "is." We take "to be" as the infinitive of "is." To put it the other way around, we involuntarily explain the infinitive "to be" to ourselves on the basis of the "is," almost as if nothing else were possible.

Accordingly, "Being" has the meaning we have indicated, which recalls the Greek conception of the essence of Being—a definiteness, then, which has not come to us from just anywhere, but which has long ruled our historical Dasein. At one blow, our search for the definiteness of the meaning of the word "Being" thus becomes explicitly what it is: a meditation on the provenance of our *concealed history*. The question, "How does it stand with Being?" must maintain itself within the history of Being if it is, in turn, to unfold and preserve its own historical import. In pursuing it, we will once again focus on the saying of Being.

CHAPTER FOUR

The Restriction of Being

JUST AS WE find a completely ordinary mode of saying Being in the "is," we also find entirely definite manners of speaking that have already become formulaic in the naming of the name "Being": Being and becoming; Being and seeming; Being and thinking; Being and the ought.

When we say "Being," we are driven, almost as if under compulsion, to say: Being *and* . . . The "and" does not simply mean that we incidentally attach and adjoin something additional but rather that we speak of something from which "Being" is distinguished: Being *and not* . . . But at the same time we mean, in these formulaic titles, something more that somehow properly belongs to Being as something distinguished from *it,* if only as its Other.

The course of our questioning up to this point has not only clarified its domain. To be sure, we have primarily taken up the question itself, the fundamental question of meta-physics, only as something passed on and proposed to us from some source. But the question has plainly unveiled itself to us in its questionworthiness. More and more, it now proves itself to be a concealed ground of our historical Dasein. It will remain this even and precisely when, self-satisfied and busy with all kinds of things, we wander around over this ground as over a thinly covered abyss ⟨*Abgrund*⟩.

We will now pursue the distinctions between Being and its Other. In doing this, we will learn that, contrary to the widely accepted opinion, Being is anything but an empty word for us. Instead, it is determined in so multifaceted a fashion that we can hardly manage to preserve this determination sufficiently. But this is not enough. This experience must be developed into a grounding experience for our future historical Dasein. So that we can participate in carrying out the distinctions in the right way from the start, we offer the following points of orientation:

1. Being is delimited against an Other and thus already has a determinateness in this setting of a limit.   [72]

2. The delimitation happens in *four* interrelated respects. Accordingly, the determinateness of Being must either be ramified and heightened or else diminish.

3. These distinctions are by no means accidental. What is held apart by them belongs together originally and tends to come together. Hence the divisions have their own necessity.

4. Therefore, the oppositions that initially strike us as mere formulas did not come up on arbitrary occasions and enter language as figures of speech, as it were. They arose in close connection with the stamping of Being whose openness became definitive for the history of the West. They had their inception with the inception of philosophical questioning.

5. The distinctions have not remained dominant only within Western philosophy. They pervade all knowing, acting, and speaking, even when they are not expressed explicitly or in these words.

6. The sequence in which we listed the terms already gives an

indication of the order of their essential connection and of the historical sequence in which they were stamped.

The two distinctions we named first (Being and becoming, Being and seeming) get formed at the very inception of Greek philosophy. As the most ancient, they are also the most familiar.

The third distinction (Being and thinking), which was foreshadowed in the inception no less than the first two, unfolds definitively in the philosophy of Plato and Aristotle, but first takes on its real form at the beginning of modernity. In fact, it plays an essential part in this beginning. In accordance with its history, this distinction is the most complex and, with regard to its intent, the most questionable. [This is why it remains for us the most worthy of question.][1]

The fourth distinction (Being and the ought) belongs thoroughly to modernity; it is prefigured only distantly by the characterization of *on* ⟨being, what is⟩ as *agathon* ⟨good⟩. Since the end of the eighteenth century, it has determined one of the predominant positions of the modern spirit toward beings in general.

7. Asking the question of Being in an originary way, in a way that grasps the task of unfolding the truth of the essence of Being, means facing the decision ⟨*Entscheidung*⟩ regarding the concealed powers [73] in these distinctions ⟨*Unterscheidungen*⟩, and it means bringing them back to their own truth.

All of these preliminary remarks should remain continually in view during the following considerations.

1. Being and Becoming

This division and opposition stands at the inception of the questioning of Being. Even today, it is still the most familiar restriction of Being through an Other; for it is immediately obvious, due to a

1. In parentheses in the 1953 edition.

representation of Being that has hardened into the self-evident. What becomes, is not yet. What is, no longer needs to become. That which "is" has left all becoming behind it, if indeed it ever became or could become. What "is" in the authentic sense also stands up against every onslaught from becoming.

Living at the turn of the fifth century B.C., Parmenides, the poetic thinker, set forth the Being of what is in contrast to becoming. His "didactic poem" has been handed down only in fragments, but these are great and essential. Here we will cite only a few verses (fragment 8, lines 1–6):

μόνος δ'ἔτι μῦθος ὁδοῖο
λείπεται ὡς ἔστιν· ταύτηι δ'ἐπὶ σήματ' ἔασι
πολλὰ μάλ', ὡς ἀγένητον ἐὸν καὶ ἀνώλεθρόν ἐστιν,
ἔστι γὰρ οὐλομελές τε καὶ ἀτρεμὲς ἠδ' ἀτέλεστον,
οὐδέ ποτ' ἦν οὐδ' ἔσται, ἐπεὶ νῦν ἔστιν ὁμοῦ πᾶν,
ἕν, συνεχές·

But there remains solely the saga of the way
(along which there opens up) how it stands with to-be ⟨sein⟩;
   for along this (way) many indications of it are given;
how Being without genesis and without decay,
complete, standing fully there alone,
without trembling in itself and not at all in need of finishing;
nor was it before, nor will it be someday,
for as the present, it is all-at-once, unique unifying united
gathering itself in itself from itself (holding itself together full
   of presentness).[2]

2. The more unconventional elements of Heidegger's translation are: 1) he renders *nun estin* as "as the present, it is," rather than as "it now is"; 2) *hen*, usually translated simply as "one," becomes "unique unifying united"; 3) *suneches*, usually translated as "continuous," is glossed as "gathering itself in itself from itself (holding itself together full of presentness)."

These few words stand there like archaic Greek statues. What we still possess of Parmenides' didactic poem fits into one slim volume, one that discredits the presumed necessity of entire libraries of philosophical literature. Anyone today who is acquainted with the standards of such a thinking discourse must lose all desire to write books.

[74]

What is said here from within Being are *sēmata*, not signs of Being, not predicates, but rather that which indicates Being itself in view of Being and from within Being. In such a view of Being we must look away from all genesis, passing away, and so on, and look beyond them in an active sense: in our seeing, we must hold them away, expel them. What is held away through the *a-* and the *oude* 〈"not" and "nor"〉 is not commensurate with Being. It has another measure.

We conclude from all this that Being indicates itself to this saying as the proper self-collected perdurance of the constant, undisturbed by restlessness and change. Even today, in accounts of the inception of Western philosophy, it is customary to oppose Parmenides' teaching to that of Heraclitus. An oft-cited saying is supposed to derive from Heraclitus: *panta rhei*, all is in flux. Hence there is no Being. All "is" becoming.

One finds nothing out of order in the occurrence of such oppositions — here Being, there becoming — because they confirm a rule that applies from the inception of philosophy onward, a rule that supposedly spans its entire history, namely that when one philosopher says A, the other says B, but when the latter says A, then the former says B. Of course, if someone asserts the opposite, that in the history of philosophy all thinkers have at bottom said the same thing, then this is taken as yet another outlandish imposition on everyday understanding. What use, then, is the multifaceted and complex history of Western philosophy, if they all say the same thing anyway? Then *one* philosophy would be enough. Everything has always already been said. And yet this "same" possesses, as its inner truth, the inexhaustible wealth of that which on every day is as if that day were its first.

Heraclitus, to whom one ascribes the doctrine of becoming, in stark contrast to Parmenides, in truth says the same as Parmenides. He would not be one of the greatest of the great Greeks if he said anything else. One simply must not interpret his doctrine of becoming according to the notions of a nineteenth-century Darwinist. Certainly, subsequent presentations of the opposition between Being and becoming never attained the uniquely self-contained self-sufficiency of Parmenides' saying. In that great era, the saying of the Being of beings contained within itself the [concealed][3] essence of Being of which it spoke. The secret of greatness consists in such historical necessity. For reasons that will become clear later on, for now we will restrict our discussion of this first division, "Being and becoming," to the guidelines we have provided.

2. Being and Seeming

[75]

This division is just as ancient as the first. The fact that these two divisions (Being and becoming, Being and seeming) are equally originary points to a deeper relation, one that remains obscure to this very day. For until now, the second division (Being and seeming) could not be developed further in its genuine form. For this, it is necessary to conceive this division originarily — that is, in a Greek way. For us, who are exposed to the modern epistemological misinterpretation, this is not easy — for us, who can respond to the simplicity of the essential only with difficulty, and then for the most part emptily.

At first the distinction appears clear. Being as opposed to seeming means what is actual as distinguished from and opposed to what is not actual — the genuine versus the ungenuine. This distinction also implies an appraisal in which Being takes precedence. As

3. In parentheses in the 1953 edition.

we say: the wonder and the wonderful ⟨*das Wunder und das Wunderbare*⟩, so, the seeming and what seems ⟨*der Schein und das Scheinbare*⟩. One often traces the distinction between Being and seeming back to the one we first discussed, Being and becoming. In contrast to Being as the constant, what seems is what at times surfaces, and just as fleetingly and unsteadily disappears again.

The distinction between Being and seeming is familiar to us, just one of the many worn coins that we exchange unexamined from hand to hand in an everyday gone flat. If it comes up, we use the distinction as a moral directive and rule of life, to avoid seeming and instead to strive for Being: "to be rather than to seem."

But as self-evident and familiar as the distinction is, we do not understand why precisely Being and seeming are originally disjoined. The fact that this happens indicates a belonging-together. What does this consist in? Above all, we need to grasp the concealed unity of Being and seeming. We no longer understand this unity because we have fallen away from the inceptive distinction, which has developed historically, and now we carry it around merely as something that, at some time, in some place, was once put into circulation.

In order to grasp the division, we must go back, here too, into the inception.

Yet if we distance ourselves from thoughtlessness and idle talk while we still have time, we can still find, even within ourselves, a trace of the understanding of the distinction. We say "seeming" and [76] know the rain and the sunshine. The sun shines ⟨*scheinen:* to appear, to seem; to shine⟩. We say: "The room was dimly lit by the light ⟨*Schein*⟩ of a candle." The Alemannic dialect uses the word *Scheinholz*—that is, wood ⟨*Holz*⟩ that glows in the dark. From depictions of saints, we are familiar with the saint's halo ⟨*Heiligenschein*⟩, the radiant ring around the head. But we also know about false saints ⟨*Scheinheilige*⟩, those who look like saints, but are not. We encounter the mock battle ⟨*Scheingefecht*⟩, a maneuver that simulates battle.

While it shines ⟨*scheint*⟩, the sun seems ⟨*scheint*⟩ to move around the earth. That the moon, which shines, is two feet wide—that just seems that way, it is just a seeming ⟨*Schein*⟩. Here we come across two kinds of *Schein* and *scheinen*. But they do not simply stand next to each other; instead, one is derived from the other. The sun, for example, can seem to move around the earth only because it shines— that is, glows and in glowing appears ⟨*erscheint*⟩, that is, makes itself manifest ⟨*zum Vorschein kommt*⟩. And in the shining of the sun as glowing and radiating, we also experience this radiation as warmth. The sun shines: it shows itself and we feel warmth. As the luster of the halo, the shining of the light makes the bearer manifest as a saint.

Considered more precisely, we find three modes of *Schein:* 1) *Schein* as luster and glow; 2) *Schein* and *Scheinen* as appearing ⟨*erscheinen*⟩, the manifestation ⟨*Vor-schein*⟩ of something; 3) *Schein* as mere seeming, the semblance ⟨*Anschein*⟩ presented by something. But at the same time it becomes clear that the second mode of *Scheinen,* appearing in the sense of self-showing, is also appropriate to *Schein* as luster, as well as to *Schein* as semblance, and not as an accidental characteristic, but as the ground of their possibility. The essence of seeming lies in appearing. It is self-showing, self-setting-forth, standing-by, and lying-at-hand. The long-awaited book has now appeared—that is, it lies at hand, it is present at hand and available. We say the moon shines; this does not just mean that it has a shine, it casts a certain brightness, but that it stands in the heavens, it is present, it is. The stars shine: in glowing they are coming to presence. *Seeming* means exactly the same as *Being* here. [Sappho's verse, *asteres men amphi kalan selannan* . . . and the poem by Matthias Claudius "Ein Wiegenlied bei Mondschein zu singen" offer a suitable opportunity to reflect on Being and seeming.][4]

4. In parentheses in the 1953 edition. See Sappho, Lobel and Page no. 34, in *Greek Lyric,* trans. David A. Campbell (Cambridge: Harvard University Press,

If we pay attention to what has been said, then we will discover the inner connection between Being and seeming. But we can grasp this connection fully only if we understand "Being" in a correspondingly originary way, and here this means in a Greek way. [77] We know that Being opens itself up to the Greeks as *phusis*. The emerging-abiding sway is in itself at the same time the appearing that seems. The roots *phu-* and *pha-* name the same thing. *Phuein,* the emerging that reposes in itself, is *phainesthai,* lighting-up, self-showing, appearing. The definite traits of Being that we have cited, if only as a list, and the results of our reference to Parmenides have already given us a certain understanding of the fundamental Greek word for Being.

It would be instructive to clarify the naming force of this word through the great poetry of the Greeks, as well. Here it may be enough to indicate that for Pindar, for example, *phua* is the fundamental characteristic of Dasein: *to de phua kratiston hapan,* that which is from and through *phua* is wholly and fully the most powerful (Olympian Ode IX, 100); *phua* means what one originally and authentically already is: that which essentially unfolds as having been ⟨*das Ge-Wesende*⟩, in contrast to the subsequently forced and enforced contrivances and fabrications.[5] Being is the fundamental characteristic of the noble and nobility (that is, what has and rests upon a high, essential provenance). In this connection, Pindar coins the phrase: *genoi hoios essi mathōn* (Pythian Ode II, 72): "may you come forth as the one who you are by learning." But for the

---

1982), 83: "The stars hide away their shining form [*eidos*] around the lovely moon when in all her fullness she shines (over all) the earth"; Matthias Claudius (1740–1815), "Ein Wiegenlied bei Mondschein zu singen" ("A Lullaby to Sing by Moonlight"), in *Sämtliche Werke* (Munich: Winkler-Verlag [1968]), 75–77.

5. The word *phua* is closely related to *phusis* and can be used as a poetic equivalent to it.

Greeks, standing-in-itself means nothing other than standing-there, standing-in-the-light. Being means appearing. Appearing does not mean something derivative, which from time to time meets up with Being. Being essentially unfolds *as* appearing.

With this, there collapses as an empty construction the widespread notion of Greek philosophy according to which it was supposedly a "realistic" doctrine of an objective Being, in contrast to modern subjectivism. This common notion is based on a superficial understanding. We must set aside terms such as "subjective" and "objective," "realistic" and "idealistic."

But now, given this more adequate grasp of how the Greeks understood Being, we must take the decisive step that will open up for us the inner connection between Being and seeming. We must attain insight into a connection that is originally and uniquely Greek but which had profound consequences for the spirit of the West. Being essentially unfolds as *phusis*. The emerging sway is an appearing. As such, it makes manifest. This already implies that Being, appearing, is a letting-step-forth from concealment. Insofar as a being as such *is*, it places itself into and stands in *unconcealment, alētheia*. We thoughtlessly translate, and this means at the same time misinterpret, this word as "truth." To be sure, one is now gradually beginning to translate the Greek word *alētheia* literally. But this is not much use if immediately afterward one again understands "truth" in an entirely different, un-Greek sense and reads this other sense into the Greek word. For the Greek essence of truth is possible only together with the Greek essence of Being as *phusis*. On the grounds of the unique essential relation between *phusis* and *alētheia*, the Greeks could say: beings as beings are true. The true as such is in being. This says that what shows itself in its sway stands in the unconcealed. The unconcealed as such comes to a stand in showing itself. Truth, as un-concealment, is not an addendum to Being. [78]

Truth belongs to the essence of Being. To be a being — this implies to be made manifest, to step forth in appearing, to set itself forth, to pro-duce something ⟨*sich hin-stellen, etwas her-stellen*⟩. Not-Being, in contrast, means to step away from appearance, from presence. The essence of appearance involves this stepping-forth and stepping-away, this hither and hence in the genuinely demonstrative, indicative sense. Being is thus dispersed into the manifold beings. These display themselves here, there, and everywhere as what is close by in each instance. *As* what appears, what is gives itself an aspect, *dokei*.[6] *Doxa* means aspect—namely, the respect in which one stands. If the aspect, corresponding to what emerges in it, is an eminent one, then *doxa* means brilliance and glory. In Hellenistic philosophy and in the New Testament, *doxa theou, gloria Dei,* is the majesty of God. To glorify, to bestow and demonstrate regard, is, in Greek, to place into the light and thereby to provide constancy, Being. Glory, for the Greeks, is not something additional that someone may or may not receive; it is the highest manner of Being. For us today, glory has long been nothing but celebrity, and as such it is a highly dubious matter, an acquisition thrown around and distributed by the newspaper and the radio—nearly the opposite of Being. If for Pindar glorifying constitutes the essence of poetry and *is* poetizing, and to poetize is to place into the light, then this by no means indicates that for him the concept of light plays a special role but simply that he thinks and poetizes as a Greek—that is, he stands in the allotted essence of Being.

We needed to show that and how, for the Greeks, appearing belongs to Being, or, more sharply stated: that and how Being has its essence together *with* appearing. This was clarified through the highest possibility of human Being, as the Greeks formed it, through glory and glorifying. Glory means *doxa*. *Dokeō* means: I

---

6. *Dokein* is usually translated "to seem," and the related noun *doxa* is often translated as "opinion."

show myself, I appear, I step into the light. What is experienced   [79]
here mainly in terms of vision and the visage, the respect in which
someone stands, is grasped more in terms of hearing and calling
⟨Rufen⟩ by the other word for glory: *kleos*. Glory is the repute ⟨Ruf⟩
in which one stands. Heraclitus says (fragment 29): αἱρεῦνται γὰρ
ἓν ἀντὶ ἁπάντων οἱ ἄριστοι, κλέος ἀέναον θνητῶν, οἱ δὲ πολλοὶ
κεκόρηνται ὅκωσπερ κτήνεα: "for the noblest choose one thing
above all others: glory, which constantly persists, in contrast to
what dies; but the many are sated like cattle."

But there is a restriction that pertains to all this, one that at the
same time shows the state of affairs in its essential fullness. *Doxa* is
the respect ⟨Ansehen⟩ in which someone stands, and in a wider
sense, the aspect ⟨Ansehen⟩ that each being possesses and displays in
its look ⟨Aussehen⟩ *(eidos, idea)*. A city offers a grand vista. The view
that a being has in itself, and so first can offer from itself, lets itself
then be apprehended at this or that time, from this or that viewpoint. The vista that offers itself alters with each new viewpoint.
Thus this view is also one that *we* take and make for ourselves. In
experiencing and busying ourselves with beings, we constantly construct views for ourselves from their look. This often happens without our looking closely at the thing itself. Along some pathways or
other, and on some grounds or other, we arrive at a view about the
thing. We construct an opinion for ourselves about it. Thus it can
happen that the view that we adopt has no support in the thing
itself. It is then a mere view, an assumption. We assume a thing to
be thus or thus. Then we are only opining. To assume or accept, in
Greek, is *dechesthai*. [Accepting remains related to the offer of appearing.][7] *Doxa*, as what is assumed to be thus or thus, is opinion.

7. In parentheses in the 1953 edition. Heidegger's *annehmen* can mean either
"assume" or "accept," so we have translated it both ways. *Dechesthai* means to
accept.

We have now reached our goal. Because Being, *phusis*, consists in appearing, in the offering of a look and of views, it stands essentially, and thus necessarily and constantly, in the possibility of a look that precisely covers over and conceals what beings are in truth—that is, in unconcealment. This aspect in which beings now come to stand is *seeming* in the sense of semblance. Wherever there is unconcealment of beings, there is the possibility of seeming, and conversely: wherever beings stand in seeming, and take a prolonged and secure stand there, seeming can break apart and fall away.

The term *doxa* names various things: 1) aspect, or respect, as glory; 2) aspect as the sheer view that something offers; 3) aspect as [80] merely looking-so, "seeming" as mere semblance; 4) a view that a person constructs for himself, opinion. This multiple meaning of the word is not looseness of language but a play with deep foundations in the mature wisdom of a great language, a multiplicity that preserves the essential traits of Being in the word. In order to see correctly from the very start here, we must guard ourselves against cavalierly taking seeming as something just "imaginary," "subjective," and thereby falsifying it. Instead, just as appearing belongs to beings themselves, so does seeming.

Let us think about the sun. It rises and sets for us daily. Only a very few astronomers, physicists, and philosophers directly experience this fact otherwise, as the movement of the Earth around the sun—and even they do so only on the grounds of a particular, although rather widespread, conception. But the seeming in which sun and Earth stand—for example, the early morning of a landscape, the sea in the evening, the night—is an appearing. This seeming is not nothing. Neither is it untrue. Neither is it a mere appearance of relations that in nature are really otherwise. This seeming is historical and it is history, uncovered and grounded in poetry and saga, and thus an essential domain of our world.

Only all the effete latecomers, with their overly clever wit, believe they can be done with the historical power of seeming by explaining it as "subjective," where the essence of this "subjectivity" is something extremely dubious. The Greeks experienced it otherwise. Again and again, they had first to tear Being away from seeming and preserve it against seeming. [Being essentially unfolds from un-concealment.][8]

Only by undergoing the struggle between Being and seeming did they wrest Being forth from beings, did they bring beings into constancy and unconcealment: the gods and the state, the temples and the tragedies, athletic competition and philosophy — all this in the midst of seeming, besieged by it, but also taking it seriously, knowing its power. Only with the sophists and Plato was seeming explained as, and thus reduced to, mere seeming. At the same time, Being as *idea* was elevated to a supersensory realm. The chasm, *khōrismos,* was torn open between the merely apparent beings here below and the real Being somewhere up there. Christian doctrine then established itself in this chasm, while at the same time reinterpreting the Below as the created and the Above as the Creator, and with weapons thus reforged, it set itself against antiquity [as paganism][9] and distorted it. And so Nietzsche is right to say that Christianity is Platonism for the people.[10]

In contrast, the great age of Greek Dasein is a unique, creative self-assertion amid the turmoil of the multiply intertwined counterplay of the powers of Being and seeming. (For the originary, essential connection between human Dasein, Being as such, truth in the sense of unconcealment, and untruth as covering-over, see *Being and Time,* §44 and §68.) [81]

For the thinking of the early Greek thinkers, the unity and antag-

8. In parentheses in the 1953 edition.
9. In parentheses in the 1953 edition.
10. *Beyond Good and Evil,* preface.

onism of Being and seeming were powerful in an originary way. However, this was all portrayed at its highest and purest in Greek tragic poetry. Let us consider Sophocles' *Oedipus Rex*. Oedipus, who at the beginning is the savior and lord of the state, in the brilliance of glory and the grace of the gods, is hurled out of this seeming. This seeming is not just Oedipus' subjective view of himself, but that within which the appearing of his Dasein happens. In the end, he is unconcealed in his Being as the murderer of his father and the defiler of his mother. The path from this beginning in brilliance to this end in horror is a unique struggle between seeming (concealment and distortion) and unconcealment (Being). The city is besieged by what is concealed in the murder of the former king, Laios. With the passion of one who stands in the openness of brilliance and who is a Greek, Oedipus goes to unveil what is concealed. In doing so, he must, step by step, place himself into an unconcealment that in the end he can endure only by gouging out his own eyes—that is, by placing himself outside all light, letting the veil of night fall around him—and then by crying out, as a blind man, for all doors to be flung open so that such a man may become revealed to the people as the man who he *is*.

But we should not see Oedipus only as the human being who meets his downfall; in Oedipus we must grasp that form of Greek Dasein in which this Dasein's fundamental passion ventures into what is wildest and most far-flung: the passion for the unveiling of Being—that is, the struggle over Being itself. Hölderlin, in the poem "*In lieblicher Bläue blühet . . . ,*" speaks this seer's word: "King Oedipus has perhaps one eye too many."[11] This eye too many is the fundamental condition for all great questioning and knowing as

11. "In Lovely Blueness . . . ," in Friedrich Hölderlin, *Poems and Fragments,* trans. Michael Hamburger, 3d ed. (London: Anvil, 1994), 717.

well as their sole metaphysical ground. The knowledge and science of the Greeks are this passion.

When today one enjoins science to serve the people, this is indeed a necessary and worthy demand, but it demands too little, and it does not demand what is authentic. The concealed will to transform beings for the openness of Dasein calls for more. In order to bring about a change in science — and this first means bringing about a change in originary knowing — our Dasein needs an entirely different metaphysical depth. It once again needs a fundamental relation to the Being of beings as a whole, a relation that is well founded and built truly. [82]

The connection between us today and everything that Being, truth, and seeming mean has been so confused and groundless and passionless for so long that even in our interpretation and appropriation of Greek poetry, we have an inkling of only a small portion of the power of this poetic saying in Greek Dasein itself. We have Karl Reinhardt to thank for the latest interpretation of Sophocles (1933), which comes essentially closer to Greek Dasein and Being than all previous attempts, because Reinhardt sees and questions tragic happenings according to the fundamental connections among Being, unconcealment and seeming. Even if modern subjectivisms and psychologisms still often interfere, Reinhardt's interpretation of *Oedipus Rex* as the "tragedy of seeming" is a magnificent achievement.[12]

I will conclude these remarks on the poetic formation of the struggle between Being and seeming among the Greeks by quoting a passage from Sophocles' *Oedipus Rex* that gives us the opportunity to establish the relation between our previous characterization

12. Karl Reinhardt, *Sophocles,* trans. Hazel Harvey and David Harvey (Oxford: Blackwell, 1979), chapter 4.

of Greek Being as constancy and our new characterization of Being as appearing.

The few verses from the last choral passage of the tragedy (verses 1189 ff.) run as follows:

τίς γὰρ τίς ἀνὴρ πλέον
τᾶς εὐδαιμονίας φέρει
ἢ τοσοῦτον ὅσον δοκεῖν
καὶ δόξαντ᾽ ἀποκλῖναι;

Who then, which man, bears more
controlled and fitting Dasein
than what suffices to stand in seeming
in order then — as one who seems — to decline?
    (namely, from standing-there-straight-in-himself)[13]

In clarifying the essence of the infinitive, we spoke of certain words that display an *enklisis,* a de-clining, falling over *(casus).* Now we see that seeming, as a variant of Being itself, is the same as falling over. It is a variant of Being in the sense of standing-there-straight-in-itself. Both deviations from Being are determined by Being as the constancy of standing-in-the-light, that is, of appearing.

[83]

It should now be clearer that seeming belongs to Being itself as appearing. Being as seeming is no less powerful than Being as un-concealment. Seeming happens in and with beings themselves. But seeming not only lets beings appear as what they really are not, it not only distorts the beings whose seeming it is; in all this it also covers itself over as seeming, inasmuch as it shows itself as Being. Because seeming essentially distorts itself in covering-over and distortion, we rightly say that appearances can be deceiving.[14] This

---

13. A more conventional translation would be: "Who then, which man / has more happiness / than what suffices to seem / and, in seeming, to decline?"
14. The German idiom is *der Schein trügt,* or "seeming deceives."

deception is part of seeming itself. Only because seeming itself deceives can it trick human beings and lead them into delusion. But self-deception is only one of many modes in which human beings move in the interlocking triple world of Being, unconcealment, and seeming.

The space, so to speak, that opens itself up in the interlocking of Being, unconcealment, and seeming, I understand as *errancy*. Seeming, deception, delusion, errancy stand in definite relations as regards their essences and their ways of happening, relations that have long been misinterpreted for us by psychology and epistemology, relations that we therefore in our everyday Dasein barely still experience and barely recognize with adequate perspicacity as powers.

It was necessary first to make clear how, on the grounds of the Greek interpretation of Being as *phusis, and only on these grounds,* both *truth* in the sense of unconcealment and *seeming* as a definite mode of the arising self-showing belong necessarily to *Being*.

Being and seeming belong together, and as belonging-together are constantly by one another, and in this by-one-another they also always proffer change from one to the other, and hence constant confusion, and hence, the possibility of aberration and mistakes. For this reason, the chief effort of thinking at the inception of philosophy—that is, in the first opening-up of the Being of beings—had to consist in controlling the urgency of Being in seeming, in distinguishing Being from seeming. This in turn demands that truth as unconcealment be brought forward against concealment, disclosing against closing-off as covering-over and disguising. Inasmuch as Being has to be distinguished from an Other and reinforced as *phusis,* Being is distinguished from not-Being, but not-Being is also distinguished from seeming. The two distinctions do not coincide.

Because matters stand in this way with Being, seeming, and [84] not-Being, three paths are necessary for the humans who stand in the midst of self-opening Being and who always relate to beings in such and such a manner according to this stance. If they are to take over their Dasein in the clarity of Being, humans must bring Being to a stand, they must endure it in seeming and against seeming, they must tear away both seeming and Being from the abyss of not-Being.

The human being must distinguish among these three paths and, accordingly, come to a decision for or against them. At the inception of philosophy, to think is to open up and lay out the three paths. This act of distinguishing puts the human being, as one who knows, upon these paths and at their intersection, and thus into constant de-cision.[15] With de-cision, history as such begins. In de-cision, and only in de-cision, is anything decided, even about the gods. [Accordingly, de-cision here does not mean the judgment and choice of human beings, but rather a division ⟨Scheidung⟩ in the aforementioned togetherness of Being, unconcealment, seeming and not-Being.][16]

The philosophy of Parmenides, as the most ancient attempt to lay out the three paths, has been passed down to us in the didactic poem we have already mentioned. We will characterize the three paths by quoting some fragments from this poem. A complete interpretation is not possible here.

Fragment 4, in translation, runs:

Come, then, I say to you: but take into keeping the word that
    you hear (about)
which paths are to be held in view as the only ones for
    inquiring.

15. *Ent-scheidung:* Heidegger stresses the root *scheiden,* which, like the Latin root of "decision," means to cut.
16. In parentheses in the 1953 edition.

The one: how it is (what it, Being, is) and also how not-Being
  (is) impossible.
This is the pathway of grounded trust, for it follows
  unconcealment.
But the other one: how it is not, and also how not-Being is
  necessary.
So this one, I declare, is a footpath that cannot be
  recommended at all,
for neither are you able to cultivate acquaintance with not-
  Being, for it cannot be brought near,
nor can you declare it with words.[17]

Here, to begin, two paths are set out sharply against each other:
1. The path to Being, which at the same time is the path into
unconcealment. This path is unavoidable.
2. The path to not-Being; it cannot be traveled, of course, but
precisely because of this, the path must be recognized as unviable,
for it leads into not-Being. The fragment at the same time gives us
the most ancient document in philosophy that shows that, together
with the path of Being, the path of Nothing must expressly be
considered, that it is consequently a misunderstanding of the question about Being if one turns one's back on Nothing with the as-
surance that Nothing obviously is not. (That Nothing is not a
being, however, by no means prevents it from belonging to Being
in its own manner.)

But meditation on the two paths mentioned entails a confrontation with a third, a path that runs counter to the first in its own
manner. The third path looks like the first, but it does not lead to

[85]

17. A more conventional translation would have "truth" instead of "unconcealment"; "is wholly unknowable" instead of "cannot be recommended at
all"; and "is impracticable" instead of "cannot be brought near." This fragment
is today usually numbered 2.

Being. Hence it provokes the semblance that it too is only a path to not-Being in the sense of Nothing.

Fragment 6 at first holds the two paths indicated in fragment 4, the one to Being and the one into Nothing, in strict opposition to each other. But at the same time, in opposition to the second way, the one into Nothing that is inaccessible and thus hopeless, a third way is indicated:

> Needful is the setting-down that gathers, as well as
>   apprehending: the being in its Being ⟨*Seiend in dessen Sein*⟩;
> For the being has Being; not-Being has no "is"; to this I bid you
>   attend.
> Above all, keep away from this way of inquiring.
> But also from the way that human beings openly prepare for
>   themselves, those who know nothing,
> the two-headed ones; for disorientation
> is the directive for their errant apprehending; but they are
>   thrown this way and that,
> both dull and blind, bewildered; the tribe of those who do not
>   distinguish,
> whose ordinance it is that the present-at-hand and not-present-
>   at-hand are the same
> and also not the same — for them the path is altogether
>   contrary.[18]

The way now mentioned is the way of *doxa* in the sense of seeming. Along this way, that which is has now this look, now that look. Here only views prevail. Human beings slide back and forth

---

18. A more conventional translation would render the opening of this fragment as "It is necessary both to say and to think that being is," and the end as "who believe that to be and not to be are the same and also not the same, and the path of all turns backward."

from one view to the other. In this way, they mix together Being and seeming.

This way is constantly traveled, so that human beings com-[86]
pletely lose themselves upon it.

It is all the more needful to know this way *as such,* so that Being
may unveil itself in and against seeming.

Accordingly, we find the indication of this third way and its
relation to the first in fragment 1, verses 28–32:

> But it is also needful (for you, who are now setting out upon
>   the way to Being) to experience all:
> the untrembling heart of well-rounded unconcealment
> as well as the views of human beings, in which there dwells no
>   reliance on the unconcealed.
> But in all this you shall also come to know how that which
>   seems persists
> in traversing all things (in its own way) as seeming,
>   contributing to the completion of all things.[19]

The third way is the way of seeming, such that on this way,
seeming is experienced *as* belonging to Being. For the Greeks, these
words had an originary and striking force. Being and truth create
their essence out of *phusis.* The self-showing of the seeming belongs
directly to Being and yet (at bottom) does not belong to it. So
what seems must also be exposed as mere seeming, over and over
again.

The threefold path provides this indication, unitary in itself:
The way to Being is unavoidable.
The way to Nothing is inaccessible.

---

19. The translation and interpretation of this passage is controversial, but
most commentators see only two paths in Parmenides' text.

The way to seeming is always accessible and traveled, but it can be avoided.

So the man who truly knows is not the one who blindly runs after a truth but only the one who constantly knows all three ways, that of Being, that of not-Being, and that of seeming. Superior knowing — and all knowing is superiority — is granted only to one who has experienced the sweeping storm on the way of Being, to whom the terror of the second way to the abyss of Nothing has not remained foreign, and who has still taken over the third way, the way of seeming, as a constant urgency.

To this knowing belongs what the Greeks in their great age called *tolma:* to dare everything with Being, not-Being, and seeming all at once — that is, to raise Dasein above itself into the decision about Being, not-Being, and seeming. On the basis of this fundamental orientation to Being, one of their greatest poets, Pindar (Nemean Ode III, 70), says: *en de peira telos diaphainetai:* in the daring test in the midst of beings, fulfillment makes itself manifest, the delimitation of what has been brought to stand and has come to stand, that is, Being.[20]

[87]

Here speaks the same fundamental orientation that shines forth from the saying of Heraclitus we have cited about *polemos* (fragment 53). Con-frontation — that is, not mere quarreling and feuding but the strife of the striving — sets the essential and the unessential, the high and the low, into their limits and makes them manifest.

What is an inexhaustible source of wonder is not only the mature sureness of this fundamental orientation to Being but also the richness of its formation in word and stone.

We conclude our elucidation of the opposition — and this also means the unity — of Being and seeming with a saying of Heracli-

20. Conventional translation: "In the test, the end shines through."

tus (fragment 123): *phusis kruptesthai philei:* Being [emerging appearance][21] intrinsically inclines toward self-concealment.[22] Being means: to appear in emerging, to step forth out of concealment—and for this very reason, concealment and the provenance from concealment essentially belong to Being. Such provenance lies in the essence of Being, of what appears as such. Being remains inclined toward concealment, whether in great veiling and silence, or in the most superficial distorting and obscuring. The immediate proximity of *phusis* and *kruptesthai* reveals the intimacy of Being and seeming as the strife between them.

If we understand the formulaic title "Being and seeming" in the undiminished force of the division for which the Greeks inceptively struggled, then we can understand not only how Being differs from and is delimited against seeming but also how Being and seeming intrinsically belong to the division "Being and becoming." What maintains itself in becoming is, on the one hand, no longer Nothing, but on the other hand it is not yet what it is destined to be. In accordance with this "no longer and not yet," becoming remains shot through with not-Being. However, it is not a pure Nothing, but no longer this and not yet that, and as such, it is constantly something else. So now it looks like this, now it looks like that. It offers an intrinsically inconstant view. Seen in this way, becoming is a seeming of Being.

In the inceptive disclosure of the Being of beings, then, becoming, as well as seeming, must be opposed to Being. Yet becoming as "arising" nevertheless belongs to *phusis*. If we understand both in a Greek manner, becoming as coming-into-presence and going-away out of presence, Being as emergent and appearing coming to

21. In parentheses in the 1953 edition.
22. Conventional translation: "Nature loves to hide."

[88]   presence, not-Being as absence, then the reciprocal relation between emerging and decaying is appearance, Being itself. Just as
becoming is the seeming of Being, seeming as appearing is the
becoming of Being.

This already lets us see that it will not do simply to reduce the
division between Being and seeming to that between Being and
becoming, or vice versa. So the question of the relation between
these two divisions must remain open for now. The answer will
depend on the originariness, breadth, and solidity of the grounding
of that within which the Being of beings essentially unfolds. And
philosophy, in its inception, did not tie itself down to particular
propositions. It is true that the subsequent accounts of its history
give this impression, for these accounts are doxographical—that is,
they describe the opinions and views of the great thinkers. But
whoever eavesdrops on the great thinkers and ransacks them for
views and standpoints can be sure of making a false move and
taking a false step, even before he has derived any result—that is,
the formula or the slogan for a philosophy. The *thinking* and the
Dasein of the Greeks struggles over a decision between the great
powers of Being and becoming, Being and seeming. This confrontation had to develop the relation between thinking and Being
into a definite form. This implies that the formation of the third
division is already being prepared among the Greeks.

3. Being and Thinking

The definitive dominance of the division between "Being and
thinking" in Western Dasein has already been pointed out more
than once. Its predominance must have its ground in the essence of
this division, in what sets it apart from the two divisions we have
mentioned and also from the fourth. And so, at the very beginning,
we would like to indicate what is proper to it. First, let us compare

this division with the two we have already discussed. In these, what is distinguished from Being comes to us from beings themselves. We find it before us in the domain of beings. We encounter not only becoming but also seeming in beings as such (consider the rising and setting sun, the oft-mentioned stick that appears broken when dipped in water, and much else of this sort). Becoming and seeming lie on the same level, as it were, as the Being of beings.

However, in the division between *Being and thinking*, not only is what is now distinguished from Being — that is, thinking — different in content from becoming and seeming, but the direction of the opposition is also essentially different. Thinking sets itself against Being in such a way that Being is re-presented to thinking, and consequently stands against thinking like an ob-ject (*Gegen-stand*, that which stands against). This is not the case in the divisions mentioned earlier. And now we can also see why this division can attain predominance. It has the superior power, inasmuch as it does not set itself between and among the other three divisions but represents all of them to itself and thus, setting them before itself, transposes them, so to speak.[23] Consequently, thinking is no longer just the opposing member in some new distinction but becomes the basis on which one decides about what stands against it, so much so that Being in general gets interpreted on the basis of thinking.

[89]

It is in this direction that we must assess the meaning of this particular division in the context of our task. For at bottom we are asking how it stands with Being, how and on what basis it is brought to stand in its essence, how it is understood and conceived and set up as definitive.

In the seemingly irrelevant division *Being and thinking* we have to recognize that fundamental orientation of the spirit of the West

23. *Vorstellen* (to represent) etymologically means to set before. *Umstellen* (to transpose) is a related word.

that is the real target of our attack. It can be overcome only *originally* — that is, in such a way that its inceptive truth is shown its own limits and thereby founded anew.

From the point at which we currently stand in the course of our questioning, we can see something further. Earlier we made it clear that the word "Being," contrary to popular opinion, has a thoroughly limited meaning. This implies that Being itself is understood in a definite way, and as something so understood, it is open to us. But every understanding, as a basic kind of opening-up, must move in a definite line of sight. This thing — for example, the clock — is closed off to us in what it is, unless we already know about something like time, reckoning with time, measuring time. Our viewpoint's line of sight must already be laid out in advance. We call this prior line of sight "perspective." Thus it will become clear not only that Being is not understood in an indeterminate way but that the determinate understanding of Being itself moves within a prior line of sight that has already been determined.

Going back and forth, slipping and sliding along this line, has become so much a part of our own flesh and blood that we neither recognize it nor even understand and pay attention to the *question* about it. Our immersion [not to say lostness][24] in the prior view and insight that sustains and guides all our understanding of Being is all the more powerful, and at the same time all the more concealed, because the Greeks themselves no longer shed light on this prior line of sight as such. For essential reasons (not due to a failure), they could not shed light on it. But the unfolding of the division between Being and thinking plays an essential part in forming and consolidating this prior line of sight in which the Greek understanding of Being already moves.

Nevertheless, we have placed this division not in the first but in

[90]

---

24. In parentheses in the 1953 edition.

the third position. At first we will try to elucidate its content in the same way as we elucidated the first two.

Once again, we begin with a general characterization of what now stands opposed to Being.

What does it mean to think? We say: *der Mensch denkt und Gott lenkt* (man proposes, God disposes: literally, human beings think and God controls). Here, to think means to devise this and that, to plan; to think about something means to set one's sights on it. "To think evil" means to intend evil; *andenken* means not to forget something. Here, thinking means memory and remembrance (*das Andenken und das Gedenken*). We use the turn of phrase: just to think something up—that is, picture it, imagine it. Someone says: I think it's turning out all right—that is, that's the way it seems to me, I look at it that way and am of this opinion. To think in an emphatic sense means to think something over, to deliberate on something, a situation, a plan, an event. "Thinking" also serves as the title for the labor and work of the one we call a "thinker." Of course, all human beings think, as opposed to animals, but not everyone is a thinker.

What do we gather from this linguistic usage? Thinking relates to what is future as well as to what is past, but also to what is present. Thinking brings something before us, *represents it*. This representing always starts of our own accord, is freely at our disposal. This freedom is not arbitrary but is bound by the fact that in representing, we think upon and think through what is represented by analyzing it, by laying it out and reassembling it. But in thinking, we not only set something forth before ourselves of our own accord, and we do not just analyze it in order to cut it apart, but we think over what is represented and follow after it. We do not simply take it just as it strikes us, but we try to find the way to get behind the thing, as we say, to experience how it stands with the thing in general. We form a concept of it for ourselves. We seek the universal.

We will at first give prominence to three of the characteristics of what is usually called "thinking" that we have listed:

[91]   1. Re-presenting "of our own accord" as a distinctively free behavior.

2. Re-presenting in the mode of analytical connection.

3. The representational comprehension of the universal.

In each case, according to the area in which this re-presenting moves, according to the degree of freedom, the sharpness and sureness of the analysis, and the breadth of the comprehension, thinking is either superficial or deep, empty or full of content, nonbinding or compelling, playful or serious.

But none of this yet shows us why it should be thinking that attains the fundamental orientation in regard to Being that we have pointed out. Thinking, along with desiring, willing, and feeling, is one of our faculties. In all our faculties and modes of behavior we are related to beings, not just in thinking. Certainly. But the distinction "Being and thinking" means something more essential than the mere relation to beings. The distinction stems from the way in which what is distinguished and divided belongs inceptively and intrinsically to Being itself. The heading "Being and thinking" names a distinction that is, so to speak, demanded by Being itself.

But in any case, such an intrinsic belonging of thinking to Being cannot be glimpsed on the basis of what we have offered so far as a characterization of thinking. Why not? Because we have not yet gained an adequate concept of thinking. But where can we get such a concept?

When we ask this, we are acting as if there had not already been a "logic" for centuries. It is the science of thinking, the doctrine of the rules of thinking and the forms of what is thought.

Furthermore, it is the one philosophical science and discipline in which the standpoints and tendencies of worldviews play little or no part. Furthermore, logic counts as a secure, trustworthy science.

It has taught the same thing since antiquity. True, one logician rearranges the structure and sequence of the various traditional doctrines; another leaves out this and that; still another makes additions from epistemology, another supports everything with psychology. But on the whole, a gratifying agreement prevails. Logic relieves us of the trouble of asking elaborate questions about the essence of thinking.

However, we would still like to raise one question. What does "logic" mean? The term is an abbreviation for *epistēmē logikē,* the science of *logos.* And *logos* here means assertion. But logic is supposed to be the doctrine of thinking. Why is logic the science of assertion?   [92]

Why is thinking determined on the basis of assertion? This is by no means self-evident. Just above, we explicated "thinking" without reference to assertion and discourse. Meditation on the essence of thinking is consequently a truly unique sort of meditation when it is undertaken as a meditation on *logos,* thereby becoming logic. "Logic" and "the logical" are simply not *the* ways to define thinking without further ado, as if nothing else were possible. On the other hand, it was no accident that the doctrine of thinking became "logic."

Be that as it may, to appeal to logic for purposes of delimiting the essence of thinking is already a questionable enterprise, because logic as such, and not just its individual doctrines and theories, is still something worthy of questioning. Thus "logic" must be put in quotation marks. We do so not because we want to abjure "the logical" (in the sense of correct thinking). In the service of thinking, we seek to attain precisely that which determines the essence of thinking, *alētheia* and *phusis,* Being as unconcealment, and this is precisely what was lost due to "logic."

When did this logic begin, the logic that still rules our thinking and saying today, the logic that from early on plays an essential part in determining the grammatical conception of language and thus the fundamental Western orientation to language in general? When does the formation of logic begin? When Greek philosophy comes to an end and becomes a matter of schools, organization, and technique. It begins when *eon*,[25] the Being of beings, appears as *idea*, and as *idea* becomes the "ob-ject" of *epistēmē* ⟨scientific knowledge⟩. Logic originated in the ambit of the administration of the Platonic-Aristotelian schools. Logic is an invention of schoolteachers, not of philosophers. And wherever philosophers took it up, it was always under more originary impulses, not in the interests of logic. It is also no accident that the great, decisive efforts to overcome traditional logic were made by three German thinkers, indeed by the greatest: Leibniz, Kant, and Hegel.

Logic, as the exhibition of the formal structure of thinking and the exposition of its rules, was first able to develop after the division between Being and thinking had already been carried out, and carried out in a definite way and in a special respect. Hence neither logic itself nor its history can ever sufficiently clarify the essence and origin of this division between Being and thinking. For its part, logic is in need of clarification and grounding as regards its own origin and the rightfulness of its claim to supply the definitive interpretation of thinking. The historical provenance of logic as an academic discipline and the particulars of its development do not concern us here. However, we must reflect on the following questions:

1. Why could something like "logic" come about in the Platonic school, and why did it have to come about?

2. Why was this doctrine of thinking a doctrine of *logos* in the sense of assertion?

3. What are the grounds for the position of power held by the

25. *Eon* is the variant of *on* that is used in the dialect of Parmenides (for instance, in Parmenides' fragment 8, quoted on p. 101).

logical, a position of power that progressively and constantly expands until it finally expresses itself in the following proposition of Hegel? "The logical (is) the absolute form of truth and, what is more, it is also pure truth itself" (*Encyclopedia* §19, WW vol. VI, 29).[26] In keeping with this position of power held by the "logical," Hegel deliberately calls "logic" the doctrine otherwise generally called "metaphysics." His "science of logic" has nothing to do with a textbook on logic in the usual style.

Thinking is called *intelligere* in Latin. It is the business of the *intellectus*. If we are struggling against intellectualism, then in order actually to struggle, we must know our opponent: that is, we should know that intellectualism is just the impoverished contemporary offshoot and derivative of a preeminent position of thinking that was long prepared and was built up by means of Western metaphysics. It is important to prune the outgrowths of contemporary intellectualism. But its position is not thereby shaken in the least, it is not even touched. The danger of falling back into intellectualism persists precisely for those who want to struggle against it. A merely contemporary struggle against contemporary intellectualism makes those who defend the rightful use of the traditional intellect seem justified. No, they are not intellectualists, but they share the same roots. This reactive flight of the spirit into the past, which stems in part from natural inertia and in part from a deliberate effort, is now becoming fertile soil for political reaction. The misinterpretation of thinking and the misuse of misinterpreted thinking can be overcome only by a genuine and originary thinking, and *by nothing else*. In order to provide a new foundation for such thinking, we must above all else return to the question of the essential relation of thinking to Being—but this means unfolding

[94]

26. Heidegger cites *Georg Wilhelm Friedrich Hegel's Werke* (Berlin: Duncker und Humblot, 1832–1845).

the question of Being as such. Overcoming traditional logic does not mean the abolition of thinking and the rule of mere feelings. Instead, it means a more originary, rigorous thinking that belongs to Being.

After this general characterization of the division between Being and thinking, we now ask more definitely:

1. How does the originary unity of Being and thinking essentially unfold as the unity of *phusis* and *logos*?

2. How does the originary disjunction of *logos* and *phusis* come to pass?

3. How does *logos* arise and gain preeminence?

4. How does *logos* (the "logical") become the essence of thinking?

5. How does this *logos,* as reason and understanding, come to rule over Being in the inception of Greek philosophy?

In accordance with the six guiding principles proposed earlier (see page 99 above), we will again follow this division in its historical origin, which also means its essential origin. Here we insist that the disjunction between Being and thinking, if it is an inner and necessary disjunction, must be founded on an originary belonging of what is divided. Thus our question about the origin of the division is also and already the question about the essential belonging of thinking to Being.

Asked historically, the question runs: how does it stand with this belonging in the decisive inception of Western philosophy? How is thinking understood at its beginning? That the Greek doctrine of thinking becomes a doctrine of *logos,* "logic," can provide us with an indication. In fact, we find an originary connection between Being, *phusis,* and *logos*. We just have to free ourselves from the opinion that *logos* and *legein* originally and authentically mean thinking, understanding, and reason. As long as we hold to this opinion, and even interpret *logos* using the later conception of *logos* as logic as our criterion, our new disclosure of the inception of Greek philosophy will lead only to absurdities. Furthermore, this conception will never give us any insight into 1) why *logos* could be separated from the Being of beings at all, and 2) why this *logos* had to determine the essence of thinking and bring thinking into opposition to Being.

Let us go straight to the decisive point and ask: what do *logos* [95] and *legein* mean, if they do not mean thinking? *Logos* means the word, discourse, and *legein* means to discourse, to talk. Dia-logue is reciprocal discourse, mono-logue is solitary discourse. But *logos* does not originally mean discourse, saying. What the word means has no immediate relation to language. *Legō, legein,* Latin *legere,* is the same word as our *lesen* ⟨to collect⟩: gleaning, collecting wood, harvesting grapes, making a selection; "reading ⟨*lesen*⟩ a book" is just a variant of "gathering" in the authentic sense. This means laying one thing next to another, bringing them together as one— in short, gathering; but at the same time, the one is contrasted with the other. This is how Greek mathematicians used the word ⟨*logos*⟩. A coin collection that one has gathered is not just a heap that has somehow been thrown together. In the expression "analogy" (correspondence) we even find both meanings side by side: the original meaning of *logos* as "interrelation" or "relationship," and its meaning as "language" or "discourse"—although in the word "correspondence" ⟨*Entsprechung*⟩ we hardly think any more of "responding" ⟨*Sprechen,* speaking⟩, just as "correspondingly," and in contrast, the Greeks did not yet necessarily think of "discourse" and "saying" in connection with *logos.*

A passage from Homer (*Odyssey* XXIV, 106) may serve as an example of the originary meaning of *legein* as "gathering." Here the theme is the encounter between Agamemnon and the slain suitors in the underworld; he recognizes them and addresses them as follows:

"Amphimedon, by what disaster have you all been plunged down into the darkness of the earth, all of you prominent and of the same age; one could hardly bring together (*lexaito* ⟨a form of *le-gein*⟩), in a search throughout a polis, such noble men."

Aristotle says (*Physics* Θ, 1, 252a13): *taxis de pasa logos,* "but every order has the character of bringing together."

We will not yet trace how the word passes from the originary meaning, which at first has nothing to do with language and word and discourse, to the meaning of saying and discourse. Here we simply recall that the word *logos* retained its originary meaning, "the relation of one thing to another," long after it had come to mean discourse and assertion.

By considering the fundamental meaning of *logos,* gathering, we have still made little progress in clarifying the question: to what extent are Being and logos originally and unitarily the same for the Greeks, so that later they can and even must be disjoined, for definite reasons?

[96] The indication of the fundamental meaning of *logos* can give us a clue only if we already understand what "Being" means for the Greeks: *phusis*. Not only have we concerned ourselves in general with Being as the Greeks meant it, but through our previous distinctions of Being from becoming and from seeming, we have circumscribed the meaning of Being ever more distinctly.

Keeping all this firmly in view, we say: Being as *phusis* is the emerging sway. In opposition to becoming, it shows itself as constancy, constant presence. This presence announces itself in opposition to seeming as appearing, as revealed presence.

What does logos (gathering) have to do with Being as so interpreted? But first we must ask: is there any evidence for such a connection between Being and logos in the inception of Greek philosophy? By all means. Once again, we will rely on the two definitive thinkers Parmenides and Heraclitus, and we will try once again to find entry into the Greek world, whose basic traits, though distorted and repressed, displaced and covered up, still sustain our own world. Again and again we must emphasize that precisely because we dare to take up the great and lengthy task of tearing down a world that has grown old and of building it truly anew, that is, historically, we must know the tradition. We must know more—that is, we must know in a more rigorous and compelling way—than all earlier ages and upheavals before us. Only the most radical historical knowledge brings us face to face with the unfamiliarity of our tasks and preserves us from a new onset of mere restoration and uncreative imitation.

We will begin to demonstrate the inner connection between *logos* and *phusis* in the inception of Western philosophy with an interpretation of Heraclitus.

Among the most ancient Greek thinkers, it is Heraclitus who was subjected to the most fundamentally un-Greek misinterpretation in the course of Western history, and who nevertheless in more recent times has provided the strongest impulses toward redisclosing what is authentically Greek. Each of the two friends Hegel and Hölderlin stands under the great and fruitful spell of Heraclitus in his own way, with the difference that Hegel looks backward and closes off, while Hölderlin gazes forward and opens up. Nietzsche has yet another Heraclitus. To be sure, Nietzsche fell prey to the commonplace and untrue opposition of Parmenides to Heraclitus. This is one of the essential reasons why his metaphysics never found [97] its way to the decisive question, although Nietzsche did reconceive the great age of the inception of Greek Dasein in its entirety in a way that is surpassed only by Hölderlin.

But it was Christianity that first misinterpreted Heraclitus. The misinterpretation already began with the early church fathers. Hegel still stands in this line. Heraclitus's teaching on logos is taken as a predecessor of the logos mentioned in the New Testament, in the prologue to the Gospel of John. The logos is Christ. Now because Heraclitus already speaks of the logos, the Greeks arrived at the very doorstep of absolute truth—namely, the revealed truth of Christianity. In a book that came my way a few days ago, we can read: "With the actual appearance of truth in the form of the God-man, the Greek thinkers' philosophical knowledge of the rule of logos over all beings was validated. This confirmation and validation is the basis for the classical status of Greek philosophy."

According to this widespread version of history, the Greeks are the classics of philosophy because they were not yet full-fledged Christian theologians. But we will see whether Heraclitus is a precursor of John the Evangelist after we have heard Heraclitus himself.

We begin with two fragments in which Heraclitus deals explicitly with *logos*. In our rendering we will deliberately leave the decisive word *logos* untranslated, in order to discern its meaning from the context.

Fragment 1: "But while *logos* constantly remains itself, human beings behave as those who do not comprehend *(axunetoi)*, both before they have heard and after they have first heard. For everything becomes a being *kata ton logon tonde*, in accordance with and in consequence of this *logos;* yet they (human beings) resemble those who have never dared anything through experience, although they attempt words and works such as I carry out, laying out each thing *kata phusin,* according to Being, and explicating how it behaves. But as for the other human beings (the other human beings as they all are, *hoi polloi* ⟨the many⟩), what they really do while awake is concealed from them, just as what they did in their sleep conceals itself from them again afterward."[27]

27. Heidegger's version of this fragment, while unusually painstaking, does not depart far from conventional interpretations. The main unconventional elements are as follows: 1) Heidegger translates *ginomenōn* as *zu Seiendem wird* (becomes a being); a more conventional version would simply have "becomes" or "is becoming." 2) *Apeiroisin,* usually translated "inexperienced," "unacquainted," or "ignorant," is rendered by Heidegger as "[having] never

Fragment 2: "Hence one must follow the Together in beings—that is, adhere to it; but whereas *logos* essentially unfolds as this Together in beings, the mass lives as if each had his own understanding (sense)."[28]

What can we glean from these two fragments?

[98]

It is said of logos: 1) constancy, lasting, is proper to it; 2) it essentially unfolds as the Together in beings, the Together of the being, that which gathers; 3) everything that happens, that is, that comes into Being, stands there in accordance with this constant Together; this is what holds sway.

What is said of *logos* here corresponds exactly to the authentic meaning of the word "gathering." But just as this word denotes both 1) to gather and 2) gatheredness, *logos* here means the gathering gatheredness, that which originally gathers. *Logos* here does not mean sense, or word, or doctrine, and certainly not "the sense of a doctrine," but instead, the originally gathering gatheredness that constantly holds sway in itself.

True, the context in fragment 1 seems to invite an interpretation of *logos* in the sense of word and discourse, and even to demand it as the only possible interpretation; for it speaks of the "hearing" of human beings. There is a fragment in which this connection between logos and "hearing" is immediately expressed: "If you have

---

dared anything through experience." This translation is etymologically sound. 3) Heidegger translates *phusis* as "Being," as he himself points out. 4) The fragment contains forms of two verbs, *lanthanō* and *epilanthanomai*, that are conventionally translated in terms of forgetting or being unaware. Heidegger translates these words in terms of concealment—no doubt in order to bring out their close etymological connection to *lēthē*, concealment, and *alētheia*, truth or unconcealment. The words in parentheses are glosses provided by Heidegger.

28. A more conventional translation would run: "Hence one must follow what is common; but while the *logos* is common, the many live as if each had his own understanding."

heard not me, but *logos,* then it is wise to say accordingly: all is *one*" (fragment 50).

Here *logos* is surely taken as something "audible." So what else is this term supposed to mean but utterance, discourse, and word — especially since at the time of Heraclitus *legein* is already in use with the meaning of saying and talking?

Thus Heraclitus himself says (fragment 73): "one should not act ⟨*poiein*⟩ and talk ⟨*legein*⟩ as if asleep."

Here *legein* in opposition to *poiein* can obviously mean nothing other than talking, speaking. Nevertheless, in those decisive passages (fragments 1 and 2) *logos* does not mean discourse and does not mean word. Fragment 50, which seems to speak especially for *logos* as discourse, gives us a clue, when it is properly interpreted, to an entirely different understanding of *logos*.

In order to see clearly and understand what is meant by *logos* in the sense of "constant gathering," we must more accurately grasp the context of the fragments we first cited.

Human beings stand before logos as those who do not grasp logos *(axunetoi).* Heraclitus often uses this word (see especially fragment 34). It is the negation of *suniēmi,* which means "bring together"; *axunetoi:* human beings are such that they do not bring together . . . what, then? *Logos, that which is constantly together,* gatheredness. Human beings remain those who do not bring it to-[99] gether, do not grasp it, do not seize it as a unity, whether they have not yet heard or have already heard. The next sentence ⟨of fragment 1⟩ explains what is meant. Human beings do not get through to logos, even if they try to do so with words, *epea.* Here word and discourse are certainly named, but precisely as distinguished from, even in opposition to, *logos.* Heraclitus wants to say: human beings do hear, and they hear words, but in this hearing they cannot "hearken" to — that is, follow — what is not audible like words, what is not *talk* but *logos.* Properly understood, fragment 50 proves precisely the opposite of what people read into it. It says: you should not cling to words but instead apprehend logos. *Logos* and *legein* already mean discourse and saying, but this is not the essence of *logos,* and therefore *logos* here is opposed to *epea,* discourse. Correspondingly, genuine hearkening as Being-obedient is opposed to mere hearing and keeping one's ears open.[29] Mere hearing strews and scatters itself in what one commonly believes and says, in hearsay, in *doxa,* in seeming. But genuine hearkening has nothing to do with the ear and the glib tongue, but instead means obediently following what *logos* is: *the gatheredness of beings themselves.* We can truly hear only when we are already hearkening. But hearkening has nothing to do with earlobes. Whoever is *not* hearkening is already always distant from *logos,* excluded from it, regardless of whether he has already heard with ears or has not yet heard. Those who merely "hear" by keeping their ears open everywhere and carrying around what has been heard are and will be the *axunetoi,* those who do not grasp. Fragment 34 tells us what they are like: "those who do not bring together the constant Together are hearers who resemble the deaf."[30]

They do hear words and discourse, yet they are closed off to what they should listen to. The proverb bears witness to what they are: those who are absently present.[31] They are in the midst of things, and yet they are away. What are human beings usually amid, and what are they away from even while they are in the midst of

29. "Entsprechend ist auch dem bloßen Hören und Herumhören das echte Hörig-sein entgegengehalten." In this passage Heidegger plays with *hören* (to hear) and *hörig* (obedient, submissive, dependent). Compare also *gehören* (to belong), as in "the essential belonging ⟨*Zugehörigkeit*⟩ of thinking to Being" (p. 130). In this passage, we translate *hörig* as "hearkening."

30. The whole phrase "those who do not bring together the constant Together" is Heidegger's rendition of the single word *axunetoi.*

31. This last sentence is Heidegger's translation of the remainder of fragment 34.

things? Fragment 72 supplies the answer: "for they turn their backs on that with which they traffic the most, *logos,* and what they run into every day appears alien to them."

The *logos* is what human beings are continually amid and what they are away from all the same, absently present; they are thus the *axunetoi,* those who do not grasp.

[100] What does the human inability to grasp consist in, when they do hear words but do not take hold of *logos?* What are they amid and what are they away from? Human beings continually have to do with Being, and yet it is alien to them. They have to do with Being inasmuch as they constantly relate to beings, but it is alien to them inasmuch as they turn away from Being, because they do not grasp it at all; instead, they believe that beings are only beings and nothing further. True, they are awake (in relation to beings), yet Being remains concealed to them. They sleep, and even what they do in their sleep is lost to them as well. Thrashing around among beings, they always take what is closest to hand as what needs to be grasped, so everyone keeps handy what lies within his grasp. One person takes hold of this, the other takes hold of that, and each person's sense follows what is his own—it is caprice.[32] Caprice prevents them from properly grasping in advance what is gathered in itself; it takes away from them the possibility of hearkening and accordingly of hearing.

Logos is constant gathering, the gatheredness of beings that stands in itself, that is, Being. So *kata ton logon* in fragment 1 means the same as *kata phusin. Phusis* and *logos* are the same. *Logos* characterizes Being in a new and yet old respect: that which is in being,

---

32. *Eigen-sinn: Eigensinn,* etymologically "own-sense," is caprice or obstinacy—the tendency to insist arbitrarily on one's own private preferences and opinions. See Heidegger's translation of Heraclitus, fragment 2, on p. 135.

which stands straight and prominently in itself, is gathered in itself and from itself, and holds itself in such gathering. The *eon*, the being, is according to its essence *xunon*, a gathered coming to presence; *xunon* does not mean the "universal" but rather what gathers everything together in itself and holds it together. For example, according to fragment 114 such a *xunon* is the *nomos* for the *polis*, ordinance [positing as placing together],[33] the inner composition of the *polis*, not something universal; not the sort of thing that floats above all and seizes none, but the originally unifying unity of what strives in confrontation. Caprice, *idia phronēsis*,[34] for which *logos* remains closed off, always takes hold only of this side or the other, and believes that it thereby has the truth. Fragment 103 says: "gathered in itself, the same is the beginning and the end in the circumference of the circle." It would be senseless to want to take *xunon* here as the "universal."[35]

For the capricious, life is just life. For them, death is death and only that. But the Being of life is also death. Everything that comes to life thereby already begins to die as well, to go toward its death, and death is also life. Heraclitus says (fragment 8): "What stands in opposition carries itself over here and over there, the one to the

---

33. "Satzung [setzen als zusammenstellen]": the bracketed phrase is in parentheses in the 1953 edition. Here Heidegger draws attention to several related words and concepts. *Nomos* in Greek means a law or convention, a way of doing things instituted by human beings. *Satzung* in German means ordinance or statute. *Setzen* and *stellen* both mean to set, put, posit, or place. The German word for a law is *ein Gesetz*, a rule that has been *set* down as binding. Heraclitus's fragment 114 begins: "If we speak mindfully we must base our strength on what is common to all, as the city on law, and far more strongly" (ξὺν νόωι λέγοντας ἰσχυρίζεσθαι χρὴ τῶι ξυνῶι πάντων, ὅκωσπερ νόμωι πόλις, καὶ πολὺ ἰσχυροτέρος).

34. "One's own understanding": Heraclitus, fragment 2.

35. A more conventional translation would render *xunon* simply as "the same" instead of "gathered in itself, the same."

other, it gathers itself from itself."[36] That which contends is gathering gatheredness, *logos*. The Being of all beings is what is most seemly ⟨*das Scheinendste*⟩ — that is, what is most beautiful, what is most constant in itself. What the Greeks meant by "beauty" is discipline. The gathering together of the highest contending is *polemos*, struggle in the sense of the confrontation, the setting-apart-from-each-other ⟨*Aus-einander-setzung*⟩ that we have discussed. In contrast, for us today, the beautiful is the relaxing, what is restful and thus intended for enjoyment. Art then belongs in the domain of the pastry chef. Essentially it makes no difference whether the enjoyment of art serves to satisfy the refined taste of connoisseurs and aesthetes or serves for the moral elevation of the mind. *On* and *kalon* ⟨"in being" and "beautiful"⟩ say the same thing for the Greeks [coming to presence is pure seeming].[37] Aesthetics is of a different opinion; it is as old as logic. For aesthetics, art is the display of the beautiful in the sense of the pleasant, the agreeable. And yet art is the opening up of the Being of beings. We must provide a new content for the word "art" and for what it intends to name, on the basis of a fundamental orientation to Being that has been won back in an originary way.

We will finish characterizing the essence of logos as Heraclitus thought it by drawing special attention to two implicit points that have not yet been brought into relief.

1. Saying and hearing are proper only when they are intrinsically directed in advance toward Being, toward logos. Only where logos opens itself up does vocabulary become word. Only where the self-

[101]

---

36. A more conventional translation of the fragment is: "That which is opposed is in agreement, and from things that differ comes the most beautiful harmony." Heidegger appears to be glossing only the opening of the fragment *(to antixoun sumpheron)*. Etymologically, *sumpheron* means "carrying together," and it can also mean "gathering."
37. In parentheses in the 1953 edition.

opening Being of beings is apprehended does merely keeping one's ears open become hearing. But those who do not grasp *logos* ἀκοῦσαι οὐκ ἐπιστάμενοι οὐδ᾽ εἰπεῖν, "are able neither to hear nor to say" (fragment 19). They are incapable of bringing their Dasein to stand in the Being of beings. Only those who are capable of this, rule over the word — the poets and thinkers. The others just reel about within the orbit of their caprice and lack of understanding. They accept as valid only what comes directly into their path, what flatters them and is familiar to them. They are like dogs: κύνες γὰρ καὶ βαΰζουσιν ὧν ἂν μὴ γινώσκωσι, "for dogs also bark at everyone they do not know" (fragment 97). They are donkeys: ὄνους σύρματ᾽ ἂν ἑλέσθαι μᾶλλον ἢ χρυσόν, "donkeys like chaff better than gold" (fragment 9). They continually deal with beings everywhere. Yet Being remains concealed to them. Being cannot be touched and tasted, can neither be heard with the ears nor smelled. Being is completely different from vapor and smoke: εἰ πάντα τὰ ὄντα καπνὸς γένοιτο, ῥῖνες ἂν διαγνοῖεν, "if all beings turned into smoke, it would be noses that would distinguish and grasp them" (fragment 7).

2. Being as logos is originary gathering, not a heap or pile where everything counts just as much and just as little — and for this reason, rank and dominance belong to Being. If Being is to open itself up, it itself must have rank and maintain it. Heraclitus's reference to [102] the many as dogs and donkeys is characteristic of this attitude, one that belongs essentially to Greek Dasein. If people today from time to time are going to busy themselves rather too eagerly with the polis of the Greeks, they should not suppress this side of it; otherwise the concept of the polis easily becomes innocuous and sentimental. What is higher in rank is what is stronger. Thus Being, logos, as the gathered harmony, is not easily available for everyone at the same price, but is concealed, as opposed to that harmony which is always a mere equalizing, the elimination of tension, leveling:

ἁρμονίη ἀφανὴς φανερῆς κρείττων, "the harmony that does not show itself (immediately and without further ado) is more powerful than the harmony that is (always) evident" (fragment 54).

Because Being is *logos, harmonia, alētheia, phusis, phainesthai* (*logos,* harmony, unconcealment, *phusis,* self-showing), it shows itself in a way that is anything but arbitrary. The true is not for everyone, but only for the strong. It is with a view to this inner superiority and concealment of Being that Heraclitus speaks that strange saying which, precisely because it seems to be so un-Greek, testifies to the essence of the Greek experience of the Being of beings: ἀλλ' ὥσπερ σάρμα εἰκῆ κεχυμένων ὁ κάλλιστος κόσμος, "the most beautiful world is like a dungheap, cast down in shambles" (fragment 124).

Sarma is the opposing concept to *logos,* what is merely cast down as opposed to what stands in itself, the heap as opposed to collectedness, un-Being as opposed to Being.

The ordinary version of the philosophy of Heraclitus likes to sum it up in the saying *panta rhei,* "everything flows." *If* this saying stems from Heraclitus at all, then it does not mean that everything is mere change that runs on and runs astray, pure inconstancy, but instead it means: the whole of beings in its Being is always thrown from one opposite to the other, thrown over here and over there — Being is the gatheredness of this conflicting unrest.

If we comprehend the fundamental meaning of *logos* as gathering and gatheredness, we must firmly establish and firmly hold to the following:

Gathering is never just driving together and piling up. It maintains in a belonging-together that which contends and strives in confrontation. It does not allow it to decay into mere dispersion and what is simply cast down. As maintaining, *logos* has the character of pervasive sway, of *phusis.* It does not dissolve what it pervades into an empty lack of opposites; instead, by unifying what contends, the gathering maintains it in the highest acuteness of its tension.

This is the place to return briefly to the question of the Christian concept of logos, particularly that of the New Testament. For a more precise account we would have to distinguish here between the synoptic gospels and the gospel of John. But in principle we can say: in the New Testament, from the start, logos does not mean, as in Heraclitus, the Being of beings, the gatheredness of that which contends, but logos means *one* particular being, namely the Son of God. Furthermore, it means Him in the role of mediator between God and humanity. This New Testament representation of logos is that of the Jewish philosophy of religion which was developed by Philo, in whose doctrine of creation logos is determined as the *mesitēs,* the mediator. Why is the mediator *logos?* Because *logos* in the Greek translation of the Old Testament (Septuagint) is the term for word, "word" in the particular meaning of an order, a commandment; *hoi deka logoi* are the ten commandments of God (the decalogue). Thus *logos* means: the *kēryx, angelos,* the messenger, the emissary who transmits commandments and orders; *logos tou staurou* is the word of the Cross. The announcement of the Cross is Christ Himself; He is the logos of salvation, of eternal life, *logos zōēs.* A world separates all this from Heraclitus.

We were attempting to display the essential belonging of *logos* to *phusis,* with the intention of comprehending, thanks to this unity, the inner necessity and possibility of their division.

But now one could almost object to our characterization of the Heraclitean logos as follows: the essential belonging of logos to Being itself is so intimate here that it is still completely problematic how the opposition between Being and logos as thinking is supposed to spring from this unity and selfsameness of *phusis* and *logos.* Certainly, that is a question, the question that we absolutely do not want to make too easy for ourselves, although the temptation to do

[103]

so is very great. But for now, we may say only that if this unity of *phusis* and *logos* is so originary, then the division must also be correspondingly originary. If this division between Being and thinking is also different in kind and different in orientation from the previous divisions, then the disjunction of the one from the other must also have a different character here. Therefore, just as we endeavored to keep our interpretation of *logos* at a remove from all later falsifications and to grasp it on the basis of the essence of *phusis,* we must also attempt to understand this happening of the disjunction of *phusis* and *logos* in a purely Greek way—that is, once again on the basis of *phusis* and *logos*. For in view of the question about the disjunction and the opposition of *phusis* and *logos,* Being and thinking, we are subject almost more immediately and obstinately to the danger of modern misinterpretation than in the interpretation of the unity of *phusis* and *logos*. How so?

[104]

When we determine how Being and thinking stand opposed to each other, we are working with a well-worn schema. Being is the objective, the object. Thinking is the subjective, the subject. The relation of thinking to Being is that of subject to object. The Greeks, so one believes, still thought of this relation in an altogether primitive way, for at the very inception of philosophy they were not yet sufficiently schooled in epistemology. One then finds nothing that demands meditation in Being and thinking's standing opposed to each other. And yet we must *question*.

What is the process of disjunction between *phusis* and *logos,* a process that follows essential laws? In order to make this process visible we must comprehend the unity and belonging-together of *logos* and *phusis* still more sharply than before. We will attempt to do so now in connection with Parmenides. We do so deliberately, for the usual opinion holds that the doctrine of logos, however one may wish to interpret it, is a peculiarity of the philosophy of Heraclitus.

Parmenides shares Heraclitus's standpoint. And where else should these two Greek thinkers, the founders of all thinking, stand if not in the Being of beings? For Parmenides, too, Being is the *hen, xuneches,* that which holds itself together in itself, *mounon,* uniquely unifying, *oulon,* the constantly complete, constantly self-showing sway, through which there also constantly shines the seeming of the one-sided and many-sided.[38] Therefore the unavoidable path to Being leads through unconcealment, yet always remains a threefold path.

But where does Parmenides talk about *logos,* not to mention what we are now seeking, the disjunction of Being and logos? If we find anything at all in Parmenides in this regard, then what we find, so it seems, is the very opposite of a disjunction. A statement has been handed down to us that Parmenides expresses in two formulations and that fragment 5 formulates as follows: *to gar auto noein estin te kai einai.* Translated roughly and in the way that has long been customary, this says: "but thinking and Being are the same." The misinterpretation of this much-cited statement is just as un-Greek as the falsification of Heraclitus's doctrine of logos.

One understands *noein* as thinking, and thinking as an activity of the subject. The subject's thinking determines what Being is. Being is nothing other than what is thought by thinking. Now because thinking remains a subjective activity, and thinking and Being are supposed to be the same according to Parmenides, everything becomes subjective. There are no beings in themselves. But such a doctrine, so the story goes, can be found in Kant and in German idealism. Parmenides already basically anticipated their doctrines. He is even praised for this progressive achievement, particularly in comparison to Aristotle, a later Greek thinker. Aristotle, in contrast

[105]

38. The words quoted are from Parmenides, fragment 8. They are conventionally translated simply as: one, continuous, single, whole.

to Plato's idealism, propounded a realism, and serves as the precursor of the Middle Ages.

This well-worn reading must be mentioned here especially—not only because it works its mischief in all historical presentations of Greek philosophy, not only because modern philosophy itself interpreted its prehistory for itself in this way, but above all because the predominance of the opinions we have mentioned has made it difficult for us to understand the authentic truth of that primally Greek statement of Parmenides. Only when we succeed in doing so can we gauge what a change has taken place, not only since modernity but since late antiquity and since the rise of Christianity, in the spiritual history of the West, and this means its authentic history.

To gar auto noein estin te kai einai. In order to understand this statement, we must know three things:

1. What do *to auto* and *te . . . kai* mean?
2. What does *noein* mean?
3. What does *einai* mean?[39]

As regards the third question, we seem to have been sufficiently instructed by what was said earlier about *phusis*. But the *noein* named in the second question is obscure, at least if we do not translate the verb right away as "thinking" and define it in the logical sense as assertion that analyzes. *Noein* means to apprehend, *nous*[40] means apprehension, in a double sense that intrinsically belongs together. On the one hand, to apprehend ⟨*Vernehmen*⟩ means to take in ⟨*hin-nehmen*⟩, to let something come to oneself—namely, what shows itself, what appears. On the other hand, to apprehend means to interrogate a witness, to call him to account, and thus to comprehend the state of affairs, to determine and set fast how

39. The conventional answers to Heidegger's questions are: (1) "the same" and "both . . . and"; (2) "thinking"; (3) "Being."
40. This noun corresponding to the verb *noein* is conventionally translated as "mind" or "intellect."

things are going and how things stand.[41] Apprehension in this double sense denotes a process of letting things come to oneself in which one does not simply take things in, but rather takes up a position to receive what shows itself. When troops take up a position to receive the enemy, then they want to meet the enemy that is coming toward them, and meet him in such a way that they at least bring him to a halt, a stand. *Noein* involves this receptive bringing-to-a-stand of that which appears. Parmenides' statement says of apprehending that it is the same as Being. We thus come to the clarification of our first question: what is meant by *to auto,* the same?

[106]

Whatever is all the same to us makes no difference to us; it is one and the same. But what sense of oneness is meant by this? It is not up to us to determine this however we like. Instead, when we are dealing with the saying of "Being," oneness must be understood in the sense that Parmenides thinks in the word *hen.* We know that oneness here is not empty one-and-the-sameness, not selfsameness as a merely indifferent all-the-sameness. Oneness is the belonging-together of that which contends. This is what is originally unified.

Why does Parmenides say *te kai?* Because Being and thinking, in the sense of contending against each other, are unified, that is, are the same *in* their belonging-together. How are we to understand this? Let us base our answer on Being, which as *phusis* has become clearer to us in various respects. Being means: standing in the light, appearing, stepping into unconcealment. Where this happens, that is, where Being holds sway, apprehension holds sway too and happens too, as belonging to Being. Apprehension is the receptive bringing-to-a-stand of the constant that shows itself in itself.

41. "Vernehmen meint sodann: einen Zeugen vernehmen, ihn vornehmen und dabei den Tatbestand aufnehmen, fest-stellen, wie es mit der Sache bestellt ist und wie es mit ihr steht." This sentence contains a series of plays on *nehmen* (to take), *stellen* (to put or set), and *stehen* (to stand).

Parmenides expresses the same statement still more sharply in fragment 8, verse 34: *tauton d'esti noein te kai houneken esti noēma:* apprehension and that for the sake of which apprehension happens are the same. Apprehension happens for the sake of Being. Being essentially unfolds as appearing, as stepping into unconcealment, only if unconcealment happens, only if a self-opening happens. In its two versions, Parmenides' statement gives us a still more originary insight into the essence of *phusis*. Apprehension *belongs* to *phusis*; the sway of *phusis* shares its sway with apprehension.

The statement says nothing directly about human beings, certainly nothing about the human being as subject, and nothing whatsoever about a subject that absorbs everything objective into something merely subjective. The statement says the opposite of all that: Being holds sway, but because it holds sway and insofar as it holds sway and appears, apprehension *also* necessarily occurs *along with* appearance. But if human beings have a part in the happening of this appearance and apprehension, then they must themselves be, they must belong to Being. *But then the essence and the manner of Being-human can be determined only on the basis of the essence of Being.*

Furthermore, if appearing belongs to Being as *phusis,* then the human, as a being, must belong to this appearing. And since Being-human amid beings as a whole obviously constitutes a distinctive way of Being, the distinctiveness of Being-human grows from its distinctive way of belonging to Being as the appearing that holds sway. But now, insofar as apprehension belongs to such appearing, the apprehension that takes in what shows itself, one may presume that this is precisely the basis for determining the essence of Being-human. Thus when we interpret this statement of Parmenides, we must not proceed by reading some subsequent or even some present-day representation of Being-human into the statement. To the contrary, the statement must first give us directions of its own accord—directions as to how Being-human is determined in accor-

[107]

dance with *the statement*—that is, in accordance with the essence of Being.

Who the human being is, according to the word of Heraclitus, first comes forth (*edeixe,* shows itself) in the *polemos,* in the disjunction of gods and human beings, in the happening of the irruption of Being itself.[42] Who the human being is—for philosophy, the answer to this problem is not inscribed somewhere in heaven. Instead:

1. The determination of the essence of the human being is *never* an answer, but is essentially a question.

2. The asking of this question and its decision are historical—not just in general, but as the essence of history.

3. The question of who the human being is must always be posed in an essential connection with the question of how it stands with Being. The question of the human being is not an anthropological question, but a historically meta-physical question. [The question cannot be asked adequately within the domain of traditional metaphysics, which essentially remains "physics."]

Therefore we may not misinterpret what is called *nous* and *noein* in Parmenides' statement according to some concept of the human being that we have brought with us, but instead we must learn to experience the fact that the Being of the human first determines itself on the basis of the happening of the essential belonging together of Being and apprehension.

What is the human being in this sway of Being and apprehension? The beginning of fragment 6, which we have met before ⟨p. 118⟩, gives us the answer: *chrē to legein te noein t'eon emmenai:* needful is *legein* as well as the apprehension, namely, the being ⟨*das Seiend*⟩ in its Being.[43]

---

42. See Heraclitus, fragment 53.
43. Conventional translation: "It is necessary both to say and to think that being is."

By no means are we allowed yet to take *noein* here as thinking. Neither is it enough to conceive of it as apprehension if we then, unwittingly and as is the custom, take apprehension as a faculty, as a mode of behavior of the human being, whom we represent to ourselves according to an empty and pale biology and psychology or epistemology. This happens even if we do not explicitly invoke such representations.

[108]   Apprehension and what Parmenides' statement says about it is not a faculty of the human being, who is otherwise already defined; instead, apprehension is a happening ⟨*Geschehen*⟩ in which humanity itself happens, and in which humanity itself thus first enters history ⟨*Geschichte*⟩ as a being, first appears — that is, [in the literal sense][44] itself comes to Being.

Apprehension is not a way of behaving that the human being has as a property; to the contrary, apprehension is the happening that has the human being. Thus Parmenides always simply speaks only of *noein,* apprehension. What is fulfilled in this saying is nothing less than the knowing entrance-into-appearance of the human being as historical (preserver of Being).[45] This saying is the determination of Being-human that is definitive for the West, and just as decisively, it contains an essential characterization of Being. In the belonging-together of Being and the human essence, their disjunction comes to light. The division "Being and thinking," which has long since become pale, empty and rootless, no longer allows us to recognize its origin unless we go back to its inception.

The type and direction of the opposition between Being and thinking are unique because here the human being comes face to

44. In parentheses in the 1953 edition.
45. The word *Verwahrer* (preserver) carries an important echo of *wahr* (true, unconcealed) that is lost in translation. It has the sense of someone who "holds true" or "proves true" to something demanding preservation.

face with Being. This happening is the knowing appearance of humanity as historical. Only after humanity became familiar as such a being was the human being then also "defined" in a concept—namely, as *zōon logon echon, animal rationale,* rational living thing. In this definition of the human being *logos* plays a part, but in a completely unrecognizable form and in a very peculiar context.

This definition of the human being is at bottom a zoological one. The *zōon* of this zoology remains questionable in many respects. However, it is within the framework of *this* definition that the Western doctrine of the human has been constructed—all psychology, ethics, epistemology, and anthropology. We have long been flailing around in a confused mixture of representations and concepts that have been taken from these disciplines.

But because the definition of the human being that supports everything is already a decline, not to mention its later interpretation, then as long as we think and question within the perspective that is laid out by this definition, we get to see nothing of what is said and what is going on in Parmenides' saying.

Yet the usual representation of humanity in all its variations is only one of the barriers that cut us off from the space in which the appearance of the human essence inceptively happens and is brought to stand. The other barrier is that even this *question* about humanity remains alien to us. [109]

Of course, there are now books with the title *What Is Humanity?*[46] But this question merely stands in letters on the book's cover. The question is not asked—and not just because one has simply forgotten to ask questions in the midst of so much book-writing but because one already possesses an answer to the question, and an

46. Heidegger refers to a work by the Catholic theologian Theodor Haecker (1879–1945), *Was ist der Mensch?* (Leipzig: Jakob Hegner, 1933).

answer that at the same time says that one is not allowed to ask at all. If someone believes the propositions expressed by the dogma of the Catholic church, that is the individual's affair and is not at issue here. But if one puts the question "What is humanity?" on the cover of one's books, even though one is *not* questioning because one does *not* want to question and *cannot* do so, this is a procedure that has forfeited in advance every right to be taken seriously. And when, for example, the *Frankfurter Zeitung* then praises such a book, in which a question is asked solely on the cover, as "an extraordinary, magnificent and courageous book," it is clear even to the blindest where we stand.

Why am I mentioning irrelevant things here in connection with the interpretation of Parmenides' saying? In itself, this sort of scribbling is certainly inconsequential and meaningless. But what is not meaningless is the crippling of all passion for questioning, a crippling that has already held us back too long. This condition confuses all standards and all stances; most of us no longer know where and between what alternatives the authentic decisions must be made, if the greatness of historical willing is to be united with the keenness and originality of historical *knowing*. Indications such as those we have given can only point to how far questioning has receded from us as a fundamental happening of historical Being. But even the understanding of the question has already slipped through our fingers. So let us now offer the essential points of orientation for thinking through what is to follow.

1. The determination of the human essence is never an answer, but is essentially a question.

2. The asking of this question is historical in the originary sense that this questioning first creates history.

3. This is the case because the question of what humanity is can be asked only in questioning about Being.

4. Only where Being opens itself up in questioning does history

happen, and with it that Being of *the human being* by virtue of which the human being ventures the confrontation with beings as such.

5. This questioning confrontation first brings humanity back to the being that it itself is and has to be. [110]

6. Humanity first comes to itself and is a self only as questioning-historical. The selfhood of humanity means this: it has to transform the Being that opens itself up to it into history, and thus bring itself to a stand. Selfhood does not mean that humanity is primarily an "I" and an individual. Humanity is not this any more than it is a We and a community.

7. Because humanity is itself as historical, the question about its own Being must change from the form "What is humanity?" into the form "*Who* is humanity?"

What Parmenides' saying expresses is a determination of the human essence on the basis of the essence of Being itself.

But we still do not know how the human essence is determined here. So far, we have simply delineated the space into which the saying speaks, and which it first helps to open up by speaking into it. Yet this general indication is still not enough to set us free from the usual representations of humanity and from the typical manner in which it has been determined conceptually. In order to understand the saying and to grasp its truth, we must at least have an intimation of something positive about Greek Dasein and Being.

From the saying of Heraclitus that we have cited several times,[47] we know that the disjunction of gods and humans happens only in *polemos,* in the confrontational setting-apart-from-each-other ⟨*Auseinander-setzung*⟩ (of Being). Only such struggle *edeixe, points out.* It lets gods and human beings step forth in their Being. Who is humanity—we do not learn this through a scholarly definition but only when humanity steps into the confrontation with beings by

47. Fragment 53.

attempting to bring them into their Being—that is, sets beings into limits and form, projects something new (not yet present), originally poetizes, grounds poetically.

The thinking of Parmenides and Heraclitus is still poetic, and here this means philosophical, not scientific. But because in this poetizing thinking, thinking has precedence, thinking about human Being also acquires its own direction and measure. In order to clarify this poetic thinking sufficiently in terms of its proper counterpart, we will now interrogate a thinking poetry of the Greeks. This poetry is tragedy—the poetry in which Greek Being and Dasein [a Dasein belonging to Being][48] were authentically founded.

[111] We want to understand the division "Being and thinking" in its origin. This is the title for the fundamental attitude of the Western spirit. In accordance with it, Being is determined from the perspective of thinking and reason. This is the case even where the Western spirit withdraws from the mere dominance of reason by wanting the "irrational" and seeking the "alogical."

As we pursue the origin of the division *Being and thinking,* we encounter the saying of Parmenides: *to gar auto noein estin te kai einai.* According to the customary translation and reading, it says: thinking and Being are the same.

We can call this saying the guiding principle of Western philosophy, but only if we attach the following note to it:

The saying became the guiding principle of Western philosophy only after it was no longer understood, because its originary truth could not be held fast. The Greeks themselves began to fall away from the truth of the saying right after Parmenides. Originary truths of such scope can be held fast only if they constantly unfold in a still more originary way—never, however, merely by applying and ap-

---

48. In parentheses in the 1953 edition.

pealing to them. The originary remains originary only if it has the constant possibility of being what it is: origin as springing forth ⟨*Ursprung als Entspringen*⟩ [from the concealment of the essence].[49] We are attempting to win back the originary truth of the saying. We first suggested the changed interpretation in our translation. The saying does not say, "thinking and Being are the same," but instead says, "belonging-together reciprocally are apprehension and Being."

But what does this mean?

The saying brings the human to language in some way. Thus it is almost inevitable that at first, the customary representation of the human is interpolated into the saying.

But this leads to a misinterpretation of the human essence as experienced in the Greek way, according to either the Christian or the modern concept of the human, or else according to a pale and diluted mixture of both.

But this misinterpretation in the direction of a *non*-Greek representation of the human is the lesser evil.

The real peril lies in utterly missing the truth of the saying from the ground up.

For it is in this saying that the decisive determination of Being-human is first accomplished. Therefore in our interpretation we must avoid not just this or that unsuitable representation of the human, but each and every one of them. We must attempt to hear only what is said. [112]

But because we are not only inexperienced in such hearing but also always have our ears full of what hinders us from properly hearing, we had to mention the conditions for properly asking who the human being is, if only in the form of a list.

But because the thoughtful determination of Being-human that

49. In parentheses in the 1953 edition.

Parmenides accomplishes is difficult to approach directly and strikes us as strange, we will first seek help and instruction by listening to a poetic projection of Being-human among the Greeks.

We will read the first choral ode from Sophocles' *Antigone* (lines 332–375). First we will hear the Greek words, so that we get some of the sound, at least, into our ears.[50] The translation runs:

Manifold is the uncanny, yet nothing
uncannier than man[51] bestirs itself, rising up beyond him.
He fares forth upon the foaming tide
amid winter's southerly tempest
and cruises through the summits
of the raging, clefted swells.
The noblest of gods as well, the earth,
the indestructibly untiring, he wearies,
overturning her from year to year,
driving the plows this way and that
with his steeds.

Even the lightly gliding flock of birds
he snares, and he hunts
the beast folk of the wilderness
and the brood whose home is the sea,
the man who studies wherever he goes.

With ruses he overwhelms the beast
that spends its nights on mountains and roams,
and clasping with wood

50. Apparently Heidegger read the Greek at this point during the original delivery of his lectures.
51. *der Mensch:* we normally translate this term as "humanity," "human beings," "humans," "the human being," or "the human," but these expressions would be unwieldy in this poetic passage.

the rough-maned neck of the steed
and the unvanquished bull
he forces them into the yoke.

Into the sounding of the word, as well,
and into wind-swift all-understanding
he found his way, and into the mettle
to rule over cities.
He has considered, too, how he might flee
exposure to the arrows
of unpropitious weather and its frosts.

[113]

Everywhere trying out, underway; untried, with no way out
he comes to Nothing.[52]
A single onslaught, death, he was unable
ever to resist by any flight,
even if in the face of dire illness
deft escape should be granted him.

Clever indeed, for he masters
skill's devices beyond expectation,
now he falls prey to wickedness,
yet again valor succeeds for him.
Between the ordinance of the earth and the
gods' sworn dispensation ⟨*Fug*⟩ he fares.
Rising high over the site, losing the site
is he for whom what is not, is, always,
for the sake of daring.[53]

---

52. The Greek that Heidegger translates in these two lines, *pantoporos aporos ouden erchetai to mellon,* can be more conventionally translated as: "resourceful in all, he meets nothing that is to come resourceless." In other words, where Heidegger sees a paradox in the sentence, most translators would see merely an expansion of the notion "resourceful in all" (*pantoporos*).
53. A more conventional translation of the previous five lines would be: "If he

Let him not become a companion at my hearth,
nor let my knowing share the delusions
of the one who works such deeds.

The following interpretation is necessarily insufficient, if only because it cannot be constructed on the basis of the whole of this tragedy, much less the poet's entire work. Neither is this the place to report on the choice of readings and the changes that have been made in the text. We will carry out the interpretation in *three phases*, and each time we will go through the whole ode in a different respect.

In the *first* phase we will especially stress what provides the inner integrity of the poem and sustains and permeates the whole, even in its linguistic form.

In the *second* phase we will follow the sequence of the strophes and antistrophes, and pace off the entire domain that the poetry opens up.

[114] In the *third* phase we will attempt to attain a stance in the midst of the whole, in order to assess who the human being is according to this poetic saying.

The first phase. We seek what sustains and permeates the whole. Actually, we hardly have to seek it. It is threefold, it assails us three times, like a repeated assault, and from the start breaks up all everyday standards of questioning and defining.

First is the beginning: *polla ta deina . . .*

Manifold is the uncanny, yet nothing
uncannier than man bestirs itself, rising up beyond him.

---

follows the laws of the earth and the gods' sworn justice he is high in the city (or: his city is high), but he is cast out from the city if he dwells with dishonor for the sake of daring."

These first two verses cast forth what the following ode as a whole will seek to capture in the details of its saying, and which it must fit into the structure of the word. The human being is, in *one* word, *to deinotaton,* the uncanniest. This saying about humanity grasps it from the most extreme limits and the most abrupt abysses of its Being. This abruptness and ultimacy can never be seen by eyes that merely describe and ascertain something present at hand, even if a myriad such eyes should want to seek out human characteristics and conditions. Such Being opens itself up only to poetic-thoughtful projection. We find no delineation of present-at-hand exemplars of humanity, no more than we find some blind and foolish exaltation of the human essence from beneath, from a dissatisfied peevishness that snatches at an importance that it feels is missing. We find no glorified personality. Among the Greeks there were no personalities yet [and thus nothing suprapersonal either].[54] The human being is *to deinotaton,* the uncanniest of the uncanny. The Greek word *deinon* and our translation call for an advance explication here. This explication is to be given only on the basis of the unspoken prior view of the entire ode, which itself supplies the only adequate interpretation of the first two verses. The Greek word *deinon* has that uncanny ambiguity with which the saying of the Greeks traverses the opposed con-frontations of Being.

On the one hand, *deinon* names the terrible, but it does not apply to petty terrors and does not have the degenerate, childish, and useless meaning that we give the word today when we call something "terribly cute." The *deinon* is the terrible in the sense of the overwhelming sway, which induces panicked fear, true anxiety, as well as collected, inwardly reverberating, reticent awe. The violent, the overwhelming is the essential character of the sway   [115]

54. In parentheses in the 1953 edition.

itself.[55] When the sway breaks in, it *can* keep its overwhelming power to itself. But this does not make it more harmless but only *more* terrible and distant.

But on the other hand, *deinon* means the violent in the sense of one who needs to use violence — and does not just have violence at his disposal but is violence-doing, insofar as using violence is the basic trait not just of his doing but of his Dasein. Here we are giving the expression "doing violence" an essential sense that in principle reaches beyond the usual meaning of the expression, which generally means nothing but brutality and arbitrariness. Violence is usually seen in terms of the domain in which concurring compromise and mutual assistance set the standard for Dasein, and accordingly all violence is necessarily deemed only a disturbance and offense.

Beings as a whole, as the sway, are the overwhelming, *deinon* in the first sense. But humanity is *deinon,* first, inasmuch as it remains exposed to this overwhelming sway, because it essentially belongs to Being. However, humanity is also *deinon* because it is violence-doing in the sense we have indicated. [It gathers what holds sway and lets it enter into an openness.][56] Humanity is violence-doing not in addition to and aside from other qualities but solely in the sense that from the ground up and in its doing violence, it uses violence against the over-whelming. Because it is doubly *deinon* in an originally united sense, it is *to deinotaton,* the most violent: violence-doing in the midst of the overwhelming.

But why do we translate *deinon* as "un-canny"?[57] Not in order

55. There is a close etymological connection among *das Gewaltige* (the violent), *das Überwältigende* (the overwhelming), and *das Walten* (the sway). See *walten* in German-English Glossary and Translators' Introduction, p. xiii.
56. In parentheses in the 1953 edition.
57. "Uncanny" translates *unheimlich,* which is based on the root *Heim,* or home. ("Canny," like the German *heimlich,* can mean "snug and cozy." The root of "canny" is "can" in the obsolete sense of "know." What is uncanny is unfamiliar, beyond our ken, and thus unsettling.)

to cover up or weaken the sense of the violent, the overwhelming and the violence-doing; quite the contrary. *Deinon* applies most intensely and intimately to human Being; thus, the essence of this Being that is determined as *deinon* should come directly into view in its decisive aspect. But then, is the characterization of the violent as the uncanny not precisely a derivative determination—that is, determined in terms of how the violent affects us—while the point is precisely to understand what the *deinon* is, as it is in itself? But we do not mean the uncanny in the sense of an impression made on our emotional states.

We understand the un-canny as that which throws one out of the "canny," that is, the homely, the accustomed, the usual, the un-endangered. The unhomely does not allow us to be at home.[58] Therein lies the over-whelming. But human beings are the uncanniest, not only because they spend their lives essentially in the midst of the un-canny understood in this sense, but also because they step out, move out of the limits that at first and for the most part are accustomed and homely, because as those who do violence, they overstep the limits of the homely, precisely in the direction of the uncanny in the sense of the overwhelming.

But in order to measure this word of the chorus about the human in its entire scope, we must at the same time consider that this word, that the human is *to deinotaton,* the uncanniest, does not intend to assign the human a particular property, as if the human were something else in addition; instead, the word says: to be the uncanniest is the basic trait of the human essence, into which every other trait must always be drawn. The saying "the human being is the uncanniest" provides the authentic *Greek* definition of humanity. We first press forward fully to the happening of un-canniness

[116]

---

58. "Homely" translates *heimisch,* meaning "domestic." "At home" translates *einheimisch*.

when we experience the power of seeming together with the struggle against seeming in its essential belonging to Dasein.

After the first verses, and with a look back in their direction, the *second* sustaining and prominent phrase is said as verse 360. The verse is the middle of the second strophe: *pantoporos aporos ep' ouden erchetai:* "Everywhere trying out, underway; untried, with no way out he comes to Nothing." The essential words are *pantoporos aporos*. The word *poros* means a going through. . . , a going over to. . . , a route. Everywhere humanity makes routes for itself; in all the domains of beings, of the overwhelming sway, it ventures forth, and in this very way it is flung from every route. Thus the whole uncanniness of the human, the uncanniest, first opens itself up; it is not just that humans try what is, as a whole, in its un-canniness, not just that *as* violence-doing they drive themselves in this way beyond what is homely for them, but in all this they first become the uncanniest, because now, as those who on all ways have no way out, they are thrown out of all relation to the homely, and *atē*, ruin, calamity, overtakes them.

We may suspect that this *pantoporos aporos* contains an interpretation of the *deinotaton*.

The interpretation is completed in the third prominent phrase, verse 370: *hupsipolis apolis*. We find that this phrase is constructed in the same way, and is even situated in the middle of the antistrophe in the same way, as the earlier *pantoporos aporos*. Yet what it says [117] points us toward another dimension of beings. Not *poros* but *polis* is named; not all the routes into the domains of beings are named, but the ground and place of human Dasein itself, the spot where all these routes cross, the *polis*. One translates *polis* as state ⟨Staat⟩ and city-state ⟨Stadtstaat⟩; this does not capture the entire sense. Rather, *polis* is the name for the site ⟨Stätte⟩, the Here, within which and as which Being-here is historically. The *polis* is the site of history, the Here, *in* which, *out of* which and *for* which history happens. To this site of history belong the gods, the temples, the priests, the celebrations, the games, the poets, the thinkers, the ruler, the council of elders, the assembly of the people, the armed forces, and the ships. All this does not first belong to the *polis,* is not first political, because it enters into a relation with a statesman and a general and with the affairs of state. Instead, what we have named is political — that is, at the site of history — insofar as, for example, the poets are *only* poets, but then are actually poets, the thinkers are *only* thinkers, but then are actually thinkers, the priests are *only* priests, but then are actually priests, the rulers are *only* rulers, but then are actually rulers. *Are* — but this says: use violence as violence-doers and become those who rise high in historical Being as creators, as doers. Rising high in the site of history, they also become *apolis,* without city and site, lonesome, un-canny, with no way out amidst beings as a whole, and at the same time without ordinance and limit, without structure and fittingness ⟨*Fug*⟩, because they *as* creators must first ground all this in each case.

The first phase shows us the inner contour of the essence of the uncanniest, the domains and extent of its sway and its destiny. We now go back to the beginning and attempt the second phase of the interpretation.

The second phase. Now we follow the sequence of the strophes in light of what has been said and hear how the Being of the human, to be the uncanniest, unfolds. We will attend to whether and how the *deinon* in the first sense is meant, whether and how the *deinon* in the second sense steps forth in unison with the first, whether and how in the reciprocal relation of both, the Being of the uncanniest builds itself up before us in its essential form.

The first strophe names the sea and the earth, each of them overwhelming (*deinon*) in its own way. To be sure, the naming of sea and earth does not intend the things it names in a merely geographical or geological way. That is how we today encounter these natural phenomena, only to paint them over with a few petty and fleeting feelings. But here, "sea" is said as if for the first time; it is named in the wintry swells in which it constantly drags up its own depths and drags itself down into them. Directly after the main and guiding saying at the beginning, the ode starts off severely with *touto kai poliou*. It sings of breaking forth upon the groundless waves, of giving up firm land. This breakaway does not take place upon the cheerful smoothness of gleaming water but amid the winter storm. The saying of this breakaway is situated in the law of motion that arranges the words and verses, just as the *chōrei* in verse 336 is placed at the point where the meter shifts: *chōrei*, he gives up the place, he heads out—and ventures to enter the superior power of the sea's placeless flood. The word stands like a pillar in the construction of these verses.

But this violence-doing breakaway into the overwhelming sea is woven together with the restless break-in to the indestructible sway of the earth. Let us mark it well: here the earth is called the highest of gods. Violence-doing, the human being disturbs the calm of growth, the nourishing and enduring of the tireless one. Here the overwhelming does not hold sway in self-devouring wildness but as that which, without toil and without tiring, from out of the superiority of the calm of great riches, ripens and dispenses what is inexhaustible and rises above all impatience. The violence-doers break into this sway, year by year they break it up with plows and drive the toilless earth into the restlessness of their toiling. The sea and the earth, the breaking forth and the breaking up, are joined by the *kai* ⟨and⟩ in verse 334, to which corresponds the *te* ⟨also⟩ in verse 338.

Let us now hear the antistrophe to all this. It names the flock of birds in the air, the animal life in the water, the bull and stallion in the mountains. The living thing, lightly dreaming, whose cycle of

[118]

life reverberates in itself and in its environs, constantly renews itself, streaming out over itself in ever new forms, and yet it remains in its own *single* route, it is familiar with the place where it spends the night and roams. As a living thing, it is fitted into the sway of the sea and the earth. Into this life that revolves within itself, its ambit, structure, and ground unfamiliar to them, humans cast their snares and nets; they tear this life away from its own order, enclose it in their paddocks and pens, and force it beneath the yoke. In one arena, breaking forth and breaking up; in the other, capturing and subjugating. —

At this point, before the transition to the second strophe and its antistrophe, we must insert a *remark* in order to ward off a widespread misinterpretation of this entire poem that lies in wait for modern humanity. We have already alluded to the fact that this is not a matter of describing and clarifying the domains and behavior of the human, who is one being among many; instead, this is a poetic projection of human Being on the basis of its extreme possibilities and limits. In this way, we have also warded off the other opinion, according to which the ode recounts the development of humanity from a wild huntsman and a traveler by dugout canoe, to a builder of cities and person of culture. These are notions from cultural anthropology and the psychology of primitives. They arise from falsely transferring a science of nature that is already untrue in itself to human Being. The fundamental error that underlies such ways of thinking is the opinion that the inception of history is primitive and backward, clumsy and weak. The opposite is true. The inception is what is most uncanny and mightiest. What follows is not a development but flattening down as mere widening out; it is the inability to hold on to the inception, it makes the inception innocuous and exaggerates it into a perversion of what is great, into greatness and extension purely in the sense of number and mass. The uncanniest *is*

[119]

what it is *because* it harbors such an inception in which, from over-abundance, everything breaks out at once into what is overwhelming and is to be surmounted ⟨*das Überwältigende, Zubewältigende*⟩.

The inexplicability of this inception is no defect, no failure of our knowledge of history. Instead, the genuineness and greatness of historical knowing lie in understanding the character of this inception as a mystery. Knowing a primal history is not ferreting out the primitive and collecting bones. It is neither half nor whole natural science, but, if it is anything at all, it is mythology. —

The first strophe and antistrophe name the sea, the earth, the animal as the overwhelming that the violence-doer allows to break into openness in all its excessive violence.

The second strophe outwardly passes from a portrayal of the sea, the earth, the animals to the characterization of the human being. But just as little as the first strophe and antistrophe speak only of nature in the narrower sense does the second strophe speak only of the human being.

Instead, what is to be named now, language, understanding, mood, passion, and building, are no less a part of the overwhelming violence than sea and earth and animal. The difference is only that the latter envelop humans in their sway and sustain, beset, and inflame them, whereas what is to be named now pervades them in its sway as that which they have to take over expressly as the beings that they themselves are.

[120] This pervasive sway becomes no less overwhelming because humans take up this sway itself directly into their violence and use this violence as such. This merely conceals the uncanniness of language, of passions, as that into which human beings as historical are disposed ⟨*gefügt*⟩, while it seems to them that it is *they* who have them at their disposal ⟨*verfügt*⟩. The uncanniness of these powers lies in their seeming familiarity and ordinariness. What they yield to humans immediately is merely the inessential, and thus they drive

humans out and keep them out of their own essence. In this way, what at bottom is still more distant and more overwhelming than sea and earth becomes something that seems to humans to be the nearest of all.

The extent to which humanity is not at home in its own essence is betrayed by the opinion human beings cherish of themselves as those who have invented and who could have invented language and understanding, building and poetry.

How is humanity ever supposed to have invented that which pervades it in its sway, due to which humanity itself can *be* as humanity in the first place? We completely forget the fact that this ode speaks of the violent *(deinon)*, of the uncanny, if we believe that the poet here is having humanity invent such things as building and language. The word *edidaxato*[59] does not mean "human beings invented" but rather: they found their way into the overwhelming and therein first found themselves — the violence of those who act in this way. The "themselves," according to what has been said, means those who at once break forth and break up, capture and subjugate.

This breaking forth, breaking up, capturing and subjugating is in itself the first opening of beings *as* sea, *as* earth, *as* animal. A breaking-forth and breakup happen only insofar as the powers of language, of understanding, of mood, and of building are themselves surmounted in doing violence. The violence-doing of poetic saying, of thoughtful projection, of constructive building, of state-creating action, is not an application of faculties that the human being has, but is a disciplining and disposing of the violent forces by virtue of which beings disclose themselves as such, insofar as the human being enters into them. This disclosedness of beings is the violence that humanity has to surmount in order to be itself first of all — that is, to be historical in doing violence in the midst of beings.

---

59. From line 356. Conventionally translated "learned" or "taught himself."

We must not misinterpret the *deinon* in the second strophe as meaning either invention or a mere faculty and quality of human beings.

Only when we grasp that the need to use violence in language, in understanding, in constructing, in building, co-creates [and this always means: brings forth][60] the violent act of laying out the paths into the beings that envelop humanity in their sway—only then do we understand the uncanniness of all that does violence. For when human beings are everywhere underway in this sense, their having no way out does not arise in the external sense that they run up against outward restrictions and cannot get any farther. Somehow or another they precisely *can* always go farther into the and-so-forth. Their not having a way out consists, instead, in the fact that they are continually thrown back on the paths that they themselves have laid out; they get bogged down in their routes, get stuck in ruts, and by getting stuck they draw in the circle of their world, get enmeshed in seeming, and thus shut themselves out of Being. In this way they turn around and around within their own circle. They can turn aside everything that threatens this circuit. They can turn every skill to the place where it is best applied. The violence-doing, which originally creates the routes, begets in itself its own un-essence, the versatility of many twists and turns,[61] which in itself is the lack of ways out, so much so that it shuts itself out from the way of meditation on the seeming within which it drifts around.

There is only *one* thing against which all violence-doing directly shatters. That is death. It is an end beyond all completion, a limit beyond all limits. Here there is no breaking forth and breaking up, no capturing and subjugating. But this un-canny thing, which sets

[121]

---

60. In parentheses in the 1953 edition.

61. In using the term *Vielwendigkeit,* which we translate with "the versatility of many twists and turns," Heidegger seems to have in mind the first line of the *Odyssey,* where Odysseus is described as *polutropos,* the man of many ways, or the man of many twists and turns, of many skills and stratagems.

us simply and suddenly out from everything homely once and for all, is not a special event that must also be mentioned among others, because it, too, ultimately, does occur. The human being has no way out in the face of death, not only when it is time to die, but constantly and essentially. Insofar as humans *are*, they stand in the no-exit of death. Thus Being-here is the happening of un-canniness itself. (The happening of uncanniness must for us be grounded inceptively as Being-here.)

With the naming of *this* violent and uncanny thing, the poetic projection of Being and of the human essence sets its own limits for itself.

For the second antistrophe does not go on to name *still* other powers but instead brings together everything that has been said so far into its inner unity. The concluding strophe takes back the whole into its basic trait. But according to what we stressed in our first phase, the basic trait of what is authentically to be said (the *deinotaton*) consists precisely in the unitary, reciprocal relation between the two senses of *deinon*. Accordingly, the concluding strophe names something threefold in its summation.

1. Violence, the violent, within which the doing of the violence-doer moves, is the whole circuit of the machination, *to machanoen*, that is delivered over to him. We are not taking the word "machination" in a derogatory sense. With this word we are thinking something essential that announces itself to us in the Greek word *technē*. *Technē* means neither art nor skill, and it means nothing like technology in the modern sense. We translate *technē* as "knowing." But this requires explication. Knowing here does not mean the result of mere observations about something present at hand that was formerly unfamiliar. Such items of information are always just accessory, even if they are indispensable to knowing. Knowing, in the genuine sense of *technē*, means initially and constantly looking out beyond what, in each case, is directly present at hand. In different

[122]

ways and on different routes and in different domains, this Being-out-beyond sets to work in advance that which first gives to what is already present at hand its relative justification, its possible determinateness, and thus its limit. Knowing is the ability to set Being into work as something that in each case *is* in such and such a way. For this reason, the Greeks call authentic artwork and art *technē* in the emphatic sense, because art is what most immediately brings Being—that is, the appearing that stands there in itself—to stand [in something present (in the work)].[62] The work of art is work not primarily because it is worked, made, but because it puts Being to work[63] in a being. To put to work here means to bring into the work—a work within which as what appears, the emerging that holds sway, *phusis,* comes to seem. Through the artwork, as Being that *is* ⟨*das seiende Sein*⟩, everything else that appears and that we can find around us first becomes confirmed and accessible, interpretable and understandable, *as a being,* or else as an unbeing.

Because art, in a distinctive sense, brings Being to stand and to manifestation in the work as a being, art may be regarded as the ability to set to work, pure and simple, as *technē*. Setting-to-work is putting Being to work *in* beings, a putting-to-work that opens up. This opening-up and keeping open, which surpasses and puts to work, is knowing. The passion of knowing is questioning. Art is knowing and hence is *technē*. Art is not *technē* merely because it involves "technical" skills, tools, and materials with which to work.

Thus *technē* characterizes the *deinon,* the violence-doing, in its decisive basic trait; for to do violence is to need to use violence

62. The 1953 edition has neither brackets nor parentheses around this whole phrase.
63. *Er-wirkt: erwirken* normally means to bring about, obtain or secure; we have formerly translated it as "bring about." But because here Heidegger is stressing the root *wirken,* to work, we render *er-wirken* as "put to work."

against the over-whelming: the knowing struggle to set Being, which was formerly closed off, into what appears as beings.

2. Just as the *deinon*, as doing violence, gathers up its essence into the fundamental Greek word *technē*, the *deinon* as the overwhelming is manifested in the fundamental Greek word *dikē*. We translate this word as fittingness ⟨*Fug*⟩.[64] Here we understand fittingness first in the sense of joint and structure; then as arrangement, as the direction that the overwhelming gives to its sway; finally, as the enjoining structure, which compels fitting-in and compliance.

When one translates *dikē* as "justice," and understands justice in a juridical-moral sense, then the word loses its fundamental metaphysical content. The same holds for the interpretation of *dikē* as norm. In all its domains and powers, the overwhelming, as regards its powerfulness, is fittingness. Being, *phusis*, is, as sway, originary gatheredness: *logos*. Being is fittingness that enjoins: *dikē*.

Thus, the *deinon* as the overwhelming ⟨*dikē*⟩ and the *deinon* as the violence-doing ⟨*technē*⟩ stand over against each other, although not as two present-at-hand things. This over-against consists, instead, in the fact that *technē* breaks out against *dikē*, which for its part, as fittingness, has all *technē* at its disposal. The reciprocal over-against *is*. It is, only insofar as the uncanniest, Being-human, happens — insofar as humanity essentially unfolds as history.

3. The basic trait of the *deinotaton* lies in the reciprocal relation of the two senses of *deinon*. The knower fares into the midst of fittingness, draws Being into beings [in the "draft"],[65] and yet can

[123]

---

64. See *Antigone*, line 369. The usual translation of *dikē* is "justice" (in German, *Gerechtigkeit*). The word *Fug* is used today only in stock phrases such as *mit Fug und Recht* (quite rightfully, quite properly). It is related to *Fuge* (joint; fugue), *Gefüge* (structure), *Fügung* (arrangement), *fügen* (enjoin, dispose), *sich fügen* (comply), *einfügen* (fit into, fit in), and *verfügen* (have at its disposal).

65. ". . . reißt [im "Riß"] das Sein in das Seiende": the two words in brackets are in parentheses in the 1953 edition. *Reißen* means to rip open, or to pull

never surmount the overwhelming. Thus the knower is thrown this way and that between fittingness and un-fittingness, between the wretched and the noble. Every violent taming of the violent is either victory or defeat. Both throw one out of the homely, each in a different way, and they first unfold, each in a different way, the dangerousness of the Being that has been won or lost. Both, each differently, are menaced by perdition. The one who is *violence-doing,* the creative one, who sets out into the un-said, who breaks into the un-thought, who compels what has never happened and makes appear what is unseen, this violence-doing one stands at all times in daring (*tolma,* verse 371). Insofar as he dares the surmounting of Being, he must risk the assault of un-beings, the *mē kalon,*[66] disintegration, un-constancy, un-structure, and unfittingness. The higher the peak of historical Dasein rises, the more gaping is the abyss for the sudden plunge into the unhistorical, which then only flails around in a confusion that has no way out and at the same time has no site.

Having come to the end of the second phase, we may ask what yet another phase is supposed to do.

The third phase. The decisive truth of the ode was brought into relief by the first phase. The second phase led us through all the essential domains of the violent and the violence-doing. The concluding strophe completes the whole by pulling it together into the essence of the uncanniest. Some details still remain to be noticed

[124]

---

forcefully or suddenly. The related noun *Riß* can mean either 1) a gap, a breach, or 2) a design, a sketch. Compare *Zusammenriß* (pulling together), two paragraphs below. In 1936 Heidegger uses the word *Riß* to describe the strife between "earth and world," a strife that is set to work in artworks: see "The Origin of the Work of Art," in *Basic Writings,* ed. D. F. Krell, 2d ed. (San Francisco: HarperSanFrancisco, 1993), 188 (where *Riß* is translated as "rift").
66. These words from *Antigone,* line 370, are conventionally translated "not beautiful," "ignoble," or "dishonorable."

and explicated more closely. This would result only in an appendix to what has been said so far, but nothing that would demand a new phase of the interpretation. If we restrict ourselves to explicating what is directly said in the poetry, the interpretation is at an end. And yet with this the interpretation stands for the first time at the inception. The authentic interpretation must show what does not stand there in the words and which is nevertheless said. For this the interpretation must necessarily use violence. What is authentic is to be sought where nothing further can be found by scientific exegesis, which brands as unscientific everything that exceeds its domain.

But here, where we have to restrict ourselves to the ode in isolation, we can dare this third phase only in a particular respect, in accordance with our primary task, and this only in a few steps. While recalling what was said in the first phase, we begin with the result of the second phase's explication of the concluding strophe.

The *deinotaton* of the *deinon,* the uncanniest of the uncanny, lies in the oppositional relation of *dikē* and *technē.* The uncanniest is not the augmentation of the uncanny to the highest degree. It is what is one of a kind, according to its kind, within the uncanny. In the opposition between beings as a whole as overwhelming and the human being as violence-doing Dasein, the possibility arises of plunging into what has no way out and has no site: perdition. But neither perdition nor its possibility first occur at the end, when the violence-doer does not succeed in a particular act of violence and mishandles it; instead, this perdition holds sway and lies in wait fundamentally in the opposition between the overwhelming and doing violence. Doing violence *must* shatter against the excessive violence of Being, as long as Being holds sway in its essence, as *phusis,* as emerging sway.

But this necessity of shattering can subsist only insofar as what must shatter is urged into such Being-here. But the human being is urged into such Being-here, thrown into the urgency of such Being, because the overwhelming as such, in order to appear in its sway, *requires* the site of openness for itself. The essence of Being-human opens itself up to us only when it is understood on the basis of this urgency that is necessitated by Being itself. Historical humanity's Being-here means: Being-posited as the breach into which the excessive violence of Being breaks in its appearing, so that this breach itself shatters against Being.

[125]   The uncanniest (the human being) is what it is because from the ground up it deals with and conserves the familiar only in order to break out of it and to let what overwhelms it break in. Being itself throws humanity into the course of this tearing-away, which forces humanity beyond itself, as the one who moves out to Being, in order to set Being to work and thus to hold open beings as a whole. Therefore the violence-doer knows no kindness and conciliation (in the ordinary sense), no appeasement and mollification by success or prestige and by their confirmation. In all this, the violence-doer as creator sees only a seeming fulfillment, which is to be despised. In willing the unprecedented, the violence-doer casts aside all help. For such a one, disaster is the deepest and broadest Yes to the overwhelming. In the shattering of the wrought work, in knowing that the work is un-fit and *sarma* (dungheap), the violence-doer leaves the overwhelming to its fittingness. But none of this takes the form of "lived experiences in the soul," in which the soul of the creator wallows, and it is absolutely not a petty feeling of inferiority; instead, it occurs solely in the manner of setting-into-work itself. The overwhelming, Being, confirms itself in works *as history*.

As the breach for the opening up of Being in beings — a Being that has been set to work — the Dasein of historical humanity is an *in-cident*,[67] the incident in which the violent powers of the released excessive violence of Being suddenly emerge and go to work as history. The Greeks had a deep intimation of this suddenness and

---

67. *Zwischen-fall:* etymologically, a between-case or fall-between.

uniqueness of Dasein, an intimation into which they were urged by Being itself, which disclosed itself to them as *phusis* and *logos* and *dikē*. It is unthinkable that the Greeks decided that they wanted to produce culture for the next few millennia of the West. In the unique urgency of their Dasein, they alone used only violence, and by doing so did not abolish the urgency but only augmented it; thus they won for themselves the fundamental condition of true historical greatness.

The essence of Being-human, as thus experienced and placed back poetically into its ground, remains closed off to understanding in its character as a mystery if understanding hastily takes refuge in some moral appraisal.

The evaluation of Being-human as overweening and audacious, in the derogatory sense, takes humanity out of the urgency of its essence — namely, to be the in-cident. Such an appraisal posits the human being as something present at hand, deposits this thing into an empty space, and appraises it according to some table of values that is attached to it externally. But it is the same sort of misunderstanding to suppose that the poet's saying is actually an implicit rejection of this Being-human, that it covertly recommends a nonviolent resignation in the sense of the cultivation of undisturbed comfort. This opinion could even find some justification in the conclusion of the ode.

[126]

One who *is* in *this way* [namely, as the uncanniest][68] should be excluded from hearth and counsel. Nevertheless, the chorus's concluding words do not contradict what it previously says about Being-human. Insofar as the chorus turns *against* the uncanniest, it says that this manner of Being is *not* the everyday one. Such Dasein cannot be discerned in just any ordinary activity and conduct. These concluding words are so unsurprising that we would have to be

68. In parentheses in the 1953 edition.

surprised if they were missing. In their defensive attitude they are the direct and complete confirmation of the uncanniness of the human essence. With the concluding words the saying of the ode swings back into its inception.

But what does all this have to do with the saying of Parmenides? Nowhere does he speak of uncanniness. He speaks, almost too soberly, only of the belonging-together of apprehension and Being. When we asked what belonging-together means, we were diverted into the interpretation of Sophocles. What help is it to us? Surely we cannot simply carry it over into the interpretation of Parmenides. Certainly not. But we must recall the originary essential connection between poetic and thoughtful saying, especially when, as here, it is a matter of the inceptive, poetizing-thinking, grounding and founding of the historical Dasein of a people. Yet above and beyond this general, essential relation, we immediately find a definite trait that is shared by the content of this poetizing and thinking.

In the second phase, in our summary characterization of the concluding strophe, we deliberately highlighted the reciprocal relation of *dikē* and *technē*. *Dikē* is the overwhelming fittingness. *Technē* is the violence-doing of knowing. The reciprocal relation between them is the happening of uncanniness.

We now assert that the belonging-together of *noein* (apprehension) and *einai* (Being), which is said in the saying of Parmenides, is nothing but this reciprocal relation. If we can show this, we will have demonstrated our earlier assertion that this saying for the first time delimits the essence of Being-human and does not accidentally happen to speak about some aspect of humanity.

[127]   In proof of our assertion, we will first carry out two more general reflections. Then we will attempt an interpretation of the saying in particular.

In the reciprocal relation between *dikē* and *technē*, as said poetically, *dikē* stands for the Being of beings as a whole. We encounter this use of the word in the thought of the Greeks even before Sophocles' time. The oldest saying that has been handed down to us, that of Anaximander, speaks of Being in its essential connection to *dikē*.

Heraclitus, likewise, names *dikē* at a point where he determines something essential about Being. Fragment 80 begins: *eidenai de chrē ton polemon eonta xunon kai dikē erin*, . . . "but it is necessary to keep in view confrontation, setting-apart-from-each-other ⟨*Auseinander-setzung*⟩ essentially unfolding as bringing-together, and fittingness as the opposed . . . "[69] *Dikē*, as the enjoining structure, belongs to the opposed setting-apart-from-each-other as which *phusis*, in emerging, lets what appears shine (come to presence) and thus essentially unfolds as Being (see fragments 23 and 28).

Finally, Parmenides himself is a definitive witness for the thoughtful use of the word *dikē* in the saying of Being. *Dikē* for him is the goddess. She guards the keys that alternately close and open the doors of day and night—that is, the keys to the ways of (unveiling) Being, (disguising) seeming, and (closed-off) Nothing. This means that beings open up only insofar as the fittingness of Being is sustained and maintained.[70] Being as *dikē* is the key to beings in their structure. This sense of *dikē* can be derived unambiguously from the thirty mighty opening verses of Parmenides' "didactic poem," which have been preserved for us in their entirety. So it

69. Conventional translation: "But it is necessary to know that war is common to all and justice is strife."
70. In the last two sentences Heidegger uses three verbs, *verwahren, wahren,* and *bewahren,* which all have a similar meaning: to preserve and safeguard. We have translated them as "guard," "sustain," and "maintain." It should be noted that the German word for "true" is *wahr.*

becomes clear that both the poetic *and* the thoughtful saying of Being name Being — that is, establish and delimit it — with the same word, *dikē*.

What we still need in order to prove our assertion in general is this. We already indicated how in apprehension, as the taking up that takes in,[71] beings as such are disclosed, and thus come forth into unconcealment. For the poet, the assault of *technē* against *dikē* is the happening through which human beings become homeless. When one is put out of the home in this way, the home first discloses itself as such. But at the same time, and only in this way, the alienating first discloses itself, the overwhelming as such. In the happening of uncanniness, beings as a whole open themselves up. This opening up is the happening of unconcealment. This is nothing other than the happening of uncanniness.

[128]   Certainly, one will object, this applies to what the poet is saying. But what we miss in the sober saying of Parmenides is what has been characterized as uncanniness.

So now we must show the sobriety of thinking in its true light. We will do so through the detailed interpretation of the saying. We say in advance: if we should show that apprehension, in its belonging-together with Being *(dikē)*, is such that it uses violence, and as doing violence is an urgency, and as an urgency is undergone only in the necessity of a struggle [in the sense of *polemos* and *eris* ⟨confrontation and strife⟩],[72] and if in addition we should demonstrate that apprehension stands explicitly in connection with logos, and this logos proves to be the ground of human Being, then our assertion that there is an inner affinity between the thoughtful saying and the poetic saying will have been grounded.

71. ". . . in der Vernehmung als dem hin-nehmenden Vor-nehmen."
72. In parentheses in the 1953 edition.

We will show three things:

1. Apprehension is not a mere process, but a de-cision.

2. Apprehension stands in an inner essential community with logos. Logos is an urgency.

3. Logos grounds the essence of language. As such, logos is a struggle and it is the grounding ground of historical human Dasein in the midst of beings as a whole.

On 1. *Noein,* apprehension, is not yet adequately conceived in its essence if we simply avoid lumping it together with the activity of thinking and even with judging. We have characterized apprehension as taking up a position to receive the appearing of beings.[73] As such, it is nothing other than setting out upon one's own, distinct way. But this implies that apprehension is a passage through the crossing of the threefold way. Apprehension can become this passage only if it is fundamentally a *de-cision for* Being *against* Nothing, and thus a confrontation *with* seeming. But such essential deciding, when it is carried out and when it resists the constantly pressing ensnarement in the everyday and the customary, has to use violence. This act of violence, this de-cided setting-out upon the way to the Being of beings, moves humanity out of the homeliness of what is most directly nearby and what is usual.

Only if we grasp apprehension as such a setting-out are we immune to the error of misinterpreting apprehending as an arbitrary human behavior, as a self-explanatory use of human spiritual faculties, or even as one more mental process that just happens to occur. Instead, apprehension is *wrested from* the usual hustle and bustle, in resistance to it. Its belonging together with the Being of beings does not come about automatically. To name this belonging-together is not merely to ascertain a fact but to indicate that strug- [129]

73. See p. 147.

gle. The sobriety of the saying is a thoughtful sobriety, for which the rigor of the concept as apprehending grasp constitutes the fundamental form of being gripped.

On 2. Earlier we cited fragment 6 in order to make visible the distinction among the three ways. At that time we deliberately postponed a closer interpretation of the first verse. Since then we have come to read and hear it in a different way: *chrē to legein te noein t'eon emmenai*. At the time we already translated it as: "Needful is the gathered setting-down as well as the apprehending of this: the being (is) Being."[74] We see that here, *noein* is named together with *legein,* apprehension with logos. In addition, the *chrē* is abruptly placed at the start of the verse. "Needful is apprehension and logos." *Legein* is named along with apprehension as a happening that has the same character. *Legein* is even named first. Here, logos cannot mean gatheredness as the fit of Being but must mean, together with apprehension, that (human) act of violence by virtue of which Being is gathered in its gatheredness. Needful is ⟨*Not ist*⟩ gathering, the gathering that belongs to apprehension. Both must happen "for the sake of Being." Here, gathering means seizing oneself when one is dispersed in the in-constant, seizing oneself again when one is sunk in confusion and seeming. But this gathering, which is still a turning away, can be carried out only by virtue of the gathering that, as a turning toward, pulls beings together into the gatheredness of their Being. Thus logos as gathering enters into urgency ⟨*Not*⟩ here and separates itself from logos as the gatheredness of Being (*phusis*). *Logos* as gathering, as human self-gathering to fittingness, first transposes Being-human into its essence and thus sets it into the un-canny, inasmuch as at-homeness is ruled by the seeming of the customary, the usual and the trite.

74. In fact, Heidegger's earlier translations (pp. 118 and 149) of this fragment are somewhat different.

It remains to be asked why *legein* is named before *noein*. The answer is that it is from *legein* that *noein* first receives its essence as apprehension that gathers.

This determination of the essence of Being-human that takes place here at the inception of Western philosophy is not brought about by picking out just any properties of the living thing "human being," in contrast to other living things. Being-human is determined by the relation to beings as such and as a whole. The human *essence* shows itself here as the relation that first opens up Being to humanity. Being-human, as the urgency of apprehending and gathering, is the urging into the freedom of taking over *technē*, the knowing setting-to-work of Being. Thus there is history. [130]

The essence of *logos* as gathering yields an essential consequence for the character of *legein*. *Legein* as gathering, determined in this way, is related to the originary gatheredness of Being, and Being means coming-into-unconcealment; this gathering therefore has the basic character of opening up, revealing. *Legein* is thus contrasted clearly and sharply with covering up and concealing.

This is demonstrated directly and unambiguously by a saying of Heraclitus. Fragment 93 says: "The lord whose soothsaying happens at Delphi *oute legei oute kruptei,* he neither gathers[75] nor conceals, *alla sēmainei,* but rather he gives indications." Gathering here stands in contrast to concealing. Here, gathering is de-concealing, revealing.

Here a simple question may well be posed: where could the word *legein,* gathering, have gotten the meaning of revealing (de-concealing) in contrast to concealing, if not on the basis of its essential relation to *logos* in the sense of *phusis?* The sway that emerges and shows itself is unconcealment. In accordance with this relation, *legein* means: to pro-duce the unconcealed as such, beings in their

75. Conventional translation: "speaks."

unconcealment. Thus *logos* has the character of *dēloun,* of revealing, not only in Heraclitus but still in Plato. Aristotle characterizes the *legein* of *logos* as *apophainesthai,* bringing-to-self-showing (see *Being and Time,* §7 and §44). This characterization of *legein* as de-concealing and revealing bears witness to the originality of this determination—and it does so all the more strongly because it is precisely in Plato and Aristotle that the decline of the determination of *logos* sets in, the decline that makes logic possible. Since then, for two millennia, these relations among *logos, alētheia, phusis, noein,* and *idea* have been hidden away and covered up in unintelligibility.

But in the inception, this is what happens: *logos* as the revealing gathering—Being, as this gathering, is fittingness in the sense of *phusis*—becomes the necessity of the essence of historical humanity. From here one need take only a single step to grasp how *logos,* so understood, determines the essence of language and how *logos* be-

[131] comes the name for discourse. Being-human, according to its historical, history-opening essence, is *logos,* the gathering and apprehending of the Being of beings: the happening of what is most uncanny, in which, through doing violence, the overwhelming comes to appearance and is brought to stand. But we heard in the choral ode from Sophocles' *Antigone* that together with the breakaway into Being, one finds one's way into the word, language.

In the question of the essence of language, the question of the origin of language surfaces again and again. One looks for an answer in the most peculiar ways. And here we have the first, decisive answer to the question of the origin of language: this origin remains a mystery—not because people up to now were not clever enough but because all cleverness and all sharp wit have mishandled the question before they even get started with it. The character of mystery belongs to the essence of the origin of language. But this implies that language can have begun only from the overwhelming and the uncanny, in the breakaway of humanity into Being. In this breakaway, language, the happening in which Being becomes word, was poetry. Language is the primal poetry in which a people poetizes Being. In turn, the great poetry by which a people steps into history begins the formation of its language. The Greeks created and experienced this poetry through Homer. Language was revealed to their Dasein as a breakaway into Being, as the formation that opens beings up.

It is not at all self-evident that language should be logos, gathering. But we understand this interpretation of language as logos on the basis of the inception of the historical Dasein of the Greeks, on the basis of the fundamental direction in which Being itself opened itself up to them, and in which they brought Being to stand in beings.

The word, the name, sets the self-opening beings out of the immediate, overwhelming assault, back into their Being, and preserves them in this openness, delimitation, and constancy. Naming does not come afterward, providing a being that is already otherwise revealed with a designation and a token called a word, but to the contrary: from the height of its originary act of violence as the opening-up of Being, the word sinks down to become a mere sign. It does so in such a way that this sign then thrusts itself before beings. In originary saying, the Being of beings is opened up in the structure of its gatheredness. This opening-up is gathered in the second sense, according to which the word preserves what is originally gathered, and thus the word governs what holds sway, *phusis*. Human beings, as those who stand and act in logos, in gathering, are the gatherers. They take over and fulfill the governance of the sway of the overwhelming. [132]

But we know that this doing violence is what is most uncanny. For the sake of *tolma*, daring,[76] humanity necessarily meets with the

76. *Antigone,* line 371.

wretched as well as with the valiant and noble. When language speaks as gathering that needs to use violence, as the taming of the overwhelming, and as preservation, then and only then, is there necessarily also loss and lack of discipline. Hence language as happening is always also chatter: instead of the opening-up of Being, it is its covering-up; instead of gathering to structure and fittingness, it is dispersion into unfittingness. Logos as language does not come about automatically. *Legein* is *needful: chrē to legein,* needful is the gathering apprehension of the Being of the being ⟨*Sein des Seiend*⟩. [From where does the urgency urge?]⁷⁷

On 3. Because the essence of language is found in the gathering of the gatheredness of Being, language as everyday discourse comes to its truth only when saying and hearing are related to logos as gatheredness, in the sense of Being. For in Being and its structure, what is, is originally and definitively already a *legomenon,* as it were: something gathered, said, spoken in advance and spoken out. Now we first grasp the full context for that saying of Parmenides according to which apprehension happens for the sake of Being.

The passage runs (fragment 8, lines 34–36):

"In themselves, apprehension and that for the sake of which apprehension happens belong together. For not without the being ⟨*das Seiend*⟩, in which it (Being ⟨*das Sein*⟩) is already spoken, will you find (reach) apprehension."⁷⁸ The relation to *logos* as *phusis* makes *legein* into the gathering that apprehends, but makes apprehension into the apprehension that gathers. In order to remain gathered, therefore, *legein* must turn away from all mere recitation, from glibness and the ready tongue. And so we find in Parmenides the sharp opposition between *logos* and *glōssa* ⟨tongue⟩ (fragment 7,

---

77. In parentheses in the 1953 edition.
78. Conventional translation: "For thinking and that for the sake of which thinking happens are the same. For not without being will you find thinking." For Heidegger's earlier translation of line 34, see p. 148.

lines 3 ff.). The passage corresponds to the beginning of fragment 6, where in relation to taking the first, unavoidable way to Being, it is said that it is needful to gather oneself to the Being of the being. Now ⟨in fragment 7⟩ we are dealing with the directive for traveling the third way, into seeming. This way leads through what is, which also always stands in semblance. This way is the customary way. Hence the man who knows must constantly tear himself away from this way into the *legein* and *noein* of the Being of the being:

> and by no means shall habit, ever so sly, force you in this way's direction, [133]
> so that you lose yourself in unseeing gaping and in clamorous hearing
> and in the ready tongue, but instead decide incisively, as gathered into one you set down before yourself the exposition of the manifold conflict,
> the exposition provided by me.[79]

Here *logos* stands in the most intimate bond with *krinein*, cutting as de-ciding, in carrying out the gathering to the gatheredness of Being. *Selective* "gleaning" (*das* auslesende *"Lesen"*) grounds and sustains the pursuit of Being and the rejection of seeming. The meaning of *krinein* includes: to select, to bring into relief, to set the measure that determines rank.

These three points carry the interpretation of the saying far enough to make it clear that Parmenides, too, in fact deals with

79. Conventional translation: "and by no means shall habit, ever so sly, force you in this way's direction, / so that you lose yourself in unseeing gaping and in clamorous hearing / and in the ready tongue, but instead judge by reason the much-contested argument / provided by me." Heidegger's three major innovations are: 1) *krinai:* "decide incisively" rather than "judge"; 2) *logōi:* "gathered into one," rather than "by reason"; 3) *poludērin elenchon:* "exposition of the manifold conflict" rather than "much-contested argument."

logos in essential respects. Logos is an urgency and in itself needs to use violence in order to fend off glibness and dispersion. Logos as *legein* stands against *phusis*. In this disjunction, logos as the happening of gathering becomes the ground that grounds Being-human. Thus we were able to claim that in the saying, the decisive determination of the human essence is first fulfilled. To be human means to gather, to gather and apprehend the Being of beings, *to take over* the knowing setting-into-work of appearance and thus to *govern* unconcealment, to *preserve* it against concealment and covering-up.

Thus in the inception of Western philosophy it is already clear that the question of Being necessarily includes the grounding of Dasein.

We can no more grasp this connection between Being and Dasein (and the corresponding question about it) by appeal to epistemological problems than we can grasp it by ascertaining, by external means, that every conception of Being depends on a conception of Dasein. [If indeed the question about Being seeks not only the Being of beings, but Being itself in *its* essence, then what is fully and explicitly required is a grounding of Dasein that is guided by this question, a grounding that therefore, and *only* therefore, gave itself the name "*fundamental* ontology." See *Being and Time,* introduction.][80]

We say that this inceptive opening up of the essence of Being-human was *decisive.* Yet it was not preserved and maintained as the great inception. This opening up had an entirely different consequence: the definition of the human being as the rational living thing—a definition that subsequently became the standard one for the West and that still remains unshaken in the prevailing opinion and attitude of today. In order to show the distance between this

[134]

80. In parentheses in the 1953 edition.

definition and the inceptive opening up of the essence of Being-human, we can contrast the inception and the end in a formulaic way. The end is revealed in the formula: *anthrōpos* = *zōon logon echon,* the human being is the living thing equipped with reason. We grasp the inception in a freely constructed formula that also summarizes our interpretation up to now: *phusis* = *logos anthrōpon echon:* Being, the overwhelming appearing, necessitates the gathering that pervades and grounds Being-human.

There, at the end, a remnant of the connection between logos and Being-human does endure, but logos has long since been externalized into a faculty of understanding and of reason. The faculty itself is grounded on the Being-present-at-hand of a living thing of a special sort, on the *zōon beltiston,* the animal that has turned out best (Xenophon).[81]

Here, at the inception, to the contrary, Being-human is grounded in the opening up of the Being of beings.

From the point of view of the customary and dominant definitions, from the point of view of modern and contemporary metaphysics, epistemology, anthropology, and ethics, which are all determined by Christianity, our interpretation of the saying must appear as a willful reinterpretation, as one that reads into the saying what an "exact exegesis" can never ascertain. That is correct. According to the usual opinion of today, what we have said is in fact just a result of that violent character and one-sidedness, which has already become proverbial, of the Heideggerian mode of interpretation. Yet here it may and must be asked: which interpretation is the true one? The one that simply takes over the perspective of its understanding because it has fallen into it, and because it offers itself as current and self-evident? Or the interpretation that puts the

81. Xenophon, *Cyropaedia,* 8.3.49.

customary perspective into question from the bottom up, because it could be and in fact is the case that this perspective does nothing to indicate *that* which is to be seen?

Certainly—giving up the ordinary and going back into questioning interpretation is a leap. Only one who takes the right running start can leap. Everything is decided by this run, for it means that we ourselves actually *ask* the questions again, and that we, in these questions, first create the perspectives. However, this does not happen in wavering arbitrariness, nor in relying on a system that has been set forth as the norm. Instead, it happens in and from historical necessity, from the urgency of historical Dasein.

[135]   *Legein* and *noein,* gathering and apprehending, are an urgency and an act of violence *against* the overwhelming, but at the same time always and only *for* it. Thus the violence-doers must time and again shrink back from this use of violence, and yet they cannot back down. In this will to surmount that at the same time shrinks back, at moments the possibility must flare up that the surmounting of the overwhelming can be fully and most certainly fought out if the concealment of Being—the emerging sway, which in itself essentially unfolds as *logos,* as the gatheredness of the conflicting— is simply preserved, and thus, in a certain way, every possibility of appearing is withheld. This audacity [which in truth is the highest recognition][82] belongs to the violence-doing of the uncanniest: to overwhelm the appearing sway by withholding all openness toward it, and to measure up to it by keeping the site of appearing closed to its almighty sway.

But for Dasein, withholding such openness toward Being means nothing other than giving up its own essence. This demands that it either step out of Being or else never step into Dasein. This is expressed once again in Sophocles, in a choral ode of the tragedy

82. In parentheses in the 1953 edition.

Oedipus at Colonus, lines 1224–1225: *mē phunai ton hapanta nika logon:* "never to have stepped into Dasein triumphs over the gatheredness of beings as a whole."[83]

Never to have taken over Being-here, *mē phunai,* is said of the human as the one who is essentially gathered together *with phusis* as *its* gatherer. Here *phusis, phunai,* is used to refer to human Being, but *logos* is used in Heraclitus's sense as the fittingness that holds sway over beings as a whole. This word of the poet expresses the most intimate relation of Dasein to Being and its opening up, for the poet's word names what is farthest from Being: not-Being-here. Here, the uncanniest possibility of Dasein shows itself: to break the excessive violence of Being through Dasein's ultimate act of violence against itself. Dasein does not have this possibility as an empty way out, but it *is* this possibility insofar as it is; for as Dasein, it must indeed shatter against Being in every act of violence.

This looks like pessimism. But it would be preposterous to label Greek Dasein with this term — not because the Greeks were somehow optimists at bottom after all, but because these assessments miss Greek Dasein altogether. The Greeks were, to be sure, more pessimistic than a pessimist can ever be. They were also more optimistic than any optimist. Their historical Dasein had not yet entered the realm of pessimism and optimism.

Both assessments, in the same way, consider Dasein in advance [136] as a business, either a bad business or one that is going well. This way of viewing the world is expressed in Schopenhauer's well-known proposition: "Life is a business that does not cover its costs."[84] The proposition is untrue not because "life" does cover its costs in the end but because life (as Being-here) is not a business at

83. Conventional translation: "not to be born surpasses all speech" (in other words, it is best never to be born). *Phunai,* "be born," is a form of *phuein,* the verb that corresponds to the noun *phusis.*
84. Cf. Schopenhauer, *The World as Will and Representation,* vol. 2, 353.

all. True, it has been one for centuries now. And this is why Greek Dasein remains so alien to us.

Not-Being-here is the ultimate victory over Being. Dasein is the constant urgency of defeat and of the renewed resurgence of the act of violence against Being, in such a way that the almighty sway of Being violates[85] Dasein (in the literal sense), makes Dasein into the site of its appearing, envelops and pervades Dasein in its sway, and thereby holds it within Being.

Logos and *phusis* disjoin, step apart from each other. But this is not yet the stepping-forth of logos. This means that logos does not yet step up to the Being of beings, does not yet come forward "versus" Being in *such* a way that logos itself [as reason][86] makes itself into the court of justice that presides over Being and that takes over and regulates the determination of the Being of beings.

This happens only when logos gives up its inceptive essence—that is, when Being as *phusis* is covered up and reinterpreted. Human Dasein then changes accordingly. The slow ending of this history, in whose midst we have long been standing, is the dominance of thinking as *ratio* (as both understanding and reason) over the *Being* of beings. Here begins the interplay of "rationalism and irrationalism," which is playing itself out to this very day, in all possible disguises and under the most contradictory titles. Irrationalism is only the weakness and utter failure of rationalism become apparent, and thus it is itself a rationalism. Irrationalism is a way out of rationalism that does not lead us out into the open but only gets us stuck *still* farther in rationalism, because it promotes the opinion that rationalism is overcome by merely saying no to it, whereas in fact it now just plays its games more dangerously, be-

---

85. *ver-gewaltigt: vergewaltigen* (root *Gewalt,* violence) means to violate, and specifically to rape.
86. In parentheses in the 1953 edition.

cause it plays them covertly and in a manner less vulnerable to interference.

It is not part of the task of this lecture course to exhibit the inner history in which the dominance of thinking [as the *ratio* of logic][87] over the Being of beings developed. Apart from its intrinsic difficulty, such an exhibition has no effective historical force as long as we ourselves have not awakened the forces of our own questioning from and for our history at this very moment of the world. [137]

Nevertheless, it is still necessary to show how on the basis of the inceptive disjunction of *logos* and *phusis,* logos secedes and then begins to establish the dominance of reason.

This secession of logos and its advance readiness to assume the position of a court of justice that presides over Being happens already within Greek philosophy. It even determines the end of Greek philosophy. We surmount Greek philosophy as the inception of Western philosophy only if we also grasp this inception in its inceptive end; for it was solely and only this end that became the "inception" for the subsequent age, in such a way that this "inception" also covered up the inceptive inception. But this inceptive end of the great inception, the philosophy of Plato and Aristotle, remains great, even if we completely discount the greatness of the way it worked itself out in the West.

We now ask: how does logos secede from and take precedence over Being? How does the decisive development of the division between Being and thinking come about? Even this history can be sketched here only in a few crude strokes. We will start at the end and ask:

1. How does the relation between *phusis* and *logos* look at the end of Greek philosophy, in Plato and Aristotle? How is *phusis* understood here? What form and role has *logos* taken over?

87. In parentheses in the 1953 edition.

2. How did this end come about? What is the real basis of the change?

On 1. At the end, the word *idea, eidos,* "idea," comes to the fore as the definitive and prevailing word for Being *(phusis)*. Since then, the interpretation of Being as idea rules over all Western thinking, throughout the history of its changes up to today. This provenance is also the basis for the fact that the great and final closure of the first phase of Western thinking, the system of Hegel, conceives of the actuality of the actual, Being in the absolute sense, as "idea" and explicitly calls it this. But what does it mean that in Plato, *phusis* is interpreted as *idea?*

In our first introductory characterization of the Greek experience of Being, *idea* and *eidos* were already mentioned alongside [138] other titles that we listed. When we directly encounter the philosophy of Hegel, or that of some other modern thinker, or medieval Scholasticism, everywhere we find the term "idea" used to name *Being;* unless we deceive ourselves, this is *unintelligible* on the basis of the *usual* representations. However, we can understand this state of affairs if we come to it from the inception of Greek philosophy. Then right away we can measure the distance between the interpretation of Being as *phusis* and its interpretation as *idea*.

The word *idea* means what is seen in the visible, the view that something offers. What is offered is the current look or *eidos* of whatever we encounter. The look of a thing is that within which, as we say, it presents itself to us, re-presents itself and as such stands before us; the look is that within which and as which the thing comes-to-presence — that is, in the Greek sense, *is*.[88] This standing is the constancy of what has come forth of itself, the constancy of

88. "Das Aussehen eines Dinges ist das, worin es sich uns, wie wir sagen, präsentiert, sich vor-stellt und als solches vor uns steht, worin und als was es an-west, d. h. im griechischen Sinne *ist*."

phusis. But this standing-there of the constant is also, from the human point of view, the foreground of what comes to presence *of itself,* the apprehensible. In the look, that which comes to presence, that which is, stands there in its whatness and its howness. It is apprehended and taken, it is in the possession of a taking-in, it is the holdings of a taking-in, it is the available coming to presence of what comes to presence: *ousia.*[89] [*Ousia,* then, can mean both the coming to presence of something that comes to presence *and* that which comes to presence in the whatness of its look.

Here is the concealed origin of the later distinction between *existentia* and *essentia.* If, in contrast, one just blindly snatches up from the tradition the now common distinction between *existentia* and *essentia,* one will never see how *existentia* and *essentia,* as well as the distinction between them, stand out from the *Being* of beings and thus can characterize it. However, if we understand the *idea* (the look) as *coming to presence,* then coming to presence shows itself as constancy in a double sense. On the one hand, the look entails the standing-forth-from-unconcealment, the simple *estin* ⟨is⟩. On the other hand, what shows itself in the look is that which looks that way, *what* stands there, the *ti estin* ⟨the what-it-is⟩.][90]

Thus, the *idea* constitutes the Being of beings. But here, *idea* and *eidos* are used in an extended sense, meaning not only what we can see with our physical eyes, but everything that can be apprehended. *What* any given being is consists in its look, and the look, in turn, presents the being's whatness (allows it to *come to presence*).

But, we will already have asked, isn't this interpretation of Being as *idea* thoroughly Greek, then? After all, this interpretation pro-

89. The Greek word *ousia,* etymologically "beingness," originally was used to mean property or holdings. In later philosophical usage it came to mean substance or essence. See pp. 64 and 207.
90. The brackets are absent in the 1953 edition. Instead, only the portion of this paragraph that follows the first sentence is parenthesized.

[139] ceeds with unavoidable necessity from the fact that Being is experienced as *phusis,* as emerging sway, as appearing, as standing-in-the-light. What else does what appears show in appearing if not its look, the *idea*? How is it that the interpretation of Being as *idea* is supposed to differ from *phusis*? Isn't the tradition completely in the right, if for centuries it has seen this Greek philosophy in the light of Platonic philosophy? The interpretation of Being as *idea* in Plato is so little a departure, much less a downfall, from the inception that instead it grasps this inception in a more unfolded and sharper way, and grounds it through the "theory of ideas." Plato is the fulfillment of the inception.

In fact, it cannot be denied that the interpretation of Being as *idea* results from the fundamental experience of Being as *phusis*. It is, as we say, a necessary consequence of the essence of Being as *emergent shining* ⟨Scheinen⟩. But in this there is no distancing, much less a fall away from the inception. Certainly not.

But if that which is an essential *consequence* is raised to the level of essence itself, and thus takes the place of the essence, then how do things stand? Then there is a fall, and it must for its part generate its own distinctive consequences. This is what happened. What remains decisive is not the fact in itself that *phusis* was characterized as *idea,* but that the *idea* rises up as the sole and definitive interpretation of Being.

We can easily assess the distance between the two interpretations if we pay attention to the difference between the perspectives in which these essential determinations of Being, *phusis* and *idea,* move. *Phusis* is the emerging sway, the standing-there-in-itself, constancy. *Idea,* the look as what is seen, is a determination of the constant insofar as, and only insofar as, it stands opposed to a seeing. But *phusis* as emerging sway is also already an appearing. To be sure. It is just that appearing has two meanings. First, appearing denotes the self-gathering event of bringing-itself-to-stand and thus standing in gatheredness. But then, appearing also means: as something that is already standing there, to proffer a foreground, a surface, a look as an offering to be looked at.

Considered in terms of the essence of space, the difference between the two types of appearing is this: appearing in the first and authentic sense, as the gathered bringing-itself-to-stand, takes space in; it first conquers space; as standing there, it creates space for itself; it brings about everything that belongs to it, while it itself is not imitated. Appearing in the second sense merely steps forth from an already prepared space, and it is viewed by a looking-at within the already fixed dimensions of this space. The visage offered by the thing, and no longer the thing itself, now becomes what is decisive. Appearing in the first sense first rips space open. Appearing in the second sense simply gives space an *outline* and measures the space that has been opened up.[91] [140]

But does not Parmenides' saying already say that Being and apprehending—that is, what is viewed and seeing—belong together? Something viewed certainly belongs to seeing, but it does not follow that having been viewed as such and alone should and can determine the coming to presence of what is viewed. Parmenides' saying precisely does not say that Being should be conceived on the basis of apprehending—that is, as something merely apprehended—but that apprehending is for the sake of Being. Apprehending should open up beings in such a way that it sets beings back into their Being, so that apprehending takes beings with regard to the fact *that* they set themselves forth and as *what*. But in the interpretation of Being as *idea,* not only is an essential consequence falsified into the essence itself, but this falsification is misin-

91. Heidegger is contrasting the verb *aufreißen* (to rip open) with the related noun *Aufriß* (an outline, diagram, architectural projection, or perspective view).

terpreted yet again—and this, too, happens in the course of Greek experience and interpretation.

The idea, as the look of that which is, constitutes *what* it is. The what-Being, the "essence" in this sense—that is, the concept of essence—in turn becomes ambiguous:

a. A being essentially unfolds,[92] it holds sway, it summons and brings about what belongs to it, including conflict in particular.

b. A being essentially unfolds as this or that; it has this what-determination.

We have indicated—though here we cannot pursue the issue further—the way in which, when *phusis* changes into *idea,* the *ti estin* (what-Being) comes forth and the *hoti estin* (that-Being) distinguishes itself in contrast to it; this is the essential provenance of the distinction between *essentia* and *existentia.* [This was the topic of an unpublished lecture course delivered in the summer semester of 1927.][93]

However, as soon as the essence of Being comes to consist in whatness (idea), then whatness, as *the* Being of beings, is also what is most in being about beings ⟨*das Seiendste am Seienden*⟩. On the one hand, whatness is now what *really* is, *ontōs on.* Being as *idea* is now promoted to the status of what really is, and beings themselves, which previously held sway, sink to the level of what Plato calls *mē on*—that which really should not be and really *is* not either—because beings always deform the idea, the pure look, by actualizing it, insofar as they incorporate it into matter. On the other hand, the *idea* becomes the *paradeigma,* the model. At the same time, the idea

92. See *wesen* in German-English Glossary.

93. In parentheses in the 1953 edition. The lecture course in question is *The Basic Problems of Phenomenology,* now available as volume 24 of the *Gesamtausgabe,* and in an English translation by Albert Hofstadter (Bloomington: Indiana University Press, 1982). The distinction between *essentia* and *existentia* is discussed in part I, chapter 2.

necessarily becomes the ideal. What is produced by imitation really "is" not, but only participates in Being, *methexis* ⟨participation⟩. The *chōrismos* has been ripped open, the cleft between the idea as what really is, the prototype and archetype, and what really is not, the imitation and likeness.[94]   [141]

Now appearing takes on still another sense on the basis of the idea. That which appears, appearance, is no longer *phusis,* the emerging sway, nor the self-showing of the look, but instead it is the surfacing of the likeness. Inasmuch as the likeness never reaches its prototype, what appears is *mere* appearance, really a seeming, which now means a defect. Now *on* and *phainomenon* ⟨what is and what appears⟩ are disjoined. This involves still another essential consequence. Because the *idea* is what really is, and the *idea* is the prototype, all opening up of beings must be directed toward equaling the prototype, resembling the archetype, directing itself according to the idea. The truth of *phusis* — *alētheia* as the unconcealment that essentially unfolds in the emerging sway — now becomes *homoiōsis* and *mimēsis:* resemblance, directedness, the correctness of seeing, the correctness of apprehending as representing.

When we properly grasp all this, we will no longer wish to deny that the interpretation of Being as *idea* stands at a distance from the originary inception. If we speak of a "fall" here, then we must insist that this fall, despite everything, still remains at a height and does not sink down to a low level. We can measure this height by the following considerations. The great age of Greek Dasein is so great — it is in itself the only classical age — that it even creates the

94. This and the following paragraph employ a number of words related to *Bild* (picture, image) and *bilden* (to form or build). These include *hineinbilden* (incorporate, or etymologically "form into"), *nachbilden* (imitate, or "form after"), *Musterbild* (model or paragon, or "model picture"), *Vorbild* (prototype, or "fore-picture"), *Urbild* (archetype, or "primal picture"), and *Abbild* (likeness, or "off-picture").

metaphysical conditions of possibility for all classicism. In the basic concepts *idea, paradeigma, homoiōsis,* and *mimēsis,* the metaphysics of classicism is delineated in advance. Plato is not a classicist yet, because he cannot yet be one, but he is the classic of classicism. The transformation of Being from *phusis* to *idea* itself brings about one of the essential forms of movement within the history of the West, not just the history of Western art.

Now we must trace what becomes of logos, in accordance with the reinterpretation of *phusis.* The opening up of beings happens in logos as gathering. Gathering is originally accomplished in language. Thus logos becomes the definitive and essential determination of discourse. Language, as what is spoken out and said, and as what can be said again, preserves in each case the being that has been opened up. What has been said can be said again and passed on. The truth that is preserved in this saying spreads in such a way that the being that was originally opened up in gathering is not itself properly experienced in each particular case. In what is [142] passed on, truth loosens itself, as it were, from beings. This can go so far that saying-again becomes mere hearsay, *glōssa.* Everything that is asserted stands constantly in this danger (see *Being and Time,* §44b).[95]

This implies that the decision about what is true now takes place as a confrontation between correct saying and mere hearsay. Logos, in the sense of saying and asserting, now becomes the domain and place where decisions are made about truth—that is, originally, about the unconcealment of beings and thus about the Being of

95. This paragraph uses several words based on *sagen* (say): *nachsagen* (say again, repeat), *weitersagen* (pass on, spread about by saying), *Hersagen* (recitation, the repetition of hearsay), *aussagen* (assert). Heidegger also plays on *wahr,* "true," when he speaks of *die verwahrte Wahrheit,* "the truth that is preserved." *Glōssa,* literally "tongue," can also mean hearsay, word of mouth (see p. 184).

beings. In the inception, logos as gathering *is* the happening of unconcealment; logos is grounded in unconcealment and is in service to it. But now, logos as assertion becomes the locus of truth in the sense of correctness. We arrive at Aristotle's proposition according to which logos as assertion is what can be true or false.[96] Truth, which was originally, as unconcealment, a happening of the beings themselves that held sway, and was governed by means of gathering, now becomes a property of logos. In becoming a property of assertion, truth does not just shift its place; it changes its essence. From the point of view of the assertion, the true is attained when saying holds on to that about which it is making an assertion, when the assertion directs itself according to beings. Truth becomes the correctness of logos. Thus logos steps out of its originary inclusion in the happening of unconcealment in such a way that decisions about truth, and so about beings, are made on the basis of logos and with reference back to it — and not only decisions about beings, but even, and in advance, about Being. Logos is now *legein ti kata tinos,* saying something about something.[97] That about which something is said is in each case what lies at the basis of the *assertion,* what lies in front of it, *hupokeimenon (subjectum).* From the point of view of the logos that has become independent as assertion, Being displays itself as *this* lying-there. [The possibility of this determination of Being is prefigured in *phusis,* as is the *idea.* Only the sway that emerges from itself can, as coming to presence, determine itself as look and lying-there.][98]

That which lies at the basis can be exhibited in asserting in various ways: as what is in such and such a state, as what is so and so large, as what is related in this and that way. Being-in-a-state,

96. Aristotle, *De Interpretatione,* chapter 4.
97. Aristotle, *De Interpretatione,* chapters 5–6.
98. In parentheses in the 1953 edition.

Being-large, Being-related are determinations of Being. Because, as ways of Being-said, they have been created out of logos—and because to assert is *katēgorein*—the determinations of the Being of beings are called *katēgoriai,* categories. On this basis, the theory of Being and of the determinations of beings as such becomes a theory that investigates the categories and their order. The goal of [143] all ontology is the theory of categories. Today it is taken to be self-evident, as it has been for a long time, that the essential characteristics of Being are categories. But at bottom, this is strange. It becomes intelligible only when we grasp that, and how, logos not only separates itself from *phusis,* but at the same time comes forth *over against phusis* as *the* standard-setting domain that becomes the place of origin for the determinations of Being.

But logos, *phasis,* the saying in the sense of the assertion, decides so originally about the Being of beings that in each case where one saying stands *against* another, where a contra-diction occurs, *antiphasis,* then the contradictory cannot *be.* In contrast, that which does not contradict itself is at least capable of Being. The old disputed question of whether the principle of contradiction has an "ontological" or a "logical" meaning in Aristotle is wrongly posed, because for Aristotle there is neither "ontology" nor "logic." Both come about only on the basis of Aristotelian philosophy. Rather, the principle of contradiction has "ontological" meaning because it is a fundamental law of logos, a "logical" principle. Thus the sublation of the principle of contradiction in Hegel's dialectic is not in principle an overcoming of the dominance of logos but only its *highest intensification.* [The fact that Hegel gives the title of "logic" to what is really metaphysics—that is, "physics"—recalls both logos in the sense of the locus of the categories and logos in the sense of the originary *phusis.*][99]

99. In parentheses in the 1953 edition.

In the form of the assertion, logos itself has become just another thing that one comes across. This present-at-hand thing is something handy, something that is handled in order to attain truth as correctness and establish it securely. So this handle for attaining truth can easily be grasped as a tool, *organon,* and the tool can easily be made handy in the proper way. This is all the more necessary the more decisively the *originary* opening up of the Being of beings has been suspended, with the transformation of *phusis* into *eidos* and of *logos* into *katēgoria.* The true as the correct is now merely spread about and spread afar by way of discussion, instruction, and prescriptions, thereby becoming ever more leveled out. Logos must be made ready as a tool for this. The hour of the birth of logic has arrived.

It was thus not without justification that the ancient philosophy of the schools collected the treatises of Aristotle that relate to logos under the title "Organon." And with this, logic was already brought to a conclusion in its basic traits. Thus, two millennia later, Kant can say in the preface to the second edition of the *Critique of Pure Reason* that logic "has not had to take a step backward since Aristotle," "nor to this very day has it been able to take a single step forward, and thus to all appearance it seems to be complete and perfected."[100] It does not merely seem so. It is so. For despite Kant and Hegel, logic has not taken a single step farther in what is essential and inceptive. The only possible step remaining is to unhinge it [that is, as the definitive perspective for the interpretation of Being][101] from its *ground* up. [144]

Let us now look over everything that we have said about *phusis* and *logos: phusis* becomes the *idea (paradeigma),* truth becomes correctness. Logos becomes the assertion, the locus of truth as correct-

---

100. *Critique of Pure Reason,* B viii.
101. In parentheses in the 1953 edition.

ness, the origin of the categories, the basic principle that determines the possibilities of Being. "Idea" and "category" will now be the two titles under which stand Western thought, action, and appraisal, under which stands all of Western Dasein. The transformation in *phusis* and *logos,* and thus the transformation in their relation to each other, is a fall away from the inceptive inception. The philosophy of the Greeks attains dominance in the West not on the basis of its originary inception but on the basis of the inceptive end, which in Hegel is brought to fulfillment in a great and final manner. Where history is genuine, it does not perish merely by ending and expiring like an animal; it perishes only *historically*.

But what happened—what must have happened—for Greek philosophy to meet this inceptive end, this transformation of *phusis* and *logos?* Here we stand before the second question.[102]

On 2. Two points should be noted about the transformation we have described.

a. It begins with the essence of *phusis* and *logos,* or more precisely, with an essential consequence—and in such a way that what appears (in its shining) shows a look, in such a way that what is said falls immediately into the domain of assertion as chatter. Thus the transformation does not come from outside but from "within." But what does "within" mean here? What is at issue is not *phusis* in itself and *logos* in itself. We see from Parmenides that both belong together essentially. Their relation itself is the ground that sustains and holds sway in their essence, their "inner core," although the ground of the relation itself initially and authentically lies concealed in the essence of *phusis*. But what kind of relation is it? What we are asking comes into view if we now bring out a second point in the transformation we have described.

102. See p. 192.

b. In each case, a consequence of the transformation is that, from the point of view both of the idea and of assertion, the original essence of truth, *alētheia* (unconcealment), has changed into correctness. For unconcealment is that inner core — that is, the relation that holds sway between *phusis* and *logos* in the originary sense. The sway essentially unfolds as coming-forth-into-unconcealment. But apprehension and gathering are the governance of the opening up of unconcealment for beings. The transformation of *phusis* and *logos* into idea and assertion has its inner ground in a transformation of the essence of truth as unconcealment into truth as correctness.

[145]

This essence of truth could not be held fast and preserved in its inceptive originality. Unconcealment, the space founded for the appearing of beings, collapsed. "Idea" and "assertion," *ousia* and *katēgoria,* were rescued as remnants of this collapse. Once neither beings nor gathering could be preserved and understood on the basis of unconcealment, only *one* possibility remained: that which had fallen apart and lay there as something present at hand could be brought back together only in a relation that itself had the character of something present at hand. A present-at-hand logos must resemble something else present at hand — beings as the objects of the logos — and be directed by these. To be sure, one last, seeming glimmer of the original essence of *alētheia* maintains itself. [The present-at-hand comes forth into unconcealment, and just as necessarily, re-presentational assertion goes forth into the same unconcealment.][103] Yet the seeming glimmer of *alētheia* that remains no longer has the sustaining strength and tension to be the determining ground for the essence of truth. And it never became such a ground again. To the contrary. Ever since idea and category have assumed their dominance, philosophy fruitlessly toils to explain the

103. In parentheses in the 1953 edition.

relation between assertion (thinking) and Being by all possible and impossible means — fruitlessly, because the question of Being has not been brought back to its adequate ground and basis, in order to be unfolded from there.

Now the collapse of unconcealment, as we briefly call this happening, does not originate from a mere deficiency, from an inability to sustain any longer that which, with this essence, was given to historical humanity to preserve. The ground of the collapse lies first in the greatness of the inception and in the essence of the inception itself. ["Fall" and "collapse" create an illusion of negativity only in a superficial exposition.][104] The inception, as incipient, must, in a certain way, leave itself behind. [It thus necessarily conceals itself, but this self-concealing is not nothing.][105] The inception that initiates can never directly preserve its initiating; it can never preserve it in the only way that it can be preserved — namely, by re-trieving it more originally in its originality. Therefore we can address the inception and the collapse of truth solely in a thoughtful re-trieval. The urgency of Being and the greatness of its inception are not merely objects for historians to observe, explain, and evaluate. This does not preclude but instead demands the possibility that this collapse be displayed as far as possible in its historical course. Here, on the path of this lecture course, *one* decisive hint must suffice.

We know from Heraclitus and Parmenides that the unconcealment of beings is not simply present at hand. Unconcealment happens only in so far as it is brought about by the work: the work of the word as poetry, the work of stone in temple and statue, the work of the word as thinking, the work of the *polis* as the site of history that grounds and preserves all this. ["Work," according

[146]

104. In parentheses in the 1953 edition.
105. In parentheses in the 1953 edition.

to what we said earlier, is here always to be understood in the *Greek* sense as *ergon*, as that which comes to presence and which is pro-duced into unconcealment.][106] The striving for the unconcealment of beings and thus of Being in the work, this striving for the unconcealment of beings, which in itself already happens only as constant antagonism, is always at the same time the strife against concealment, covering-up, against seeming.

Seeming, *doxa*, is not something external to Being and unconcealment but instead belongs to unconcealment. But *doxa* is also ambiguous in itself. On the one hand, it means the view in which something proffers itself, and on the other hand it means the view that human beings have. Dasein settles into such views. They are asserted and passed on. Thus *doxa* is a type of logos. The dominant views now obstruct our own view of beings. Beings are deprived of the possibility of turning themselves *toward* apprehension, appearing on their own right. The view granted by beings, which usually turns itself toward us, is distorted into a view upon beings. The dominance of views thus distorts beings and twists them.

"To twist a thing" is called *pseudesthai* by the Greeks. The struggle *for* the unconcealment of beings, *alētheia*, thus becomes the struggle *against* the *pseudos*, against twisting and distortion. But the essence of struggle implies that the one who struggles becomes dependent on his opponent, whether he conquers him or is defeated by him. So because the struggle against untruth is a struggle against the *pseudos*, then the struggle for truth, in contrast to the *pseudos* against which one is struggling, becomes the struggle for the *a-pseudes*, the undistorted, the untwisted. [147]

With this, the originary experience of truth as unconcealment is endangered. For the undistorted is reached only when apprehend-

106. In parentheses in the 1953 edition.

ing and comprehending turn to beings without twisting, straight on—that is, when apprehending and comprehending are directed by beings. The way to truth as correctness lies open.

This happening of the transformation of unconcealment, by way of distortion, to undistortedness and from this to correctness, must be seen together with the transformation of *phusis* into *idea*, of *logos* as gathering into *logos* as assertion. On the basis of all this, the final interpretation of Being that is secured in the word *ousia* works itself out and works itself to the fore. *Ousia* means Being in the sense of constant presence, presence at hand. Consequently, what really is is what always is, *aei on*. What is continuously coming to presence is what we must go back to, in advance, in all comprehending and producing of anything: the model, the *idea*. What is continuously coming to presence is what we must go back to in all *logos*, asserting, as what always already lies at hand, the *hupokeimenon, subjectum*. What always already lies at hand before us is, from the point of view of *phusis*, of emergence, what is *proteron*, the earlier, the *a priori*.

This determination of the Being of beings characterizes the way in which beings stand against all comprehending and asserting. The *hupokeimenon* is the forerunner of the later interpretation of the being as object.[107] Apprehension, *noein*, is taken over by logos in the sense of the assertion. It thus becomes the apprehending that, in determining something as something, analyzes it, thinks it through by taking it through,[108] *dianoeisthai*. This analysis by means of assertions, *dianoia*, is the essential determination of the

---

107. *Gegenstand* (object) etymologically means "that which stands against."
108. *durch-nimmt, durchvernimmt:* the word that Heidegger uses to translate *noein, Vernehmen* (apprehend), is related to *nehmen*, to take. *Durchnehmen* (analyze, examine) etymologically means "to take through." It is thus a good translation of *dianoia*, etymologically the kind of *noein* that goes through.

understanding in the sense of the representing that makes judgments. Apprehending becomes understanding, apprehending becomes reason.

Christianity reinterprets the Being of beings as Being-created. Thinking and knowing come to be distinguished from faith *(fides)*. This does not hinder the rise of rationalism and irrationalism but rather first prepares it and strengthens it.

Because beings have been created by God—that is, have been thought out rationally in advance—then as soon as the relation of creature to creator is dissolved, while at the same time human reason attains predominance, and even posits itself as absolute, the Being of beings must become thinkable in the pure thinking of mathematics. Being as calculable in this way, Being as set into calculation, makes beings into something that can be ruled in modern, mathematically structured technology, which is *essentially* something different from every previously known use of tools. [148]

That which is, is only that which, when correctly thought, stands up to correct thinking.

The main term for the Being of beings—that is, its definitive interpretation—is *ousia*. As a philosophical concept, the word means constant presence. Even at the time when this word had already become the dominant conceptual term in philosophy, it still retained its original meaning: *hē huparchousa ousia* (Isocrates) is present-at-hand assets.[109] But even this fundamental meaning of *ousia* and the track it lays out for the interpretation of Being could not maintain itself. *Ousia* immediately began to be reinterpreted as *substantia*. This meaning remains current in the Middle Ages and in modernity up to now. Greek philosophy is then interpreted retroactively—that is, falsified from the bottom up—on the basis of the

109. Isocrates, *To Demonicus,* chapter 19 and chapter 28.

dominant concept of substance; the concept of function is only its mathematicized degeneration.

It remains to be seen how, starting with *ousia* as the term that is now definitive for Being, the divisions we have discussed before between *Being and becoming, Being and seeming* are also conceived. Here we immediately recall the schema of the divisions that are in question:

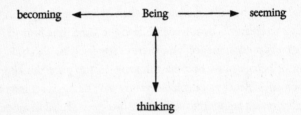

What stands over against becoming as its opposite is continuous endurance. What stands over against seeming as mere semblance is what is really viewed, the *idea*. As the *ontōs on* (what really is), the *idea* is furthermore what endures continuously, as opposed to mutable seeming. But becoming and seeming are not determined only by *ousia;* for *ousia,* in turn, is still definitively determined by its relation to logos, judgment as assertion, *dianoia.* Accordingly, becoming and seeming are also determined by the perspective of thinking.

From the point of view of the thinking that makes judgments, which always starts from something that endures, becoming appears as not-enduring. Not-enduring shows itself at first, within what is present at hand, as not staying in the same place. Becoming [149] appears as change of place, *phora,* local motion. Change of place becomes the definitive phenomenon of motion, in the light of which all becoming is then to be comprehended. When the dominance of thinking comes to the fore, in the sense of modern mathematical rationalism, no other form of becoming whatsoever is recognized other than motion in the sense of change of place. Wherever other phenomena of motion show themselves, one attempts to grasp them on the basis of change of place. Change of place itself, motion, is for its part now conceived only in terms of $c = s/t$.[110] Descartes, the philosophical founder of this way of thinking, ridicules every other concept of motion in his *Regulae*, number XII.[111]

Just as becoming, in accordance with *ousia*, is determined by thinking (calculating), so is the other opposite to Being, seeming. It is the incorrect. The basis of seeming is the distortion of thought. Seeming becomes mere logical incorrectness, falsehood. Only on this basis can we completely gauge what the opposition of thinking to Being means: thinking extends its dominance [as regards the definitive determination of essence][112] over Being, and at the same time over what is opposed to Being. This dominance goes *still* farther. For at the moment when logos in the sense of the assertion assumes dominance over Being, when Being is experienced and conceived as *ousia*, Being-present-at-hand, the division between Being and the ought is also in preparation. The schema of the restrictions of Being then looks like this:

110. That is, *celeritas = spatium/tempus,* or velocity = distance/time.
111. "Again, when people say that motion, something perfectly familiar to everyone, is 'the actuality of a potential being, in so far as it is potential' [Aristotle, *Physics,* III, 1, 201a10], do they not give the impression of uttering magic words which have a hidden meaning beyond the grasp of the human mind? For who can understand these expressions? Who does not know what motion is? Who would deny that these people are finding a difficulty where none exists?" Descartes, *Rules for the Direction of the Mind,* in *The Philosophical Writings of Descartes,* trans. John Cottingham et al., vol. 1 (Cambridge: Cambridge University Press, 1984), 49.
112. In parentheses in the 1953 edition.

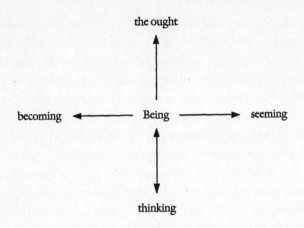

4. Being and the Ought

If we use our diagram as a guideline to represent this division, it goes in still another direction. The division between *Being and thinking* is drawn downward. This indicates that thinking becomes the ground that sustains and determines Being. The division be-[150] tween *Being and the ought,* however, is drawn upward. This suggests that whereas Being is grounded in thinking, it is surmounted by the ought. What this means is that Being is no longer what is definitive, what provides the measure. But is it not the idea, the prototype? Yes, but precisely because of their character as prototypes, the ideas no longer provide the measure. For as that which offers a look, and thus in a certain way is something that is *(on),* the idea, as such a being, demands in turn the determination of *its* Being—that is, once again *a single* look. According to Plato, the idea of ideas, the highest idea, is the *idea tou agathou,* the idea of the good.

The "good" here does not mean what is orderly in the moral sense, but the valiant, which achieves and can achieve what is proper to it. The *agathon* is the standard as such, what first grants Being the potency to unfold essentially as *idea,* as prototype. What grants such potency is the primally potent. But now, insofar as the ideas constitute Being as *ousia,* the *idea tou agathou,* the highest idea, stands *epekeina tēs ousias,* beyond Being.[113] Thus Being itself, not in general but as *idea,* comes into opposition to something else to which it itself, Being, remains assigned. The highest idea is the archetype of the prototypes.

We need no far-reaching discussions now in order to make it clear that in this division, as in the others, what is excluded from Being, the ought, is not imposed on Being from some other source. Being itself, in its particular interpretation as idea, brings with it the relation to the prototypical and to what ought to be. As Being itself becomes fixed in its character as idea, it also tends to make up for the ensuing degradation of Being. But by now, this can occur only by setting something *above* Being that Being never yet is, but always *ought* to be.

Our only goal here has been to shed light on the essential origin of the division between Being and the ought, or on what is at bottom the same, the historical inception of this division. Here we will not trace the history of the unfolding and transformation of this division. Let us mention just *one* more essential point. In all the determinations of Being and of the divisions we have mentioned, we must keep one thing in view: because Being inceptively is *phusis,* arising-unconcealing sway, it itself exhibits itself as *eidos* and *idea.* This exposition is never based exclusively or even primarily on philosophical exegesis.

It became clear that the ought arises in opposition to Being as soon as Being determines itself as idea. With this determination,

113. Plato, *Republic* 509b.

[151]   thinking as the logos of assertion (*dialegesthai*) assumes a definitive role. Thus, as soon as this thinking achieves dominance in the modern age, as self-sufficient reason, the real development of the division between Being and the ought is made ready. This process is completed in Kant. For Kant, beings are nature—in other words, whatever can be determined and is determined in mathematical-physical thinking. The categorical imperative, which is determined both by and as reason, is opposed to nature. Kant more than once explicitly calls it the ought, considering the relation of the imperative to what merely is, in the sense of merely instinctive nature. Fichte then explicitly and especially made the opposition of Being and the ought into the fundamental framework of his system. In the course of the nineteenth century, definitive precedence is attained by that which is, in Kant's sense—that which can be experienced according to the sciences, which now include the sciences of history and economics. Due to the predominance of beings, the ought is endangered in its role as standard. The ought must assert its claims. It must attempt to ground itself in itself. Whatever wants to announce an ought-claim in itself must be justified in doing so on its own basis. Something like an ought can emanate only from something that raises such a claim on its own, something that in itself has a *value*, and itself *is* a *value*. Values as such now become the ground of the ought. But because values stand opposed to the Being of beings, in the sense of facts, they themselves cannot *be*. So instead one says that they are valid. Values provide the measure for all domains of beings—that is, of what is present at hand. History is nothing but the actualization of values.

     Plato conceived of Being as idea. The idea is the prototype, and as such it also provides the measure. What is easier now than to understand Plato's ideas in the sense of values, and to interpret the Being of beings on the basis of the valid?

     Values are valid. But validity is still too reminiscent of validity for a subject. In order to prop up yet again the ought that has been raised to the level of values, one attributes a Being to values themselves. Here, Being *at bottom* means nothing other than the coming to presence of what is present at hand. It is just not present at hand in as crude and tangible a way as tables and chairs are. With the Being of values, the maximum in confusion and deracination has been reached. Yet because the expression "value" is starting to look worn out, especially because it also plays a role in economic theory, one now calls values "totalities." With this term, however, just the spelling has changed—although when they are called totalities it is easier to see what they are at bottom—namely, half-measures. But in the domain of the essential, half-measures are always more fatal than the Nothing that is so terribly feared. In 1928 there appeared the first part of a collected bibliography on the concept of value. It cites 661 publications on the concept of value. Probably by now there are a thousand. All this calls itself philosophy. In particular, what is peddled about nowadays as the philosophy of National Socialism, but which has not the least to do with the inner truth and greatness of this movement [namely, the encounter between global technology and modern humanity],[114] is fishing in these troubled waters of "values" and "totalities." [152]

Yet we can see how stubbornly the thought of values entrenched itself in the nineteenth century when we see that even Nietzsche, and precisely he, thinks completely within the perspective of the representation of values. The subtitle to his projected main work, *The Will to Power,* is *Attempt at a Revaluation of All Values.* Its third book is headed: *Attempt at a New Positing of Values.* Because Nietzsche was entangled in the confusion of the representation of values,

114. This phrase is printed in parentheses in all the German editions, but it was almost certainly added when Heidegger prepared this text for publication. For details, see our introduction.

because he did not understand its questionable provenance, he never reached the genuine center of philosophy. But even if some future thinker should reach the center again—we today can only labor to pave the way—he will not avoid entanglement either; it will just be a different entanglement. No one can leap over his own shadow.

*   *   *   *

We have questioned our way through the four divisions *Being and becoming, Being and seeming, Being and thinking, Being and the ought.* Our discussion was introduced with a list of seven points of orientation.[115] At first it seemed as though this were just an exercise in thought, a distinction among arbitrarily juxtaposed terms.

We will now repeat the points in the same formulation and see to what extent what we have said has maintained its direction according to these points of orientation and has reached the insight we were seeking.

1. In the divisions we have considered, Being is delimited against an Other, and thus already has a determinateness *in* this re-strictive setting of a limit.

[153]   2. The delimitation happens in four simultaneously interrelated respects. Thus the determinateness of Being must correspondingly be ramified and heightened.

3. The distinctions are by no means accidental. What is held apart by them belongs together originally and tends toward a unity. Hence the divisions have their own necessity.

4. Therefore the oppositions that initially strike us as mere formulas did not come up on arbitrary occasions and enter language as figures of speech, as it were. They arose in the most intimate con-

---

115. See p. 99. Heidegger's two formulations of the seven points are not exactly the same.

nection with the definitive Western stamping of Being. They had their inception with the inception of philosophical questioning.

5. Yet these distinctions have not remained dominant only within Western philosophy; they pervade all knowing, acting, and speaking, even when they are not expressed explicitly or in these words.

6. The sequence in which we listed the terms already gives an indication of the order of their essential connection and of the historical sequence in which they were stamped.

7. *Asking* the question of Being in an originary way, in a way that grasps the task of unfolding the truth of the essence of *Being*, means facing the decision regarding the concealed powers in these divisions, and it means bringing them back to their own truth.

Everything that before was merely declared in these points has now been brought into view, *except* what is claimed in the last point. And it contains nothing but a demand. In conclusion, we must show that this demand is justified and its fulfillment is necessary.

This demonstration can be carried out only in such a way that at the same time, we cast an eye once again over the entirety of this "introduction to metaphysics."

Everything is based on the fundamental question that we raised at the beginning: "Why are there beings at all instead of nothing?" The first unfolding of this fundamental question forced us into the prior question: how does it stand with Being as such?

At first, "Being" appeared to us as an empty word with an evanescent meaning. This appeared to be one ascertainable fact among others. But in the end, that which apparently was not open to question, which apparently was no longer questionable, proved to be *what is most worthy of questioning*. Being and the understanding of Being are not a present-at-hand fact. Being is the fundamental hap-

pening, the only ground upon which historical Dasein is granted in [154
the midst of beings that are opened up as a whole.

But we experience this most question-worthy ground of historical Dasein in its worth and its rank only if we put it into question. Accordingly, we posed the prior question: How does it stand with Being?

The references to the common yet ambiguous usage of the "is" convinced us that the talk of the indeterminateness and emptiness of Being is erroneous. Instead, the "is" determines the meaning and the content of the infinitive "to be," and not vice versa. Now we can also comprehend *why* this must be so. The "is" serves as the copula, as the "little connecting word" (Kant) in the assertion. The assertion contains the "is." But because the assertion, *logos* as *katēgoria*, has become the court of justice over Being, the *assertion* determines Being on the basis of the "is" that is proper to *assertion*.

Being, from which we set out as an empty label, must therefore have a definite meaning, contrary to this semblance of emptiness.

The determinateness of Being was brought before our eyes by the discussion of the four divisions:

Being, in contradistinction to becoming, is enduring.

Being, in contradistinction to seeming, is the enduring prototype, the always identical.

Being, in contradistinction to thinking, is what lies at the basis, the present-at-hand.

Being, in contradistinction to the ought, is what lies at hand in each case as what ought to be and has not yet been actualized, or already has been actualized.

Endurance, perpetual identity, presence at hand, lying at hand — all at bottom say the same: *constant presence, on* as *ousia*.

This determinateness of Being is not accidental. It grows out of the determination[116] under which our historical Dasein stands by virtue of its great inception among the Greeks. The determinateness of Being is not a matter of delimiting a mere meaning of a word. It is *the* power that today still sustains and dominates *all our* relations to beings as a whole, to becoming, to seeming, to thinking, and to the ought.

The question of how it stands with Being also proves to be the question of how it stands with our Dasein in history, of whether we *stand* in history or merely stagger. Seen metaphysically, *we are staggering*. Everywhere we are underway amid beings, and yet we no longer know how it stands with Being. We do not even know that we no longer know it. We are staggering even when we mutually assure ourselves that we are not staggering, even when, as in recent times, people go so far as to try to show that this asking about Being brings only confusion, that it has a destructive effect, that it is nihilism. [This misinterpretation of the question of Being, which has been renewed since the rise of existentialism, is new only for the very naive.]

[155]

But where is the real nihilism at work? Where one clings to current beings and believes it is enough to take beings, as before, just as the beings that they are. But with this, one rejects the question of Being and treats Being as a nothing *(nihil)*, which in a certain way it even "is," insofar as it essentially unfolds. Merely to chase after beings in the midst of the oblivion of Being—that is nihilism. Nihilism thus understood is the *ground* for the nihilism that Nietzsche exposed in the first book of *The Will to Power*.

In contrast, to go expressly up to the limit of Nothing in the *question* about Being, and to take Nothing into the question of

---

116. *Bestimmung* here can also mean destiny, vocation, or dispensation.

Being—this is the first and only fruitful step toward the true over-coming of nihilism.

But the discussion of the four divisions shows us that we must go *this* far in pursuing the question about Being as what is most worthy of questioning. That *over against which* Being is limited— becoming, seeming, thinking, the ought—is not just something that we have thought up. Here, powers are holding sway that dominate and bewitch beings, their opening up and formation, their closing and deformation. Becoming—is it nothing? Seeming—is it nothing? Thinking—is it nothing? The ought—is it nothing? By no means.

But if all that stands *over against* Being in the divisions is *not* nothing, then it *itself* is *in being,* and in the end is in being even more than what is taken as in being in accordance with the restricted essential determination of Being. But in what sense of Being *is in being,* then, that which becomes, that which seems, thinking, and the ought? By no means in *that* sense of Being from which they set themselves apart. But this sense of Being is the one that has been current since antiquity.

Thus the concept of Being that has been accepted up to now does not suffice to name everything that "is."

Being must therefore be experienced anew, from the bottom up and in the full breadth of its possible essence, if we want to set our historical Dasein to work as historical. For those powers that stand against Being, the intricately interwoven divisions themselves, have long determined, dominated, and pervaded our Dasein and keep it in confusion regarding "Being." And so from the originary questioning of the four divisions there grows the insight that Being, which is encircled by them, must itself be transformed into the encompassing circle and ground of all beings. *The* originary divi-

[156]

sion, whose intensity and originary disjunction sustains history, is the distinction between Being and beings.

But how is this distinction to happen? Where can philosophy start to think it? Yet here we should not talk about a start, but instead we should *re*-accomplish it; for it *has* been accomplished in the necessity of the inception under which we stand. It was not in vain that, in discussing the four divisions, we dwelled relatively long on the division between Being and thinking. Even today it is still the ground that sustains the determination of Being. The thinking that is guided by *logos* as assertion provides and maintains the perspective in which Being is viewed.

Hence if Being itself is to be opened up and grounded in *its* originary distinction from beings, then an originary perspective needs to be opened up. The origin of the division between Being and thinking, the disjunction of apprehension and Being, shows us that what is at stake here is nothing less than a determination of Being-human that springs from the essence of Being *(phusis)* that is to be opened up.

The question about the essence of Being is intimately linked to the question of who the human being is. Yet the determination of the human essence that is required here is not a matter for a free-floating anthropology, which at bottom represents humanity in the same way as zoology represents animals. The question about human Being is now determined in its direction and scope *solely* on the basis of the question about *Being*. Within the question of Being, the human essence is to be grasped and grounded, according to the concealed directive of the inception, as *the site* that Being necessitates for its opening up. Humanity is the Here that is open in itself. Beings stand within this Here and are set to work in it. We therefore say: the Being of humanity is, in the strict sense of the word, *"Being-here"* ("Da-sein"). The perspective for the opening up of

Being must be grounded originally in the essence of Being-here as such a site for the opening up of Being.

The entire Western tradition and conception of Being, and accordingly the fundamental relation to Being that is still dominant today, is summed up in the title *Being and thinking*.

[157]   But *Being and time* is a title that can in no way be coordinated with the divisions we have discussed. It points to a completely different domain of questioning.

Here, the "word" time has not merely been substituted for the "word" thinking; instead, the essence of time is determined according to other considerations, fundamentally and solely within the domain of the question of Being.

But why time, precisely? Because in the inception of Western philosophy, the *perspective that guides* the opening up of Being is time, but *in such a way* that this perspective *as such* still remained and had to remain concealed. If what finally becomes the fundamental concept of Being is *ousia,* and this means constant presence, then what lies unexposed as the ground of the essence of stability and the essence of presence, other than time? But *this* "time" still has not been unfolded in its essence, nor can it be unfolded (on the basis and within the purview of "physics"). For as soon as meditation on the essence of time begins, at the *end* of Greek philosophy with Aristotle, time itself must be taken as something that is somehow coming to presence, *ousia tis.* This is expressed in the fact that time is conceived on the basis of the "now," that which is in each case uniquely present. The past is the "no-*longer*-now," the future is the "not-*yet*-now." Being in the sense of presence at hand (presence) becomes the perspective for the determination of time. But time does not become the perspective that is especially selected for the interpretation of Being.

In such a meditation, "Being and time" means not a book but the task that is given. The authentic task given here is what we do not know; and insofar as we know this *genuinely* — namely *as* a given task — we always know it only in *questioning*.

Being able to question means being able to wait, even for a lifetime. But an age for which the actual is only whatever goes fast and can be grasped with both hands takes questioning as "a stranger to reality," as something that does not count as profitable. But what is essential is not counting but the right time — that is, the right moment and the right endurance.

> For the mindful god
> does detest
> untimely growth.
> — Hölderlin, fragment from the period of "The Titans"
> (IV, 218)[117]

117. Heidegger cites Friedrich Hölderlin, *Hölderlin: Sämtliche Werke,* ed. Norbert v. Hellingrath et al. (Berlin: Propyläen-Verlag, 1923). See "But When the Heavenly . . .," in Hölderlin, *Poems and Fragments,* trans. Michael Hamburger, 3d ed. (London: Anvil, 1994), 571.

German-English Glossary

This glossary allows readers to trace our translations of important German terms and to explore some of their original senses. We provide brief explanations for some words; these should be considered not rigid definitions but indications of the range of meaning that is associated with these words. We have also cross-referenced terms that are related in etymology or in meaning, as Heidegger often expects his audience to perceive such connections. Where we have used more than one English word to render a German word, the most common rendering is listed first. In the case of words that are used sparingly, we have listed the pages on which they appear.

Note: Page numbers refer to the pagination of the Niemeyer editions of the text, provided in the margins of this translation.

Abbild	likeness (141). See also *Bild*
Abbilden	reproduction (48). See also *Bild*
Abgrund	abyss. See also *Grund*

Ablauf	process (66). See also *Vorgang*
Abwandlung	inflection (in grammatical context); variation (108)
Abwesen	absence (87). See also *wesen*
allgemein	universal
Allgewalt	almighty sway. See also *walten*
Alltag	everyday life (58)
alltäglich	ordinary
Anblick	view; aspect (26); look (51); viewpoint (89); vista (79). See also *sehen*
Andere, das	Other. We have capitalized Heidegger's special usage of *das Andere* and its variants to indicate the various attempts to restrict Being according to some "Other" — namely, becoming, seeming, thinking and the ought (see 71).
Anfang	inception. An inception, for Heidegger, is not merely the starting point of a process but an origin of a historical epoch that continues to have significance throughout that epoch.

Related words

anfangen	initiate
anfangend	incipient (145)
anfänglich	inceptive; initial

Anschein	semblance. An illusion, a deceitful appearance. See also *Schein*
Ansehen	aspect; respect. The word can mean both an appearance of something and renown or prestige. Both senses are combined on 78–80. See also *sehen*

Ansicht	view (79, 81, 85–86, 88, 146); view upon beings (146). See also *sehen*
anwesen	come to presence. Heidegger uses a wide variety of words in connection with presence, which he interprets as the fundamental meaning of Being for the Greeks (see 154).

Related words

Anwesen	coming to presence
An-wesen	coming-to-presence (47); pre-sencing (55)
Anwesende, das	that which comes to presence
Anwesenheit	presence

See also *Gegenwart; gegenwärtig; Gegenwärtigkeit; präsentieren, sich; Schein; vorhanden; Vorhandenheit; Vorhandensein; vorkommen; vorliegen; vor-liegen; wesen*

aufgehen	emerge. Along with abiding *(verweilen)*, emerging is one of the two main traits of *phusis* as Heidegger sees it. See 11.
aufgehend	emerging; emergent
Aufgeschlossenheit	openedness (15). See also *offen*
Aufhebung	sublation (143). In Hegel, to sublate a concept or position is to overcome it while preserving its limited truth within a higher truth.
Aufnahme-stellung	position to receive (105, 128)
aufnehmend	receptive (105–106)
aufreißen	tear open (80); rip open (140). See also *Riß*

Aufriß	contour (117); outline (140). See also *Riß*
aufschließen	disclose. See also *offen*
Augenpunkt	viewpoint (79). See also *sehen*
Augenschein	look of things (4). See also *sehen, Schein*
Auseinandersetzung	confrontation. *Auseinandersetzung* is Heidegger's own translation of the Greek word *polemos* (war), an important theme explored in this work. In terms of its etymology, the German word means a setting-out-and-apart-from-one-another, and it underlies Heidegger's understanding of phenomena as diverse as truth, history, and politics. In everyday German, *Auseinandersetzung* has a range of meanings, including clash, discussion, debate, argument, or a settling of accounts. Sometimes, Heidegger hyphenates this word in various ways to emphasize the disentangling or oppositional action of *Auseinandersetzung:*
	Aus-einander-setzung: confrontational setting-apart-from-each-other (110)
	Aus-einandersetzung: con-frontation (47)
	See also *Satz; Satzung; setzen; Setzung*
auseinanderstreben	strive in confrontation (139, 142)
auseinandertreten	disjoin; step apart
Auseinandertreten	disjunction
Auslegung	interpretation; exposition (150)
auslesen	select
Aussehen	look (46). See also *sehen*
Aussehensweisen	modes of appearance (50). See also *sehen*
Aussicht	view granted by beings (146). See also *sehen*

Bedeutung	meaning. See also *Sinn*
befragen	interrogate. See also *fragen*
begründen	found. See also *Grund*
Bereich	domain
bergen	hold within it (32); possess (79). See also *unverborgen*
Besinnung	meditation
Bestand	subsistence (26); substance (69). See also *stehen*
beständig	continuous (147, 148). See also *stehen*
Beständigkeit	stability (157). See also *stehen*
bestehen	subsist (69, 124); undergo (80, 128). See also *stehen*
bestimmen	determine; define
bestimmt	definite; determinate
Bestimmung	determination; definition; vocation (29)
bewältigen	surmount. See also *walten*
Bild	picture. Through a series of plays on this word, Heidegger suggests a genealogy and critique of the representational understanding of truth, which he traces back to the Platonic theory of "forms." See esp. 140–142.

Related words

bilden	to form
Bildung	formation

See also *Abbild; Abbilden; hineinbilden; Musterbild; Nachbild; Umbildung; Urbild; Vorbild; vorbilden*

bleiben	remain; stay; endure
Bleiben	endurance (148, 154); enduring (154)
Blick	view. See also *sehen*

Blickbahn	perspective (108, 134, 139, 144, 148, 152, 156–157; line of sight (89). See also *sehen*
Blickfeld	point of view (134). See also *sehen*
Bodenständigkeit	rootedness (30)
brauchen	use; need to use (115, 132, 133); require (124). The German verb can mean either "to use" or "to need."
Dasein	Dasein. See Translators' Introduction. See also *Sein*
Da-sein	Being-here. See also *Sein*
dichten	poetize
Dichten	poetry
Dichtung	poetry
durchnehmen	analyze (147). See also *zergliedern* (analyze)
durchwalten	pervade in its sway. See also *innehaben; walten*
Durchwaltende, das	pervasive sway (102, 120)
echt	genuine
eigenständig	autonomous (7); self-standing (54). See also *stehen*
eigentlich	authentic, real; really, actually. We have translated this word as "authentic" at points where it could carry some of the weight of the concept of *Eigentlichkeit* (authenticity) in *Being and Time;* at other points it is simply an emphatic modifier, like "real" in its everyday English usage.
einfügen	fit into. See also *Fug*
einheimisch	at home. See also *unheimlich*
entbergen	display (79). See also *unverborgen*

ent-bergen	de-concealing (130). See also *unverborgen*
entbergend	unconcealing. See also *unverborgen*
Ent-borgenheit	de-concealment (16). See also *unverborgen*
entfalten	unfold
entscheiden	decide. For Heidegger, decision is to be understood in terms of a fundamental "cutting" or "division" *(Scheidung)*. See esp. 84.

Related words:

entscheidend	decisive
Ent-scheidung	de-cision

See also *Scheidung; Unterscheidung*

Entschlossenheit	resoluteness
Ent-schlossenheit	open resoluteness. The hyphenation suggests the meaning "un-closedness." See *Being and Time*, §60. See also *offen*
entspringen	originate
entstehen	come about; originate (92). See also *stehen*
ent-stehen	stand forth, arise (12); arise and stand forth (48). See also *stehen*
Entstehen	genesis (13, 73, 74). See also *stehen*
Ereignis	event (90, 121). This word becomes crucial for Heidegger in the *Contributions to Philosophy* (1936–1938), but it is used in its ordinary sense in *Introduction to Metaphysics*.
erfragen	inquire into. See also *fragen*
Erkenntnis	knowledge. See also *Kenntnis*. See 16–17 and 122 for the contrast between the two terms.
Erkenntnistheorie	epistemology

Erlebnis	lived experience (125)
ernötigen	necessitate. See also *Not*
eröffnen	open up. See also *offen*
Eröffnung	manifestation (44). See also *offen*
erscheinen	appear. It is important to keep in mind that for Heidegger, appearing pertains to Being itself; appearing is not originally the antagonist of Being. See esp. 76–78. See also *Schein*
Erscheinung	appearance; phenomenon (13, 18, 149); manifestation (12). See also *Schein*
erschließen	disclose. See also *offen*
Erschwerung	burdening (9, 34)
erstehen	arise. See also *stehen*
erwirken	bring about; gain; work out (65)
er-wirken	put to work (122)
Existenz	existence (49). See also *Sein*
Fortriß	tearing-away (125). See also *Riß*
fragen	ask; question. See also *befragen; erfragen*
Fug	fittingness; dispensation (113). With the constellation of words related to *Fug*, Heidegger is trying to articulate the sense in which structures of meaning "fit" together as engendered by the encounter of Being with Dasein. See 123.

Related words

Fuge	joint (123); fit (129)
fügen	enjoin; dispose (120)
fügen, sich	comply
Fügung	arrangement

See also *einfügen; Gefüge; Unfug; verfügbar; verfügen*

Geborgenheit	safety (4, 6). See also *unverborgen*
Gediegenheit	perdurance (74)
Gefüge	structure. See also *Fug*
Gegensatz	contradiction; opposite; opposition
Gegenteil	opposite
Gegenwart	the present (34, 73); present (55). See also *anwesen*
gegenwärtig	present. See also *anwesen*
Gegenwärtigkeit	presentness (69). See also *anwesen*
Geist	spirit. The German word has a very broad sense; it refers to the qualities that raise human beings above other animals and enable them to have culture, history, and thought.
geistig	spiritual
Gerede	chatter (132, 144)
geschehen	happen

Related words

Geschehnis	happening
Geschichte	history
geschichtlich	historical
Geschichtswissenschaft	historical science; the science of history (33)
Geschick	destiny

See also *Schicksal*

Gesicht	visage (46, 79, 139); aspect (60)

Related words

Gesichtskreis	purview (14, 15, 157); perspective (111)

	Gesichtspunkt viewpoint (79)
	See also *sehen*
Gesollte, das	what ought to be (150, 154). See also *Sollen, das*
Gestalt	form
gestalten	to form. See also *bilden; verunstalten*
Gewalt	violence. The German word does not always have the connotation of arbitrariness of the English "violence," and sometimes it could also have been translated as "force." See Translators' Introduction.
	Related words

Gewalten	violent forces (48, 120)
gewaltig	violent; mighty (58, 119, 127)
gewaltsam	violent
Gewalt-tat	act of violence
gewalt-tätig	violence-doing
Gewalt[-]tätigkeit	violence-doing; doing violence

See also *walten*

Ge-Wesende, das	that which essentially unfolds as having been (77). See also *wesen*
Gewesene, das	what has been (30, 34); what is past (90). See also *wesen*
gleich	identical (20, 25, 35, 154). See also *selbe*
gleichgültig	indifferent
Grenze	limit
Grund	ground; reason; foundation; *im Grunde* = at bottom; fundamentally. See Translators' Introduction.

Related words

grund-	grounding; funda-mental; basic
Gründung	grounding; founda-tion
Grundzug	basic trait

See also *Abgrund; begründen*

Habe	holdings (138)
handhaben	to handle (143). See also *vorhanden*
handlich	handy (143); tangible (151). See also *vorhanden*
heimisch	homely. See also *unheimlich*
Herkunft	provenance
Herrschaft	dominance. See also *Vorherrschaft*
herrschen	rule; prevail
Hersagen	hearsay (99, 142). See also *sagen*
herstellen	produce
her-stellen	pro-duce (48, 78, 130, 146). The hyphenation suggests the meaning "to set forth."
hervor-bringen	pro-duce (13)
Hinblick	view (32, 74). See also *sehen*
hineinbilden	incorporate (140). See also *Bild*
hineinschauen	view into (48). See also *sehen*
hineinsehen	see into (48). See also *sehen*
hin-nehmen	taking-in (138). *Hinnehmen* ordinarily means to take or accept.
Hinsicht	respect; aspect (35, 115, 126); *hinsichtlich* = with respect to; *im Hinsehen auf* = in view of (74). See also *sehen*
hören	hear; hearken (99)
hörig	obedient; hearkening (99)
innehaben	pervade. See also *durchwalten*

Interpretation	exegesis (124, 134, 150). See also *Anslegung*
Irre	errancy (28, 83). See also *Verirrung*
Kampf	struggle; *sich erkämpft* = struggles itself forth (47)
Kenntnis	information (16–17, 37, 54, 122). See also *Erkenntnis*
Kluft	chasm (80)
Kraft	force; strength (15, 29, 145); energy (16, 36)
Leistungssinn von x	sense of what x can achieve (7–9)
Leitsatz	guiding principle (94, 111). See also *Satz*
Logos	logos
λόγος	*logos.* Heidegger sometimes writes this word in Greek letters and sometimes uses a transliteration. We have italicized it when it is written in Greek letters in Heidegger's text.
Machenschaft	machination (121–122)
Macht	power
Mann	man. See also *Mensch*
Maß	measure
maßgebend	definitive; standard-setting; providing the measure
Maßstab	standard
Mensch	human beings; humanity; the human being; the human; man (97, 112, 114); *Normalmensch* = average man (28). This is the generic, gender-neutral term. See Translators' Introduction.
Menschsein	Being-human

Muster	model (147)
Musterbild	model (140). See also *Bild*
Nachbild	imitation (140–141). See also *Bild*
náchsagen	say again (141–142). See also *sagen*
Nennkraft	naming force
Nichtdasein	not-Being-here (135–136). See also *Sein*
Nichtige, das	nullity (18)
nichts; Nichts	nothing
Nichts, das	Nothing. See Translators' Introduction.
Nichtsein	not-Being; *nicht-sein* = not-to-be (49). See also *Sein*.

Not urgency; predicament (62). *Not tut, Not ist* = is needful. *Not* means a situation of distress, emergency, or urgent need. In the 1930s Heidegger often says that all necessity *(Notwendigkeit)* is grounded in urgency *(Not)*.

Related words

nötig	necessary; required
nötigen	urge; compel
notvoll	dire (113)
Notwendigkeit	necessity

See also *ernötigen*

offen open. For Heidegger, the questions of Being and truth are also the question of openness: that is, how is it that an open region opens up, within which we can stand open to the unconcealment of beings as such?

Related words

offenbar	revealed; open

offenbaren	reveal
Offenbarkeit	openness (16–17, 64–65, 72, 81, 115, 119)
offenbarmachen	reveal
Offenbarung	revelation (5, 44)
Offene, das	the open (23)
Offenheit	openness (124, 131, 135)
offenkundig	manifest (15); evident (102)

See also *Aufgeschlossenheit; aufschließen; Ent-schlossenheit; eröffnen; Eröffnung; erschließen; verschließen*

optisch	optical (49). See also *sehen*
Ort	place; locus
Perspektive	perspective (89). See also *sehen*
präsentieren, sich	present itself (138). See also *anwesen*
Rang	rank. See also *Vorrang; Vorrangstellung*
Rede	discourse
reden	to talk
reißen	draw (123). See also *Riß*
Riß	draft (123). See also *aufreißen; Aufriß; Fortriß; reißen*
sagen	say
	Related words
Sage	saga (55, 73, 80)
Sagen	speech; speaking (55); discourse (74)

See also *Hersagen; Sprache; sprechen; Spruch; weitersagen*

sammeln	gather. Heidegger interprets Greek *logos* as gathering: see 95.
Satz	sentence; proposition; statement. See also *Auseinandersetzung; Leitsatz*
Satzung	ordinance (13, 85, 100, 113, 117). See also *Auseinandersetzung*
schauen	to view. See also *sehen*
Scheidung	division. See also *entscheiden*
Schein	seeming; illusion (2, 19, 48); light (76). According to Heidegger, seeming was not originally separate from Being but was part of the self-manifestation or "shining" of beings (see 76–78). Occasionally Heidegger does use the word *Schein* to mean a *deceptive* manifestation; on these occasions we translate it as "illusion." However, his usual word for a deceptive manifestation is *Anschein* (semblance).

Related words

scheinen	seem; shine (76, 104, 127, 139, 144); shine forth (51, 54)
scheinend	seemly (100)

See also *Anschein; anwesen; Augenschein; erscheinen; Erscheinung; sehen; Vorschein; zum Vorschein bringen; zum Vorschein kommen*

scheitern	shatter
Schicksal	fate. See also *geschehen*
sehen	see; *von x her gesehen* = from the point of view of x. Heidegger explores the phe-

nomenon of seeing, in the broadest sense, through a wide variety of words. Seeing as a human activity corresponds to the self-showing of beings or Being (see *anwesen; Schein*). See also *Anblick; Ansehen; Ansicht; Augenpunkt; Augenschein; Aussehen; Aussehensweisen; Aussicht; Blick; Blickbahn; Blickfeld; Gesicht; Gesichtskreis; Gesichtspunkt; Hinblick; hineinschauen; hineinsehen; Hinsicht; hinsichtlich; optisch; Perspektive; schauen; Sicht; sichten; Sichtweite; Übersicht; Vorblick; Vorblickbahn*

seiend in being. This is a verbal adjective describing something that *is*. The reader must hear "being" in the translation here in a manner distinct from *a* being in the sense of an entity or thing. See also *Sein*

Seiend, das the being (85, 98, 100, 107, 129, 132); "*das Seiend*" = the in-being (23). When Heidegger employs *das Seiend* in his discussions of the pre-Socratics, this very uncommon usage parallels the ambiguous Greek expression *to on* or *to eon* (see 23–24). Sometimes the Greek and German expressions seem to refer to beings as such, sometimes they seem to refer to Being, and sometimes their meaning is indeterminate. See also *Sein*

Seiende, das; Seiendes beings; what is; that which is. See Translators' Introduction. See also *Sein*

Sein Being. That by virtue of which all beings as

such become accessible to us. For further explanation, see Translators' Introduction. Related words

Seiendheit	beingness (23–24)
seiend werden	come into being
sein	be; to be; to-be (73). This is the infinitive form of the verb.
Seinsvergessenheit	oblivion of Being (14–15, 19, 155)

See also *Dasein; Da-sein; Existenz; Nichtdasein; Nichtsein; seiend; Seiend, das; Seiende, das, Seiendes; Un-seiende, das; Unseiendes, Unsein; Vorhandensein*

selbe	same. What is "the same" is not necessarily identical *(gleich):* see 106.
Selbigkeit	selfsameness (103, 106)
selbstverständlich	self-evident
setzen	set; set up; put; posit. See also *Auseinandersetzung*
Setzung	positing (13, 152). See also *Auseinandersetzung*
Sicht	view (9). See also *sehen*
sichten	to view (139–140, 148, 156). See also *sehen*
Sichtweite	vista (8). See also *sehen*
Sinn	sense; *Sinn des Seins* = meaning of Being. The phrase "meaning of Being" is well-established in English translations of Heidegger; in other contexts, we have translated *Sinn* as "sense" in order to distinguish it from *Bedeutung* (meaning).

Sitten	mores (13)
soll	should
Sollen, das	the ought. See also *Gesollte, das*
Sprache	language. See also *sagen*
sprechen	speak. See also *sagen*
Spruch	saying. See also *sagen*
Sprung	leap. See also *Ursprung*
Stand	stand; stance (114); status (47). See also *stehen*
ständig	constant. See also *stehen*
Ständigkeit	constancy. See also *stehen*
Stätte	site. See esp. 117.
stehen	to stand. See also *Bestand; beständig; Beständigkeit; bestehen; eigenständig; entstehen; ent-stehen; Entstehen; erstehen; Stand; ständig; Ständigkeit; Verstand; Verständigkeit; verstehen*
stellen	place; pose; set
Stellung	orientation; position
Streit	strife (47, 87, 146)
Übergewalt	excessive violence (119, 124, 125, 135). See also *walten*
Übermacht	superior power (89, 118)
Übersicht	overview (8). See also *sehen*
überwältigen	overwhelm. See also *walten*
Umbildung	transformation; transfiguration (51). See also *Bild*
umdeuten	reinterpret
umwalten	envelop in its sway (119, 121, 136). See also *walten*
Unfug	unfittingness (123, 132); un-fit (125). See also *Fug*

unheimisch	homeless (127). See also *unheimlich*
unheimlich	uncanny. Heidegger's word for the Greek *deinon* (see especially 114–117). The word might also be rendered as "unsettled"; it is a condition in which one is not at home (*Heim*).
	Related words
	unheimisch homeless (127)
	See also *einheimisch; heimisch*
Un-seiende, das	un-beings (123)
Unseiendes	an unbeing (122)
Unsein	un-Being (102). The *un-* in these three words connotes not just negation but badness or wrongness. See also *Sein*
Unterscheidung	distinction. See also *entscheiden*
unverborgen	unconcealed. For Heidegger, *truth* is an event of unconcealment in which beings become accessible and understandable to us. This unconcealment is not the discovery of particular, factual "truths" but rather the establishment of the structures of meaning whereby such discoveries themselves become possible. See also *bergen; entbergen; ent-bergen; entbergend; Entborgenheit; Geborgenheit; verbergen*
Unverborgenheit	unconcealment. See also *wahr*
ur-	primal; originary
Urbild	archetype. See also *Bild*
Ursprung	origin
	Related words
	Ur-sprung originary leap (5)
	ursprünglich original; originary

Ursprünglichkeit   originality
See also *Sprung*

verbergen   conceal. See also *unverborgen*

Verfall   decline

verfügbar   available. See also *Fug*

verfügen   have at its disposal. See also *Fug*

Vergangene, das   what is past (33). See also *Gewesene, das*

vergewaltigen   violate (136). See also *walten*

Verirrung   aberration (83). See also *Irre*

vernehmen   apprehend. Heidegger's translation of the Greek *noein* (see 105).

Vernehmung   apprehension

Vernichtung   annihilation (12, 29)

versagen   withhold (135)

Versagen   failure

versammeln   gather. See also *sammeln*

verschließen   close off. See also *offen*

Verstand   understanding. See also *stehen*

Verständigkeit   astuteness (35). See also *stehen*

verstehen   understand. See also *stehen*

verunstalten   deform (11, 33, 140, 155). See also *gestalten*

verwalten   govern (131, 133, 142). See also *walten*

Verwaltung   governance (132, 145). See also *walten*

verweilen   abide. Along with emerging *(aufgehen)*, abiding is one of the two main traits of *phusis* as Heidegger understands it. See 11.

verwirklichen   actualize; realize. See also *wirklich*

Volk   people. See Translators' Introduction.

Vollendung   fulfillment. See 46.

Vorbild   prototype (45, 48, 50, 141, 150, 151, 154). See also *Bild*

vorbilden	prefigure (72, 142). See also *Bild*
Vorblick	prior view (90, 114). See also *sehen*
Vorblickbahn	prior line of sight (89–90). See also *sehen*
Vorfrage	preliminary question (32)
Vor-frage	prior question. "How does it stand with Being?" See 25.
Vorgang	process
Vorgehen	procedure
vorhanden	present at hand
Vorhandenheit	presence at hand (147, 154, 157)
Vorhandensein	Being-present-at-hand (38, 134, 149). See also *anwesen; Sein*
Vorherrschaft	predominance. See also *Herrschaft*
vorkommen	present itself (31, 56); can be found (25). See also *anwesen*
Vorkommnis	occurrence (3, 4, 38)
vorliegen	lie at hand (65, 76, 147, 154). See also *anwesen*
vor-liegen	lie before us (36); lie at hand before us (147). See also *anwesen*
Vorrang	precedence (110, 137, 151). See also *Rang*
Vorrangstellung	preeminent position (93)
Vorschein	manifestation. See also *Schein*
Vorschein bringen, zum	make manifest. See also *Schein*
Vorschein kommen, zum	manifest itself; make itself manifest (76). See also *Schein*
vorstellen	represent
vor-stellen	re-present; set forth (140). This spelling suggests the root meaning, "to set before."
Vorstellung	representation; notion (49, 51, 74, 77, 119). In its narrow sense, this word refers to a particular, "representational" under-

standing of truth and thinking: see 90–91. We have translated it as "notion" when it carries a broad, vague sense, much like the everyday English use of "idea."

vorwaltend	prevailing (137). See also *walten*
wahr	true
Walten	sway
walten	to hold sway. See Translators' Introduction.

See also *Allgewalt; bewältigen; durchwalten; Gewalt; Gewalten; gewaltig; gewaltsam; Gewalt-tat; gewalt-tätig; Gewalt[-]tätigkeit; Übergewalt; überwältigen; umwalten; vergewaltigen; verwalten; Verwaltung; vorwaltend*

weitersagen	pass on (141, 146). See also *sagen*
Wesen	essence
wesen	essentially unfold. In modern German, the noun *Wesen* means "essence," but the archaic or poetic verb *wesen* can mean "to be," "to live," or "to dwell"; vestiges of this verb are found in forms of the modern German *sein* (to be), such as *gewesen* (been). Through his use of *wesen*, Heidegger seeks to evoke a sense of essence that is not a What, an *idea*, but rather an aspect of Being: a happening, a process, an unfolding. For this reason, we translate *wesen* as "essentially unfold."

See also *Abwesen; anwesen; Anwesen; Anwesen; Anwesende, das; Anwesenheit; Ge-Wesende, das; Gewesene, das; Sein*

Widerstreit	antagonism (81, 146); conflict (133, 140). See also *Streit*
widerwendig	contrary; conflicting (135)
wieder-holen	repeat and retrieve (29); re-trieve (146). For an elucidation of this concept, see *Being and Time*, §74.
Willkür	arbitrariness (19, 115)
wirklich	actual
Wissen	knowledge; knowing
Würde	worth
würdigen	deem worthy (63)
zergliedern	analyze (90, 105). See also *durchnehmen*

Acknowledgments

We would like to offer our thanks to the scholars and readers who have helped us with this translation, although we must take full responsibility for the results. We owe a debt first of all to Ralph Manheim, whose own pioneering translation we frequently consulted. Also of great assistance have been the Spanish translation by Angela Ackermann Pilári, the Italian by Giuseppe Masi, and especially the French translation by Gilbert Kahn. Joseph J. Kockelmans lent us very helpful advice in the early stages of our work, and Daniel Dahlstrom, Clare Pearson Geiman, Charles Guignon, Theodore Kisiel, Susan Schoenbohm, Thomas Sheehan, and Dieter Thomä suggested refinements as we proceeded. We are particularly thankful to Charles Scott and his students at Penn State University, who made use of a draft for a class and who passed on remarks based on their careful reading.

Index

people *(Volk)*, xiv, 9, 12, 40, 41, 49, 52, 54, 113

perdition *(Verderb)*, 172, 173

perspective *(Blickbahn)*, 124 (line of sight), 151, 187–188, 194, 201, 208, 213, 219–220

perspective *(Perspektive)*, 124

Philo Judaeus, 143

philosophy, 9–14, 27–28, 45, 90

phusis: as appearing, 10, 75, 106, 110, 147–148, 194; and apprehension, 148; as Being, 14–19, 64, 106, 119; as beings, 14, 17, 18; and concealment, 121; as emergent-abiding sway, xiii, 15–16, 64, 66, 194; and *idea,* 192–194, 196; and *logos,* 132–144, 171; narrowing of its meaning, 17–18, 66; and nature, 14–16, 18, 64, 66; and truth, 107, 119

physics, 16, 19, 90, 149, 200, 220

Pindar, 106, 108, 120

Plato: on becoming, 69–70; on Being and thinking, 100; and end of philosophy, 191; on the good, 210–211; and *idea,* 111, 194, 198, 212; and *logos* as logic, 182; Nietzsche on, 111; on noun and verb, 60, 70; and ontology, 43; and Parmenides, 145–146; *Phaedrus,* 18; *Republic,* 211n; *Sophist,* 60; on space *(chōra),* 69–70; on *technē,* 18; *Timaeus,* 69–70; and value, 212

poetry *(Dichten, Dichtung):* Greek, 15, 108, 154, 183; mentioned, 50, 65, 167, 204; and philosophy, 28, 141, 176

polemos, 64–65, 120, 149, 153, 177, 178. *See also* confrontation

polis, 162–163, 141, 204

positivism, 49

possibility, 32

presence *(Anwesenheit)*, coming to

presence *(Anwesen)*, presentness *(Gegenwärtigkeit):* as Being, 64, 96, 132, 192–193, 206, 207, 216, 220, 225; in Parmenides, 101; and time, 220; and *Wesen,* 75–76

presence at hand *(Vorhandenheit)*, Being-present-at-hand *(Vorhandensein)*, 187, 206, 209, 216, 220

present *(Gegenwart)*, 47, 76, 101

prior question *(Vorfrage)*, 35, 44, 77, 215

pro-ducing *(Her-stellen)*, 66, 108, 181, 205

pro-ducing *(Hervor-bringen)*, 18

prototype *(Vorbild)*, 66, 69–70, 197, 210, 216

ptōsis, 62–63, 67

race *(Rasse)*, 49

rank *(Rang):* and Being, 87, 141; destruction of, 48; and *logos,* 65, 185; and philosophy, 11, 28; of why-question, 2, 5, 7

rationalism, 190, 207

realism, 146

reason *(Vernunft)*, 52, 130, 154, 187, 190–191, 207, 212

Rectoral Address, 52

Reinhardt, K., 113

religion, 50, 143. *See also* Christianity; God; gods

representation *(Vorstellung)*, 34, 84, 125–126, 203

resoluteness *(Entschlossenheit)*, 22–23

re-trieval *(Wieder-holung)*, 41, 204

rhēma, 60–61

rootedness *(Bodenständigkeit)*, 42

Russia, 40, 48, 52

Sappho, 105

Scholasticism, 192

Schopenhauer, A., 66, 189